MORYA *and* YOU

WISDOM

MORYA
and YOU
WISDOM

MARK L. PROPHET
ELIZABETH CLARE PROPHET

SUMMIT UNIVERSITY PRESS®

Gardiner, Montana

MARK L. PROPHET

ELIZABETH CLARE PROPHET

For information, contact
The Summit Lighthouse, 63 Summit Way, Gardiner, MT 59030 USA
Tel: 1-800-245-5445 or 1 406-848-9500
TSLinfo@TSL.org
SummitLighthouse.org
www.SummitLighthouse.org/El-Morya/
www.ElMorya.org

Library of Congress Control Number: 2019942243
ISBN: 978-1-60988-310-2 (softbound)
ISBN: 978-1-60988-311-9 (eBook)

SUMMIT UNIVERSITY ☙ PRESS®

The Summit Lighthouse, Summit University, Summit University Press, ☙, Church Universal and Triumphant, Keepers of the Flame, and *Pearls of Wisdom* are trademarks registered in the U.S. Patent and Trademark Office and in other countries. All rights reserved

Cover portrait by John Paul, by agreement with Inner Artz LLC

22   21   20   19   1   2   3   4

CONTENTS

PROLOGUE

What is wisdom? The inner meaning of the word is *wise dominion*. It's the ability to steer the course of affairs in such an enlightened and divinely inspired way that it brings about a deep sense of satisfaction for all parties concerned.

The ascended master El Morya excels in this ability to wield the faculties of the mind as a splendid reflector of the mind of God. For this reason he's known by many wondrous names: the Zen master; the mercurial master; the master with the Gemini mind; and the one whose mind is like the diamond-shining mind of God.

Understanding El Morya's nature as a lord of wisdom takes us back far into the past. Not surprisingly, though Morya now works extensively with the evolutions of Earth, his origin hearkens back to the planet Mercury.

Mercury and Venus, the ascended masters tell us, were once inhabited by beings much like the people living on Earth. In those bygone days, these two planets did not yet have the hot, inhospitable environments that characterize them now. Whereas lovely Venus was a focus for the flame of love, Mercury was a platform for the development of the mind.

The ancient story goes that at one point in Mercury's long history, things went terribly wrong as the intergalactic battle between Good and Evil extended its nefarious influence to this small planet, just as it did on Earth. El Morya himself explains what happened:

> In that planetary body, the issue of light and darkness was present. Here, where the sign of Gemini is the mind of God for action in concentration, the perversion of the light was in the mechanical creation of a robot in imitation of the Gemini mind. Absolute travesty against the Almighty! And yet, the fallen ones carried off their scheme —and it seemed for a time that they would carry the day!
>
> They created, then, a robot manifestation with a superficial ability to deal with mundane information but lacking the depth of the prongs of love/wisdom that come forth out of the threefold flame. This, then, seemingly practical yet highly spiritually impractical robot began to overrun that civilization. The challenge to sons and daughters of God was to use . . . the Gemini mind to confute, refute, denounce, *bind* and remove from Mercury those manifestations—an absolute usurpation of the creation of the Almighty One.
>
> As we saw the challenge and as we were taught by God Mercury, we knew that unflinching devotion to the will of God, the drawing within of energy to the diamond point of the Self, the wielding of the sword of blue flame, and the mastery of the action of fohatic keys would result in the victory.

As the master recounts this ancient struggle on Mercury, it's becoming clear how his very consciousness and sense of determination were shaped by participating in the heroic effort to reclaim the planet as a place of light. He continues:

> Now then, it was out of our deep desire to free evolving souls upon Mercury (who were no match for the robot creation) that we developed our adeptship in the will of

God. Absolute perversions of absolute power demand the counteraction by the intensity of Great Central Sun Magnet energies. You will recall that the victory of Jesus Christ gave to him that power of heaven and earth, the wherewithal to defeat the enemy at his call.

God gave to us, as we fought the battle of worlds on Mercury, that energy, that power—only because we were willing to balance the threefold flame, to pursue wisdom and wisdom's might, to intensify such love in every cell and in the flame of every cell, so that our auras were so saturated with love that there was no possibility for the misqualification of one erg of God's power through any form of tyranny whatsoever.[1]

What, then, is this Gemini mind that has become El Morya's hallmark? For one thing, it's the opposite of the mechanized, robotic mind that Morya spoke about. But more specifically, it's the *balanced* mind that expresses the wholeness and the fullness of the divine consciousness.

Elizabeth Clare Prophet, who with her husband Mark Prophet received Morya's messages collected in this book, explains that "any division, any schism within the self—the warring of one's members, the dividing of the desire body and of the mind—will take from you this wholeness, this oneness."[2]

When the masters speak about becoming one with the universal mind, they refer to the ability of the mind of God to move through us freely so that we have no separate consciousness from God. We must understand that the mind that we use, even in our daily affairs, is God's mind working through us. The brain is not the generator of that mind, explains Elizabeth Clare Prophet, it's simply "a chalice for certain programming, certain skills that we must perform in a given embodiment, a tool for a certain training and awareness. . . .

"Through the brain, through the nervous system, through

the chakras, through the heart, we tune in to the universal mind of God and we find that what we can do and be—the point of action—far exceeds the capacity of the brain, which has more to do with maneuvering in the physical environment than it has to do with the probing of universal life."

In short, the mind of God operates independently from the physical form. As Mrs. Prophet puts it, "Because the brain is not an adequate vessel for the mind of God . . . there is an arcing and a skipping over the brain into the very soul awareness, which is soul consciousness, into the very heart. And there is an instantaneous knowing based on an instantaneous Be-ness in the presence of God."[3] This is exactly the point where Master Morya would bring us.

To be sure, it's important to understand that the Gemini mind is not simply an abstraction, a nice-to-have spiritual treasure that's not really useful in real life. To the contrary. Developing the Gemini mind allows us to think as Morya thinks and do as Morya does. It's a necessity, a condition for fully integrating with the mercurial master and making ourselves useful to him. No one says it better than Morya himself in this dictation where he speaks about the process of the chela or disciple bonding to his own diamond heart:

> Blessed hearts, the bonding process is a sealing much the way there is a vulcanization in the processing of rubber. Blessed hearts, that sealing is that bonding. Therefore to achieve it you must understand the Path and its consequences. . . .
>
> You do not have to walk the earth in the sense of being a karma-being, a person burdened and limited. Shout the fiats! Internalize the light! And let this celebration of another birthday be a celebration of many candles lit around the world who have said, "This is the end of it! I will have no more to do with my human creation!

I will *stomp* on it! I will *drive it* out! I will not be off guard. I will not catch myself in those valleys of derision whereby my own God is derided as I dally in the nonsense of self-pity and indulgence."

Can't you feel in these words the master's fierce determination to help us become what he himself already is? Morya's love for our souls is so great that he finds it difficult to wait for the hour of our victory. It's hard for him to see us struggle endlessly against the dictates of our higher nature and simply take so very long to cast off our finite beliefs about who we really are. He urges us to make haste:

> Blessed ones, you must reassess your leap! You can leap much farther than you think. But you truly allow yourself to remain in such limited states that, I must say, my patience does run out. And I become impatient! And then I simply quit the place where you are, for I cannot wait another moment. For life calls me everywhere upon this planet and I must be there.
>
> And I am where the piercing of the Gemini mind may reach the very heart of the mind of the chela, where quick as a flash of light you catch my thought and then you do not dally in implementing it but you *know* it is my thought, for you *know* my vibration. You do it. You act upon it. And you know what is the process of receiving divine direction from your Guru heart to heart and mind to mind.

All it takes to learn to receive the sendings from his heart, says Morya, is to make ourselves receptive to his word in body, soul and mind.

> You must have the opening. The *ears* must be opened! The *pores* must be opened! The *chakras* must be opened! And you must have a listening *heart!* You must have a

listening *mind!* You must have space where I can speak to you and you can recognize my ray as distinct from the babble of all of the . . . astral voices that promise you this and that and easier paths and easy rewards.[4]

Clearly, El Morya is calling his students to come up higher than where he finds them in the highways and byways of life.

In this second volume of dictations by the incomparable master from Mercury, you'll delve deeply into his profound thoughts on the mind of God that he himself has made his own. May his words inspire you to pursue the Gemini mind and the divine wisdom whereof he speaks!

Carla Groenewegen
Summit University Director

CHAPTER 1

The Presence is ever at hand.
The Presence is over you with its bright and
shining radiance at all hours of the day and night.

THE PERFECTION IN YOUR HEART IS GOD

I am come this morning carrying the radiation of the Brothers of the Diamond Heart and all who love goodwill. You have heard it said, the will of God is good. You have believed in your minds that the will of God is good. But our chelas have not always acted in their feeling worlds or acted even in the outer activity of their being with the perfection which they have spoken of and which they have adored. And for this reason I come to you this morning, beloved ones, to call to your attention the fact that the Great Law was given to you in order that you might march forward with it into perfection. The Law was not given to you merely as a document to examine and be idly curious about. The Law was not given to you in order to give you some particular specific good feeling, although it is true that the Law ought to do so if it be obeyed. The Law was given to you in order to give you your eternal freedom. And the Law is the Law of God written within your own heart.

When you outpicture the will of God in everyday living, you are manifesting the perfection of God and you are pleasing the ascended masters and those who love the purposes of the Father. Beloved ones, when you do not outpicture the perfection of the eternal spheres but you yield to the impulses of shadowed substance and all of the forces of negativism which are rampant upon earth, you are only hindering the manifestation of the beautiful, eternal plan, which is now waiting to be revealed to all mankind.

ADORE THE PERFECTION OF YOUR PRESENCE

Beloved ones, the so-called mystery of being is no mystery to us. We who see directly into the face of our own mighty I AM Presence—we who commune daily because we have become one with it, with the Presence of Life—find no mystery there except the infinite mysteries of God, which are revealed by an orderly, progressive method even to the saints and ascended beings. But there is no mystery to our actual coming forth, for we know the face of the Father and we ever behold the face of his good and pure will.

Beloved ones, I cannot censure those among you whose hearts are so pure that you have continually and faithfully adored your Presence daily for many years. Nor can I censure those who are in ignorance, nor would I censure anyone; but I would speak out in order to inspire you to change the future where the outer has not outpictured the perfection that is within your heart. The perfection that is within your heart is God. The goodness of God must be reckoned with as the most vital force in your lives. And yet, beloved ones, many people pay far more attention to outer conditions than they do to the importance of adoring the perfection of their Presence.

THE PRESENCE IS EVER AT HAND

I am most grateful to see you here this morning, for after the outpouring at Easter I expected that the students would find a tremendous magnet to draw them to these meetings and that they would realize that these meetings are not held merely to give you a pacification or to pacify the outer selves. They are held, beloved ones, in order to give us a focus and a platform where we can pour out our radiation to you and through you into the world of form and out into this city and to bless all mankind with a great spiritual love of God, the will of God, the power of the sacred fire and every good blessing which the Law will permit you to receive.

The Presence is ever at hand. The Presence is over you with its bright and shining radiance at all hours of the day and night. But, beloved ones, regardless of the fact that the great magnificent Presence of Life stands over you, I still find that some of the students wake up during the night and have a sense of oppression or depression or doubt or fear. Beloved ones, you must stop to realize that this is as though there were a cloud before the face of the Sun of your Presence.

You must realize that the Presence with its light is ever shining behind that cloud of maya and shadow and darkness and oppression. And you must dissipate that by calling to Archangel Michael and to those of our octave to blaze our tangible power—the sword of blue flame, the power of the sacred fire—through that cloud and to dissipate it. You must take dominion over your worlds! You must learn to exercise the authority which you have been given by God and realize that only by exercising that authority shall you arise as sons of God and daughters of the light and of the sacred fire to your rightful estate, where you have a knowledge of all mysteries.

AN EVER-PRESENT COSMIC DRAMA OF EXISTENCE

There is nothing then curious, there is nothing then hidden, there is nothing then secret pertaining to the average mysteries of the kingdom of God that you will not know. You will know, beloved ones, all that the Great Law requires you to know in order to make your ascension. Now, this is a specific and important point. It is absolutely impossible for anyone upon this planet before they have made their ascension to have all knowledge. Even we, beloved ones, in our octave of eternal perfection do not know all that the Father has in store, for he chooses to unveil and to reveal continually new and transcendent mysteries to the ascended masters. And therefore, there is no ultimate anywhere in the universe.

But, beloved ones, you must remember that the requirement of the Law is that you know all that is necessary in order for you to make your ascension. And therefore, when you call to your omnipresent, omniscient Presence of Life, you must realize that it has the power to give you exactly the portion of its perfection of knowing that is required to set you free. And it is not necessary for the universe to give you one iota more of its energy than that which will set you free, for once you are free to rise untrammeled and unfettered into the octaves of light you can find for yourselves how to unlock every doorway of secret knowledge that you may require because of the need to unfold and expand your own specific service to life from the higher octaves.

O beloved ones, so many have had the feeling that after they passed on into the higher octaves that life would then automatically carry forward and that there would no longer be any need for them to render any specific service. Well, let them think again, beloved ones. For we have ascended long ago and we are still rendering a service to the light and, by the grace of Almighty God, we expect to continue to do so forever. For this universe is flooded—literally flooded—with planets and stars and systems of worlds and great galaxies, and the plans of the Father are from everlasting unto everlasting. And therefore, we believe and know that the infinite light of God will unfold before our spiritually opened eyes an ever-present cosmic drama of existence that shall go on through the eternal cycles forever and forever.

And we, therefore, have no fear of an end or a suddenness coming where we will cease to be, for we ever perceive a transcendent and unveiled, all-knowing perfection from the mind of God. And you too, right now while you are unascended, if you will, can enter into that and throw off the fetters of existence, the fetters that have kept you bound far too long.

RISE IN THOUGHT
AND FEEL YOURSELF ASCENDING

And you can ascend into your perfection in thought even before you have ascended into your perfection by actually raising the physical body until the atoms thereof become atoms of pure light—weightless, deathless, celestial, immortal, the cosmic fire soaring through your being. And therefore, you will be able to rise in thought prior to that time and you will assist your ascension by so doing.

Beloved ones, how would you like to try, for many weeks ahead, the ceremony of thinking of yourselves each morning when you rise from your beds as though you were going to make your ascension and then, facing the rising sun, feel yourselves as the Christ upon the mountain making your ascension[1] into light? How would you like to try this exercise, beloved ones? Feel your bodies ascending. Try to envision what your thoughts might be and how you would feel if you were ascending into the immortal perfection of God.

Then, beloved ones, after you find that you have not made your ascension and you are still anchored to the earth, you may go forth and face your problems with somewhat the spirit of a dragon slayer. And you will be able to slay those dragons of existence which have plagued you far too long because you will have a sense of what shall come to you and the great perfection that is going to be showered upon you by Almighty God, who, in all love, created each child of light in order to give him the exaltation of his ascension in light that every atom of his body, every precious cell of light might be so flooded with the effulgent, transcendent radiance of God that it will shine like the sun. And each atom then might be raised up and the whole ascend in perfect light as the Christ did, to be received out of human sight into the realms invisible, into the octaves of light,[2] to come from that invisible realm at will, to manifest—as Saint Germain and the great ascended masters did and do—to mankind and to bless them, to heal them, to raise this civilization to a pinnacle of great achievement.

Beloved ones, all this can be, for it is the will of God for you. It is good! And it is real and pure and true and can be known. It can be achieved. It can be entered into. It is within your reach. It is not a fruit that cannot be obtained, but it is one that can be obtained by you who hear my voice this morning and all who choose to accept the perfection of God, the voice of many waters,[3] which speaks to mankind and says to all, "Come, let all who are athirst come and drink of the water of Life freely."[4]

In the holy name of freedom, from the Darjeeling Council tables, I thank all of you. I bless you this morning with a sense of eternity, brought down into the realm of time, because you are beings of eternity, not ephemeral creations of time.

Thank you and good morning.

May 6, 1962
Theosophical Hall
Washington, D.C.
Mark L. Prophet (MLP)

CHAPTER 2

The hour is at hand when wisdom shall be treasured,
when the simplicity of wisdom shall be recognized
as the complexity of God.

FLY INTO THE HEART OF THE SUN

The mist upon the mountain clears.
The luminous orb of the golden sun
Stands forth to the eyes of the beholder.

I AM come to those who travel in weariness
To bring refreshment at the fount of goodwill,
To bring awareness
To those whose yearnings and strivings are valiant
Of the facts that heaven has not forsaken mankind
As they relentlessly journey
Across the trackless desert sands.

The plane of being, the plane of reason,
The plane of *no* achievement
Must be considered in the light of attainment.
The mountains ahead are challenges.

Let men deride the power of Truth;
It is as a gnat passing through the air.
Let men pursue a game of chess;

The hand of God is the trump.
Let men in vain labor;
The Most High God shall laugh as the waves
Shall lap over their castles of sand
And lap them up.
They shall be dissipated, and nothing shall remain
But a smoothening upon the beach
And hollow places in the sand
Where the sitters scan the sky with a vain sense.

The hour has come when virtue and loveliness
And the essence of the rose must be treasured.
Those who, as scorpions, carry stings must beware,
Lest the lion walking the street shall devour them
And they shall be no more than a meal
For the wild beasts.
The hour has come when the throne of Christ
Must be established in every heart.

Let those who will pursue
The vanity of delusion do so!
So much hauteur, so much pride, so much vanity
Shall bring them speedier to judgment.
They shall find that the ways to our abode are cut off
When they seek to pursue the ways of the spoiler
And prefer them to the path of Truth.
They shall knock and the door shall be closed.
They shall call and no answer shall come!
They shall strive and it shall be in vain.

Let those who realize and recognize
The unguents of life as necessary for healing
Apply them before the wound has destroyed the flesh
And the canker has gnawed the very vitals.

We say to all today:
The enigmas that have puzzled mankind's minds
Cannot be solved in the simple ways of the earth
But can be solved in the simple ways of the heart.
For the earth is the earth
And the heart is the heart.
And the heart is within the earth.
And yet the fire of life blazes forth
In the center thereof,
And the center thereof contains this fire
Which shall not be extinguished—nay!
For upon Zion shall the light descend.
And the light shall expand!
And all nations shall behold
The Shekhinah glory of the Lord.
The power of the first ray is abroad in the land.
And it carries order, as heaven's first law,
In its vibratory action.

Let men beware of simplicity
When that simplicity is vanity.
Let them beware of complexity
When that complexity is vanity.
Let them learn to strive to escape from the cage,
From the hand of the spoiler, and from the vain.
Let them fly into the heart of the sun!
They shall not singe their wings—
If those wings be infused
With the asbestos power of the Spirit.

I say, then, in this age
When you wait for some word from on high,
When your hearts hunger and thirst after righteousness,
Know that the power of truth

Is ever around you and within you.
You, by the straining of recognition,
Shall come to an awareness of God.
You shall cast aside the old mantles.
They shall be consumed by the flame!
From your memory they shall vanish.
And all that is light and the will of God
Shall replace them.

The hour is at hand when wisdom shall be treasured,
When the simplicity of wisdom shall be recognized
As the complexity of God,
When men shall see their dreams coming forth
As reality suddenly appearing.
For their dreams shall be dreams of light,
Spun from the radiance of the sacred fire
And purposed according to the plan.
Then will all things come to purity,
For the plans of men are often not the plans of God.

We stand now in Darjeeling
Awaiting the coming of the archer.
We wait now the coming of the perfect bowmen
Who, in their bending and their suppleness,
Shall see clearly the eye and the mark
And shall cast forth the arrow as unto perfection.
We await the strivings of the spirit.
We await the purifying of the vessels.
We await the evaluation of the treasure.

We say unto all:
Pursue truth.
Let it escape you not.

Peace and blessings
From the fire on the mountain.
The day is to the swift and the strong.

Let all then cast off their burdens.
Let all become pursuers.
Let all become esteemers.
Let men cherish righteousness.
Let them eschew evil.
Let vanity be abandoned.
Let the old carcasses rot upon the desert.
Let the bones bleach.
And let men perceive that which hath value.

Then shall the essence of the Spirit
Stand arrayed in form.
And from the veil, the spiral shall come forth.
And lo! the master appeareth as in the air,
And all is well.

For he who beholdeth
Shall also behold within himself,
And it shall come to pass
That the outer spell of vanity shall be broken
Because the way to the temple shall be known.

Thank you and good morning.

January 17, 1965
Dodge House
Washington, D.C.
MLP

CHAPTER 3

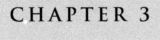

*The orbits of the earth, each one, are intended
to be the markings of cyclic accomplishment,
and each turn of the planet upon its axis
is intended to be the turning of the wheel of life
one step nearer the manifestation of perfection.*

CHAPTER 3

THE JAR OF FREEDOM

As the chant of the *Yasna*[1] rings in the ears of their devotees, so there comes to my mind visions of the sacred fire angels chanting the holy Om to the will of God.

I greet you this day from Darjeeling, flooded with love for the first ray and for the thrust for a worthy purpose that has been manifest among you. Calumny and vilification of the divine ideal can never permanently retain any vestige of ill effects when the divine image is raised on high as an icon of light. Light shall rise above darkness and pervade all. Light shall strengthen the bonds of brotherhood. Light shall perceive light from afar, and union and strength and God's will shall be enhanced.

Visions of loveliness and of perception have flooded the minds of the saints. What of those who would be saints but are bereft of the necessary application? We come this day to once again call to your attention the need for diligence in application. For without application, the best saints would not rise, and their garments would be weights and would pull them down through the flow of gravity and the attraction of descent from lofty purpose.

We envision, then, this day a cutting off of the lines that are attached to the weights of the world's thought. We advocate freedom from despair. We advocate freedom from self-purposes that have not become divine, from ideas that are nonillumination; and thus, because they are nonillumination, they are no ideas at all, but they are the concepts of mortality which have not produced in all generations one ounce of freedom.

Peace, blessed ones. The will of God is intense but sheer love when understood. The will of God is defense against all that would impute to thee those actions which are not the supreme purposes made manifest through thy form and thought. Thy thought does indeed affect thy form, and thy form can also affect thy thought. For the convergence of influences is often little understood, and the source of infections is little recognized by those who are thwarted in their every lofty pursuit by the vanities of mortal delusion, which they cling to as though they were passports into the highest realms.

INATTENTION TO GOD'S HOLY PLAN

When will mankind learn to recognize the savage infiltration that they submit to within their own mind, thinking it is reality, when we know full well that the purity of God would deliver them from the subtle and at times obvious, yet always crass interferences with the holy plan?

The holy plan has suffered as the result of man's inattention. The holy plan has suffered as a result of man's defection and of those purposes which are so far beneath the dignity of the Divine as to be nonexistent in our realm. They have no existence whatsoever to us; yet we speak of them because, though they be gnats and flies which infest the lower domain, they seem to concern those who insist upon being different than the ascended host, perhaps only for the sake of being different. They therefore suffer all the results of their defections from reality and complain withal, more so than all others. Yet these have had opportunity after opportunity and have let the opportunities pass without recognition of the great strength that comes from the summoning of the holy will to divine order, to the acceptance of the supreme call.

Now then, I am apprised of all that men are wont to do, and I recognize how that today in the world of form there are movements afoot that distort the wondrous blessings of Christianity throughout the world and would rob mankind of that birthright through an action of a few men of the cloth who desire to alter the structure in a very base way, in order that they might be thought wise as interpreters of the holy plan. These men of the cloth have actually submitted to the infiltration of jazz music within the sanctuary. They have permitted to come into Holy Church those vibratory actions of mortal destructivity and dissonance which stem from the very dissolute activities of witchcraft centered in Louisiana and in New Orleans.

I therefore call to your attention that hierarchy are determined to let them carry forth in this manner until, by the waves of contradistinction, mankind will see the contrast and will thus desire to free themselves from such false shepherds who, in the name of earthly wisdom and position or title, will somehow or other seek to impose upon mankind a further weight of destructivity. Rest assured they shall not prevail. Nevertheless, some have paid them heed and they have persisted in their own realm in continuing an action which has not brought them nigh the body of Christ but has brought them nigh the corpse of mortal delusion, which will always strew forth the ravages of death and decay where resurrection and righteousness and life ought to be honored.

IMPORTANCE OF COSMIC HONOR

Now, gracious ones, having given you some admonishments, I come also to carry and to bear from Darjeeling a holy prayer of influence for all of you that have come under my tutelage now for many a year in this area. I come that you might sense Morya's love for all that you have done for the protection of America and for the bringing about of those cosmic miracles of ascended master love that have gone forth from our bourn into the realm of earth's domain to refresh the weary traveler.

We come, then, this day bearing the flame of the divine will. We come to convey. We come to strengthen. We come to bring you the succor of heaven and to assert it for all time to come. Your nation is our nation. For out of this great calling, the calling of America, has come a fountain of freedom to the world. The pageant of all nations is manifestly blessed by all that liberty which has been cradled among you.

The past may be prologue, but the future is yours to carve. And therefore, as we come to you this day, we say: Be mindful of the pages of the future. Revel not in past delusion. Be not steeped in that or in delusion. Shun and avoid earthly confusion and the substance that has dried up the bones. Recognize that the life force of Almighty God that beats your heart is to give you freedom now. But you must seize it! You must seize every opportunity, and you must recognize the strength of honor.

There are those today who have no honor and are unaware of it. There are those today who have honor and are aware of it. And there are those who have no honor and are aware of it. Let all beware of a condition of being without honor. The thoughtform for the year, released to you by the Lord of the World and ensconced and raised above you, is the holy vision of "Peace with Honor."[2]

The great master of Luxor, beloved Serapis Bey, warned of the destructive activities directed at America. We come today and now—before winter solstice, before Christmas, before the coming of the full flood tide of the angels that at this season gladden the hearts of men—to say unto you that you must, if you are to retain your freedom in this great nation, pay greater heed to the ascended masters and to the Great Law of life manifesting from our octave as cosmic honor.

When men hold a vision of honor, they are as knights of old summoned round our board. They will heed the words, then, of this old bard, and they will know that every ounce of energy dispensed to you and retained within the precious bottle of concentrated self is yours to command for good. When wasted or poured upon the earth in pursuit of vanity and without holy purpose, it becomes a millstone round about thy neck, for each ounce must be redeemed. I think the stones at Stonehenge themselves are small by comparison to the weights that some have placed round about their neck through human discord directed at those little ones of God who place themselves wholly within his loving care.[3]

HOLD THE IMMACULATE CONCEPT OF THE ASCENDED MASTERS

I should not wish, were I embodied among you, to be guilty of the responsibility of having wrought a work of condemnation of any part of life. Therefore, I wish to clear the air for all of you and all connected with this activity concerning the statement that the ascended masters have condemned. Our actions are for the purposes of breaking up mortal crystallization and our words are designed to blast you loose from those positions of lethargy which would be your downfall, that you may become acclimatized to the atmosphere nigh the portals of heaven.

In the name of all creation, I say to every one of you, do you think for one moment that heaven is like earth in its present state? Are you so deluded as to conceive for a moment that discord exists in our octave? It does not! And therefore, whether Saint Germain or Mother Mary or the Great Divine Director or one of the archangels speak to you, it makes no difference. We are not in argument or discord with one another. We do not hotly seek to pursue some status among you whereby one of you will say, "Oh, Morya is coming again with all his pomposity!"

I tell you, precious ones, and I tell you truly, that among the student body there have been individuals who have actually attributed to us those qualities of mortal mien. Therefore it is most important and significant this day that I call to your attention that in your spiritual revels, you will recognize the need to hold the vision of the immaculate concept of the ascended masters. When we choose to practice any form of levity or sobriety, if we choose to adopt a mood with a thrust for a purpose, it is sometimes perhaps a bit entertaining but it is not intended to drain you of energy or to cause you to criticize us. For to do so would be folly indeed.

Our entire life's energy now spent is being renewed momentarily by the power of God in a thrust for a purpose in his service. How, then, gracious ones, can you even imagine that we, who have given our all, would be denied our all? All that we have given is now ours forever. For although we have given it away, it has been renewed as a fountain of immeasurable strength, a great pillar that comes against the earth and pushes the earth in its round through space into the arms of God.

The orbits of the earth, each one, are intended to be the markings of cyclic accomplishment, and each turn of the planet upon its axis is intended to be the turning of the wheel of life one step nearer the manifestation of perfection. The carnal mind in its intense spirit of delusion is always ready to impute, even to the ascended masters, human qualities, as though we ourselves would actually function now in the ascended state as we once did before our ascension. But I wish to deny that we functioned in a human way before our ascension. For in those immediate years before our ascension and even in embodiments preceding that, most of us were well upon the trail of light and were seeking with all of our heart to bring forth the very perfection of Almighty God into outer manifestation.

Do you know, precious ones, that an individual once proclaimed in our name that we were temperamental; and there went forth a proclamation in the name of Kuthumi to the effect that he was concerned because he was not invited to sit at a seat placed for other ascended masters in a certain home.

I would like to call to your attention that to impute to the ascended masters qualities of imperfection is the same act that men of little faith have imputed unto God. They have imputed unto God human qualities throughout the centuries and have felt that with a flash of lightning and the roar of thunder, with the quaking of the earth, the wrath of God was manifest.

They have not understood that their own energy flowing forth, qualified with human discord, entered into elemental life and was retained there as the cause of great suffering to the elementals—as a groaning that could scarcely be uttered, retained unto the uttermost limits of cosmic mercy, and then released at last as the only means of saving the planet from utter destruction.

When mankind understand the cause of calamity, when they understand the causes behind the actions, they will no longer condemn heaven. They will recognize the responsibility is solely affixed upon themselves, upon their errors of thought, and upon the concepts that have been fostered upon them by a recalcitrant priesthood, by high priests of darkness, and by residual forces of negation which remained untransmuted upon the planet in some darkened corner or recess of time or space.

BARRIERS TO THE CAUSE OF GOODWILL ON EARTH

And now, gracious ones, as I gaze upon the minarets here at Darjeeling, as I see the gleaming white marble so unlike and yet like the Taj Mahal, as I see our art treasures resplendent in hope of the will of God, how I would share with you some glimpse of all that herein remains as a monumental achievement to the Temple of Good Will. How I would share with you the soft carpets of our retreat. How I would share with you the musical tinkle of our fountain. How I would share with you the pleasant hours by the fireside, contemplating the immortal purpose.

How I would share with you myself and all that God has wrought through me. How I would share with you the love of the shining faces round about our council table. How I would share with you the deliberations of our council. How I would share with you the communion of saints and the communion with heaven. How I would share with you the mighty pillar of goodwill, the great blue flame that pulsates upon our altar. How I would share with you every gift of goodwill, this season and eternally.

Yet there exists a barrier which must be broken down by each one. We have sent forth the invitation. Men have thought to respond and have not. They have held themselves back in fear of loss. They have been interested in progress without willingness to do the necessary. They have fostered a spirit of doubt within themselves and nourished it at times when they needed just a spark more of faith to turn the balances. They have seen iniquity where love existed, and they have fancied acts of love existed where iniquitous purposes have manifested. They have not always correctly judged or understood our purposes.

And therefore, in spite of all that we have done and regardless of all that we have said, mankind have not made the desired progress—either in the eyes of self or the eyes of God. And the Lord who liveth and seeth all confirmeth this thusly to you today, that you may know that in the days ahead you must secure a greater domain within the realm of God's holy will for yourselves by the wedding of self to the great cosmic purpose, by the dedicating of self to understanding, by gracious acknowledgment of our mercy.

And you know, precious ones, it is a great pity that we must often concern ourselves with those who are moths, when the valiant ones press so close within the flame with the shining armor that penetrates the flame. Yet we must sometimes do so, for there are those who do not hesitate to come into our realm without the realization of the strength of our octave, without the understanding of their own strength or lack thereof, and without the necessary application.

We do not, precious ones, in many cases deny them opportunity. We unfortunately are not able to convince them of our reality or sincerity so that they can also be convinced of their own reality and sincerity and thus, by reason of the cosmic yoke, find it within themselves to live and to do as God intends without fear and without doubt. For it is doubt, precious ones, that creates a closing door in the face of everyone to whom we would bring our message of goodwill. And it is doubt in the eternal purposes or rewards that causes mankind to desire to hold the hand of the finite self lest some temporal pleasure escape them.

Pitiful creatures of the dark! Must they wander forever in the realm of shadow? Can they conceive that all that life has wrought is for destruction? Can they conceive that all that life has wrought is for man's downfall? Can they not perceive the hands of infinite love that encompass them all round about? What more must God do? He is as a magician. Having produced a bag of tricks and the full complement thereof, he is asked to exceed himself. And yet, in this great activity of cosmic diathermy, mankind find it within themselves to question God's activity that would heal them, purify them, and change them.

Why is this so? They are as waders at the beach. They go to their ankles and then see a wave a thousand feet away and run for the shore. They flee when none pursue; and they desire safety and shall lose it. For unless they are willing to plunge into the deep of Almighty God, they can never know the love of his Sonship, the love of his oneness, the love of his compassion—not in all eternity. So all that we would share with you is prevented by human barriers from coming forth into manifestation.

One by one we have removed barriers from the expansion of this activity. And this, too, should be an act of faith that you have all seen. And you ought to rejoice, one and all, at that which has been done and continue to make your thrust for a purpose, continue to serve the cause, the First Cause of goodwill on earth unto men.

Precious ones, we do not need you, from the standpoint of self-sufficiency. We are self-sufficient in the ascended state without you. God needs you in order to spread the message of goodwill and to create matrices of assistance to unascended mankind who have not yet come to an understanding of freedom and the need to pursue it.

SHUN INFILTRATION OF UNHOLY ENERGIES

The hound of heaven, then, pursues mankind through you, and the karmic pattern unfolding upon earth with all of its activity of calamity does, at times, shake the foundations of mankind's faith until they become more pliant, more willing to yield, desiring more to unravel the mysteries of life, and thus able to come up a step higher. They are not always content to part with their delusions, however. For with the rise upon the stairs, they still hold on to the railing below and seem to feel that if they do not, they might have unhappiness as a result.

I wish to speak this simply, precious ones, because the simplicity is born of need. Complex ideas and statements couched in the greatest words, which we have often used—words of superior rhetoric—are not always understood. One of the chelas here made the comment to this messenger in the past that I had often spoken in almost the Zen style through Nicholas Roerich. I have spoken thusly also through this messenger. I find it necessary to adopt many styles—in imitation, perhaps, of the many styles of my auditors and in order that I may reach through and break up the crystallized patterns of human thought.

You have a saying upon earth, "The end justifies the means"— and it cannot be used by you, for to do so is destructive. But in our octave, the end justifies the means indeed, for all that we would do is benign. We, having clean escaped from among you, cannot become entangled again by your activity. And therefore, all that we do is for your admonishment and protection. It is an activity of love, as God himself was wont to do. And you, precious ones, if you wish to thrust an anchor within the veil, will recognize that you can act from that motiveless state where the one motive is all that is and thus perform for your fellowmen those acts of cosmic virtue which will help to set them free from every form of mortal bondage, because it is an activity motivated not by the expectation of gain but by the blessed release of freedom's flame into their world and into the world to return men back to the heart of God.

There is some great blessing in being motiveless insofar as human thought goes. For, oh, what a motivated generation this is. And if I could curl my lip, I would do so today with absolute scorn at this generation! They do not even wish to open their mouth and say "Good morning" without the expectation of some form of salutation that will flatter themselves. And the light of God shining from a thousand hills gives them the hope of God to pass on as the bread from heaven! And our bread is the Sacred Eucharist! It unites God and man as one! And you cannot unite darkness and light; therefore you must transmute the darkness in men and in yourselves and bring yourselves, come full circle, to his domain.

You cannot thwart the cosmic purposes by the actions of mortal thought and feeling above, but you can certainly delay it here below as you have done. There is only one way to avoid it in the future, and that is to shun the sinister infiltration of those energies which you know, as you receive them, are unholy. When you receive unholy energies in thought and feeling, you *know* that they are unholy! And yet you do it! You do not reject it!

Perfect it, then. Understand it. Be wise.
Mount as eagles through the sky,
Blazing symmetry of shining star—
The oneness of God that comes from afar,

Calling to you, "Awake and view
The supreme way of life for the very few!"
I would enfold the many now
And see them take the first-ray vow:
To do thy will, O God, I come
Out from the blazing Central Sun.
Magnificent in purity,
I AM the bond to keep the free
Forever one with God's own might
To hold the victory for the right.

Secure I AM in God domain,
Forever free from mortal stain.
My victory's won by God's own will—
I'll hold that torch upon the hill.
I'll let it fall nevermore!
I AM the light to even the score
And see that for the good He's done,
Our God is honored in the Son.

I AM God's will, the dawn of right!
I AM God's will, the strength of might!
I AM God's will that frees you all.
I honor Him. To you, I call:
O come and let us mold anew
A cosmic pathway for the few
And widen then the highway bold
That many may come and accept his mold—
The Christ of God, the Mighty One,
The blazing armor of the Son,
The shining strength to make us all
His chosen people now and forever.

Come, then, to Eden's portal
And see the Tree of Life!

Eat its fruit,
Hold to its root.
Are you a green shoot?
I hope so.

'Tis Christmas soon. What adventure is in the concept centered
round this ideal?

Like a great wheel the cycles turn
And first-ray energy in me burns!
I'll penetrate that shroud you wear—
Just keep on coming right where I AM
And you will know that Morya knows
To strike a blow for God
And freedom to the earth!

God has spoken in the silent spaces
Where I speak not,
For he is interested in freeing
This generation from every blot.
For not one jot or tittle
Of the world's delusion shall pass
Until they have made right
All this confusion en masse.
And if you think, perhaps, that I drink
Of some mortal delusion myself,
Keep looking at that which comes forth
Into manifestation in the coming days,
And see if you will not feel like changing your ways.
I hope you will and think you will,
But, then, of human life I've had my fill
In bygone days and sometimes said,
"Perhaps the hand of God should snuff it all,
As a candle out, and start anew."

You know, precious ones, in a dull moment of poetry in a past embodiment, I once said, "They drag their snout." I think they do, and I think 'tis time to end it. You may not think my message appropriate for the Christmas season in your mortal ways, but if you could see the jar I desire to create for your freedom in higher ways, you would extend hands of gratitude to me—and I would give them all to thee, O God! For this generation deserves to be free.

I have made a thrust for a purpose.
This entire activity here,
Centered round about our government dear—
O America, Saint Germain's prize,
Must go on into the skies
And rise and rise and rise
Until its children, cultures, all
Become the radiant splendor for which we call.
It must, it shall, it will be done.
It is his will for each one.
And ye are few that hear me now,
But all the earth shall one day vow
To God to serve the ray I do.
For ere they find their freedom's hue,
They must bow the knee to Christ above
And serve the cause of holy love.

This is the patience of the centuries, stretching cross the barren sands, measured oasis by oasis, until at that wonderful conjunction of life, the framed Holy Mother, blest by archangels and angels alike, heralded by shepherds and lovingly honored through the centuries, becomes nigh unto the door of every man and every woman and every mother's son upon the planet. You cannot exclude any.

Thank you, and may your sandals become winged sandals of light as you put off mortal dross. And then you shall walk upon my carpet here at Darjeeling and not a stain will you leave. For you, too, as we do, shall hold these thoughts of freedom for all.

Thank you. Good-bye, fond ones. From this place we have launched our wonderful activity of light into orbit. And now we go to prepare a place for you, that where I AM, there ye may be also.[4] This is God's will. Peace and blessings in the name of God, forever and forever and forever.

May I hold you dear to my heart here. Remember the Lord all of thy days.

I thank you and bid you a pleasant good afternoon.

December 12, 1965
Beacon's Head
Vienna, Virginia
MLP

CHAPTER 4

You are sharing the great beams of divine grace.
And as these fragments of God flow through your life
they will flush out therefrom all that is density
and shadow and you will become airy beings
that can kindle the great fires of fohat
in the world and the universe.

CHAPTER 4

THE GIFT OF DIVINE GRACE

As I survey the wondrous intent of God for his creation—the love-delight that he has dropped through nature upon mankind and the magnificent purity of his love whereby he is ever the Great Giver and seldom the receiver—I am amazed at the recalcitrance of mankind and at their disbelief in the grandeur of his concepts for themselves.

How quickly indeed do mankind accept the epitaph "sinner." How quickly indeed do they claim for themselves the worst status of being created by God and yet being determined to fall beneath the weight of the slightest mortal condemnation.

What *immortal* condemnation have mankind received? The only denunciation that man has received from God is simply that which is inherent within the beauty of himself. The very beauty of God and the beauty of nature, with the infinite power of his love and the expanse of his mind, is ever a repudiation of all that is inherent within the domain of puny mortality.

I say to you that mankind ought to be tired of their own caterwauling! I say to you today that they ought to seek to make a sweet home of light wherever they are. For right where they are, God is. And where God is, there abides the spirit of infinite harmony.

We know that there are any number of lame excuses that mankind frame, saying, "If this were so, *that* would be so." You need not exert yourself to permissiveness in that which you allow. If you will but understand that life is not dependent upon "this" and "that," then you will understand that it is dependent upon your acceptance of the grand design and upon your contentedness therein. For when mankind are discontented with the search for God, to whom shall they turn? As was spoken of old by the apostles, "To whom shall we go? Thou hast the words of eternal life."[1]

You must understand, then, gracious ones, that the framing of a "home sweet home," whether unascended or ascended, is an act of divine grace. And when life does not manifest for you below as it was intended to manifest, and when that which is Above does not seem to manifest below, it is time for a plea to God for more divine grace.

Grace is the gift of God, but it must be received by mankind and *acknowledged* by mankind as the dominant power of their life. So long as mankind are content with lesser images and so long as they are *dis*content with lesser images, in both cases there is a vacuum that often acts. This may seem a bit contradictory. But if you will ponder the enigma, I am sure you will understand that there are times when one case is true and there are times when the other applies.

You must understand, gracious ones, that the powers of light that have often shaken mankind have done so in order to relieve them of the density of their own imponderability. You must understand that mankind are often heavy and weighed down with thoughts of their many difficulties whilst the Most High is waiting, by the wind of the Holy Spirit, to disperse those thoughts, one and all, and to say to that speck of dust that is misqualified energy: "Never shalt thou be anymore!"

For God will free this soul to stand clothed before him and to be anointed with the oil of rejoicing and compassion for the little self—that little self that is often wedded to conditions that are so determinate in bringing about a condition of unhappiness, whereas God, in his infinite love and capacity to love, is ever the great bestower of grace upon all life according to man's capacity and desire to receive it.

It is almost amusing (if it were not so serious) to consider that there are men who fear to ask God for divine grace lest they lose the power to do their own stubborn will. They feel, in actuality and in the density of their own mortal reason, that their own way is best. And they question and doubt concerning a state of consciousness that they have never known in human form and that they seldom understand, even when they do know in part.

You must understand, dear ones, that I am referring here to the fact that mankind do not understand the heavenly life! They understand, in part, mortal life, and they pass through the shrouds of its density from time to time, appearing to have a moment of rejoicing upon the stream of time. But they are often surfeited with themselves and with others, and they are bored, precious ones, because experiences seem to move too slowly for their comprehension.

They await the coming of higher things with some mixture of feelings. There are times when they welcome it, when they are weary of the world and its bondage. But there are other times when they seem to be having a good time and are most anxious to avoid contact with the powers of Deity, seeming to feel that there is no real affinity between the higher powers and themselves.

They seem to fear contact with God, as if God would rob them of the illusions of life and of their petty enjoyments thereof. Let me tell you, precious ones, that this fear of having contact with God is such an evil statement for mankind to make concerning themselves. If they would only understand the need to unravel the mysteries of God, they would soon clearly see that the concepts of mankind are absolutely wrong and that they are steeped in pride and vanity, which can never give mankind their freedom.

Now, then, in this age of great enlightenment when the world seems to be so wise, why is it that such a struggle seems to ensue within the domain of individuality, within the domain of spiritual serving, and also within the realm of mortal affairs, where we are bringing to mankind the gift of their freedom? Why does conflict continue?

Precious ones, there are a multitude of reasons for the continuation of conflict, but none of them have any validity in the eyes of God, who is the master of harmony. Actually, the gift of freedom is a most magnificent and generous offering on the part of Almighty God, who has offered to convey to mankind, in the midst of all of their density and lack of gratitude, the precious gifts of life and opportunity.

Mankind are continually being granted new offerings from on high, while they do not often use the ones they have already received. And sometimes—unintentionally, of course, but nevertheless in fact—mankind do spurn the offerings of God and heaven. For that which is unused by mankind will indeed pass from the screen of their consciousness.

THE LAW OF ATTRACTION

When mankind are given a gift and do not appropriate it, there is no doubt that we are aware of the fact that herein is the neglect of the law of giving and receiving. It is often the result of a neglect that has occurred in the past that brings about a repetition of neglect in the future. And yet all such neglect, when accumulated, brings about a cutting off of divine grace.

Thus mankind find that they cannot receive and understand divine law simply because they have not made the necessary effort to do so in the past. This may seem for a moment to be unjust, but it is not, I assure you. Yet on the other hand, is it not clearly recorded that "For whosoever hath, to him shall be given, and he shall have more abundance; but whosoever hath not, from him shall be taken away even that he hath"?[2]

This is the law of attraction, precious ones. Those who have not, have other conditions—conditions of negation. They have attracted these conditions of negation to themselves, and thus the preponderance of their life is made up of negative impulses. The great lodestone of their being, then, consists of negation and thus they attract more of negation to themselves, for this is the sum substance of that which they consist.

Those who have divinity and grace, because there is a preponderance of divine grace in their world, are the recipients of more grace. For the lodestone or magnet of life is always that which is in excess or that which is in total manifestation.

You must understand, then, that in order to receive more of God, you must appropriate that which you have already been given. As you expand the gifts and graces of life, you will receive more and more of divine grace. And eventually, because of this preponderance of grace, negation will flee from your life and you will find that you will overcome the things that you have longed to overcome. This is simply because you have kept on keeping on and because you have been consistent and have acted with worthy purpose.

RESPOND TO WHAT IS REAL

Unfortunately, men and women do not realize what a small span a lifetime is in the great realms of infinity. By comparison it is but a dot—yea, a half a dot or a quarter dot—and in some cases it is but a speck. Yet I say to you, precious ones, that you must understand that the span of life is most gracious if appropriated correctly. And if you will qualify life with the right attitudes of divine grace and with a receptivity and willingness to serve, there is always a continuation of the outpouring of opportunity and grace.

Many of you who are here have responded again and again in the past to the ministrations of grace. But there have been moments when the sun of your being was eclipsed in your world, and in those moments of darkness and shadow certain shames have crept into your world and into your affairs.

You must understand the need, precious ones, to balance these shames, now and forthrightly. This is so that you may come to a state of concord with Almighty God and with the ascended masters, which precludes the possibility of you ultimately losing your ascension but [instead makes it possible for you to] receive it expeditiously. Simply put, this means, precious ones, that if you should fail to win your ascension today, then you will win it tomorrow—which is much better than in some dubious hereafter.

I think, then, that if you will pause to consider the effect of your own acts upon your own world, you will realize that almost all, if not all, of the vicissitudes of life that have come to you have resulted from your own accumulation of human scum.

Now, I recognize that the words "human scum" do not seem to be pretty words, but I am certain that they are most descriptive. And thus it may be vivifying to your mind to realize how it is that many of the things that mankind hold dear are in reality the offscouring of all things and all human activity whatsoever. And to us who have apprehended divine grace, the many things that mankind hold dear are seen as but a pittance in contrast to that divine grace and scarcely worthy of note.

Yet mankind are often affrighted by conditions in their own mind, and to them they hold reality and hold it as error. We ask you to hold reality as *actuality*, as that which *is*. "Reality," as perceived by mankind, is usually error because that which seems to be real unto them is not. Therefore actuality is seldom realized, for the veil does not go up before their eyes but remains as human density and error. This perpetuates the shrouds of darkness that enclose the human soul and cuts off the light of its own happiness and grace.

YOU WILL KNOW YOURSELVES AS DIVINE

We come, then, today, in order to alert you to these conditions—not to keep you in them, not to perpetuate these conditions, but to give you the mighty sword of life that will cut you free from all that binds you and that will bring you to a realization of infinite grace.

The brothers here at Darjeeling survey the world in many ways. They survey the world as God intends it, and they stand back with a gasp of praise and admiration that actually spans the realm of infinity. Their praise goes from the beginning to the ending of all cycles. But then they survey the world as man is living in it, and they turn away and avert their gaze and say to one another, "I can scarcely bear to look."

I can well understand this. For those of us who have sometimes and somewhat acted in the manner of a scavenger, helping mankind to release themselves from their own offscouring, we have often, even from the ascended state, had to engage in sessions of utilizing some of the great flames of freedom after we have come freshly from the realm of mortal affairs.

I tell you, you may have washed your hands because you felt they were dirty, but we have washed our hands knowing that they were clean, wondering if perhaps they could be soiled because of the debris in which we have found ourselves—debris [that surrounded us] as we sought to free mankind from conditions that we were scarcely aware of when we ourselves were embodied upon the planet.

You must understand, then, that we do have compassion for your situations, and I think a *total* compassion. Nevertheless, we would like you to have compassion for yourselves so that you will understand that none of these conditions are necessary.

I do not care what state of consciousness those in the world may view you from. I do not care how they may consider your life. If you consider your life as the manifestation of infinite perfection and you hold with that absolutely, I assure you that it will make a difference and that one of these days your eyes will open and you will know yourselves as Divine. You will understand that Eden— the paradise of God, the realities of God—is always present with you and has always been with you. You simply have allowed, as a great gulf, the shadows of mortal thought and feeling to stand between you and the Reality that has always been your True Self.

You must understand, then, that this is somewhat difficult for mankind to comprehend, for they do not understand the things that they cannot touch and handle with their hands and with their mortal senses. They prefer the forms of reasoning that are customary upon the planet, and they do not understand how it is that God transcends all reason and yet can be understood to a degree *by* reason. For he himself has said, "Come now, and let us reason together."[3]

So then, precious ones, there *is* a degree of comprehension of Almighty God and of the infinite laws of cosmos that can be received and entered into by mortal understanding. But it is limited in each lifestream, some possessing the capacity to go further than others, and therefore it is not reliable for those who search for infinite expressions.

Those who search for the Infinite must understand the need to shed finite reasoning, or at least to set it aside until the hand of God—the hand that composed all life in manifestation—is able to remove the scales from the eyes of men[4] and to let them see clearly, as God does. Then at that moment there is a lessening and even a thinning of the karmic veil, and men see the gleams of God's holiness penetrating through the mortal gloom.

GOD IS YOUR VICTORY

This is our desire: To chase the encircling gloom, to disperse the shadows and darkness, to make flee the ghosts of mankind's own self-created fantasy. All this is also our desire:

That the face of God may come forth by his power,
That the face of God may come forth this very hour,
That the face of God may strengthen all,
That the faith of God may answer calls made in faith to him,
That life be made free from sin and the concept thereof,
That mankind perceive the grace of him who loves them all
As expressing over all
So that love may be all
Even as it is in all.

Understand, then, gracious ones, that we do not care for mortal puns, nor do we care for mortal opinions, nor do we care what individuals may think of us. We know what we have received, and we know him in whom we have believed. Therefore when you are like us, you will find less concern in your mind for the world at large insofar as mortal opinion is concerned. Yet you will carefully execute your every act so as to cast no stone in your brother's pathway, nor stumbling block. But you will be ever willing to assist, in the right way, all those whom we love and even those who love us not.

For all mankind are destined by Almighty God to receive the best gifts of which they are capable of receiving, their own capacity being the limiting factor that prevents them from achieving understanding in this hour. Understand, then, that with the passing of time many will find, through view and review, that they can change their minds and that they too can accept the light that removes the blinders from their own vision.

You know, precious ones, that inherent within words are magnificent concepts. For even the word *vision* holds within it the magnificent concept of *v*ictory for the *i*ndividual *son* of God— *victory* + *son*—*v-i-s-o-n*—*vision*. You must understand, then, that God is your victory and that the beloved ascended master Mighty Victory chose the name "Victory" because of the great God-quality inherent within that name, and God himself appended the appellation to the very being of Mighty Victory.

All of these qualities—and they can be numbered and counted by man—are qualities of God. And all of these qualities can be bestowed upon anyone, upon any son who will receive them. Therefore, all mankind may proudly wear the appellation of "Victory" and all mankind may wear the appellation of "Freedom" if they will but externalize from the heart of God those qualities thereof.

How many individuals do you think have had "gold fever," precious ones, and have gone out into the world in search of material gold? I tell you, if they were to develop one-tenth of the enthusiasm that they have for the pursuit of mortal riches by pursuing the treasures of heaven, they would manifest ten times as much benefit.

LET GO OF SELF-CONDEMNATION

Do you understand how the Law works—the law of your being?

I think you understand this in part. But there are many parts of your own selves that are not clear unto yourselves. Therefore the search must be continued. But how strange it is that those who are steeped in the dye of intellectualism are often quick to state that they have apprehended all things, whereas those who are less wise in mortal ways are often able to understand by faith that which the minds of men cannot comprehend by the power of intellect.

We urge, therefore, that all despise no gift or grace of mortal opportunity, nor honor of person or place, but that all understand that the divine ideal is to let go of all mortal thoughts that have caused men and even angels to cringe. Let all understand that the divine ideal is to heal by the balm of infinite love the great schism that divides men from one another and from God—understanding, then, the need to let go of all of the awful seeds, of weeds, of contemplation of mortal deeds.

Now then, what do I mean by this? Let us examine it a little more clearly. Let us take the number of activities there are in the world. Multiply these activities by the number of people in the world, and imagine the weight—the preponderous and ponderous weight that is actually resting upon the consciousness of mankind as human evil deeds. A review and view of these activities [show us that these] will never give mankind their freedom.

Precious ones, the weight of condemnation upon any will never give mankind their freedom. You can condemn the world or you can condemn your fellowman who is close to you in proximity, and neither act will result in your freedom. The Son of God came not into the world to condemn the world but to save the world![5]

If you, then, are indeed a son of God, you are not here to condemn the world itself but you are here to save the world. In some cases, precious ones, this requires a lifestream to point out to those in the world at large the weight of self-condemnation that they have imposed upon themselves!

This does not mean that a son of God must be perceived as an angel of light, as one who never speaks a word whatsoever that seems to be corrective. This does not mean that at all. Precious ones, it means the alerting of mankind when necessary to their own inherent weaknesses. But it must be done in a good and proper manner so that the souls of mankind may understand that there is no *divine* condemnation of the soul of man in the act, nor even any human or personal condemnation, but only a pointing out to the individuals that the acts that they do are condemnatory in themselves and therefore are not a part of the life pattern but of the death pattern, which cannot inherit eternal life.

When mankind understand this, they will be more willing, you see, to understand God's laws. For they will perceive that God is not in any way interested in punitive action so much as he is interested in the mending of flaws so that his laws are upheld because they are just and righteous and true. When this is understood by mankind and accepted throughout all areas of their consciousness and life, it is as marvelous as a regenerative tonic that causes mankind to just let go of that condemnation.

To let go of all of the weight of the condemnation of the world is a magnificent thing. But unless you let go of the condemnatory acts and attitudes that you hold toward yourself, you will definitely find that you will continue to attract to yourselves those qualities of negation that you have in the past condemned in others.

You must therefore enter into a total catharsis so that the Darjeeling Council may stand back and applaud your acts. For we will. We will applaud your acts when we see that you are not condemning any part of life. And then, if you will remember the simple little song used so often in Sunday schools throughout the land and in songs even by children, "Brighten the Corner Where You Are,"[6] you will understand that as a son of God you have a need to shine. This is not the shining of intellectual brilliance nor even the shining of personal arrogance. It is not even the shine of do and derring,* but it is the shine of heaven sharing.

BUILD YOUR PYRAMID OF BEING

You must understand that you are sharing the great beams of divine grace, the *be-ams* of Reality that are within you. You are letting the fragments of God flow through you. And as these fragments of God flow through your life, they will flush out therefrom all that is density and shadow, and you will become airy beings that can kindle the great fires of fohat in the world and in the universe. The power of victory will come forth, and the power of personal achievement and attainment will also come forth. The light of yourself will be brilliant, and it will be God's light shining forth from within you.

This is a great thrust for a purpose. It is an entering into Reality. It is the shedding of all the dismal and abysmal concepts that have made mankind dense and unhappy through the centuries. And we would be so happy to see you, one and all, as just how you

---

*derring-do: daring action

would look at that moment when finally the last shred, the last trump has sounded.[7]

You must understand that I am so eager to let these words tumble out into your octave that it is almost a happenstance that I occasionally leave out a small phrase here or there. For the blessed one through whom I am speaking is scarcely able to keep apace with the rapidity of my mind as I continue to pour out upon you my instruction and my hope for you as sons of freedom and as sons of Morya.

You must understand that as Morya's sons, you are divine masons. You are remembering the old patterns that God has engraven in the heavens. You are taking into your hand the great Masonic trowel and you are cementing the chief cornerstone to the very earth where you desire to build your edifice of Being.[8] Then each stone, laid alongside the chief cornerstone, is patterned after that cornerstone that was made eternal in the heavens, and the plumb line is utilized to make certain that your building is straight and true.[9]

You must understand that the Eye of God is over it all and that the purposes are to build a pyramid of divine activity, where the base thereof is square and the apex thereof is triangular, and where you have at last attained to a point where the Eye of God in the capstone is able to survey all of your creation as it is laid upon the square—acts of virtue wrought in holy prayer.

Mankind today, in their lack of understanding of that which is their own, are often prone to misunderstand the old Masonic laws. And therefore I hope that I have shed some light upon this subject even this day. For condemnation has often been wreaked by the Church upon the Masonic fraternity and upon other deeds of men, which were simply not understood. And many today in that fraternity have not understood, even scarcely one iota, all that has been conveyed in symbology's lore unto their consciousness.

And so it is with the Church and so it is even with life;
It is a lack of understanding that generates strife.
For men in ignorance have indeed wrought evil deeds.
And thus the Master said, "Father, forgive them, for they
    know not what they do."[10]
Let us instead, today, say we will enlighten the few
And all that can be added thereto
Until the few become the many
And the world is filled with illumined souls
Who will understand their own and God's great goals.

Precious ones of the light of freedom, precious friends of Saint Germain, precious friends of truth and of God, your labor ought not to be in vain. Therefore, build wisely upon that foundation which you have honored in the beginning with your attention, and let nothing rob you of your birthright immortal.

Remember, all that which toils for divine grace is able to foil the Tempter's purposes. And you must do so; you must overcome personally. That we have won our freedom is not enough to assure you your own. You must attain individually. And therefore we stand to assist, as we have in the past, and we help those who have missed as well as those who have passed.

You see, then, precious ones, there is always the ever-present attitude of divine grace. But you, individually speaking and in the bond of this individualized earth life, have a limited span in which to accomplish the plan. Therefore, I think that idle moments ought to be put to good use. Don't you? I think that life ought to be sought as a means of proving the beneficence of Almighty God —not to *disprove* his beneficence but to *approve* of it by faith, which Abraham manifested, which was in the old prophets, which was in the Master Jesus, and which is in every son of heaven.

This is not a diminuation* of the divine intent. If all mankind manifested the divine intent, think you that God would

---
diminuation: Fr. translates "diminution" (decrease)

be robbed blind? I think not. For God is the bestower, and he is only robbed when mankind rob themselves of his precious gifts of divine intent.

I thank you, and I trust that you will all be a bit more heaven-bent.

I thank you.

July 24, 1966
La Tourelle
Colorado Springs, Colorado
MLP

CHAPTER 5

*The banner of every retreat of the
Great White Brotherhood shall fly its flags. . . .
Light shall burst as the sun in its splendor
as ten thousand suns unto the planet.
New hope shall fill the heart chalices of the faithful.*

CHAPTER 5

THE WILL OF GOD IS A CHARGE OF RADIANCE FROM AFAR

What tides of decay dismember mankind! How they are swept away again and again from those lofty moorings of the Spirit, which encourage men to seek the portals of heaven even while the glitter and glamour of the outer-world consciousness below seems to present to their being a treasure incomparable.

We who understand the precious sparkling diadems of spiritual magnetism are well aware that there is indeed no comparison between mortality and immortality. But those who are wedded to mortality, who see through the lens and screen of mankind's imperfection, are again and again dashed upon the rocks and shoals of mortal numbness.

We come, then, to awaken mankind from the lethargy of the senses. We come to call to their attention that the will of God is good, that it is a charge of radiance from afar that draweth nigh unto the heart and mind in order to create therein a response to the ministrations of the Deity, the Master Potter who molds the clay so that he may deify it and make of that clay creation the creative manifestation of himself.[1]

Let men, then, be aware that out of the darkness comes forth a great light because the light has the power to expand into the darkness and to show forth therein that life is teeming with abundance because God *is*.

Because God *is,* you *are!* And because *you are* and because *God is,* Reality is born! And the sunburst of that first flash of consciousness in the domain of the individual is the doorway to great opportunity. But when this opportunity is lightly cast aside for the baubles and trinkets of life, what think ye the Lords of Karma will say when they peruse the record of the individual and find that again and again this individual has expressed preference for outer-world conditions?

Shall we then find some measure of recompense that will allow us to grant unto mankind renewed opportunity, when his pathway is strewn with rejected opportunities again and again?

I cite, then, the responsibility of individuals to peruse for themselves the eternal records and to understand, by reading those precious records, that there are no outer circumstances that are not governed by the law of man's being.

Mankind again and again profess that they desire to expand the wisdom of their own God intent, but again and again they turn toward the outer-world conditions as though they were real, and they reject the internal security of the Polestar of Being as though it were unreal.

THE REAL AND THE UNREAL

I, El Morya, Chohan of the First Ray, bearing dedication to the great will of God, carry forth to you this day the God feeling of eternal security which comes from that peace and goodwill that is borne from the heart of God.

This is reality! It is the reality of the divine revelation that pulls back the covering curtains and veils that mankind have created over the face of Nature, revealing the wonderful kingdom of Nature as God's own. And ye, as a part thereof, find no longer that Nature is a raging, roaring thing that is seeking to devour you, but it is that which ye were originally given divine dominion over—divine dominion to command the wind and the waves and to say, "Peace, be still,"[2] and then to behold as Nature obeys.

This *is* the dominion of the Christed ones! It is the dominion of those who have sought and found their own God-reality and who have understood the need for constancy of expression whereby they may *pursue* the divine Path until it becomes the only tangible reality of existence. When men do this, they are not bereft of the tides of grace! They are not covered by shrouds of darkness! But they have cracked the Cosmic Egg,[3] and the sunlight of the eternal Presence shines through!

Cognition of the will of God is the forte, then, of the God-realized man. And they that dwell in outer darkness—where there is gnashing of teeth and pain,[4] where banality and unhappiness hold sway—must understand that this occurs because they have permitted it!

We know that man does not have the strength to be able to resist evil except he draw that strength from the Divine Source. But there is no excuse for man to permit himself to be cast beyond the pale of spiritual existence and into the domain of encrusted insecurity of mortal thought and feeling, with its constant round of ceaseless struggles for existence and happiness.

God lives! And he lives in you! But you must nourish the seeds of his flame and the memory of his covenant in a greater measure *by far* than you have accepted the crushing burden of the world and the senses of the world. *Yet it is to the world that men turn as though it were real, and it is from God that men turn as though he were unreal!*

Thus long ago, when it was the desire of the great Lords of Karma to teach mankind and to do so through a living teacher, and when the selection was made in the Theosophical Order for that one to be Mr. Krishnamurti,[5] the desire was that Mr. Krishnamurti would expound the ideal of the Real as opposed to the false. Unfortunately, certain ones were able to captivate and confuse that precious soul, and so once again the powers of darkness that sought to sift as wheat[6*] were able to express through this chosen advocate the qualities of untruth. This was in refutation of the great tides of ascended master truth and law, which came forth in the original *At the Feet of the Master.*[7]

WHEN MANKIND FALLS SHORT OF THE MARK

Thus it has been down through the centuries, when thundering from great heights came the tomes of immortal life, that individuals have been sifted as wheat while others have pointed at these individuals as a thing upon the side of the pit and have said, "There stands or lies Lucifer."[8] This [situation] is understandable, for the kingdom of God is a *prize*—the greatest prize that can come to any. Therefore the dangers are great and the pitfalls many. But those of the outer-world consciousness are not consumed by their own fashions, for they are a part of that sea of slime that engulfs hearts and turns them from the great tides of cosmic reality.

Those who are a part of this outer-world consciousness do not seem to be enmeshed in struggle at all. For within the framework of reference that is their own Lilliputian world, they live and die as mice and men,[9] playing out the small dramas of their individual expressions as though it were a cosmic drama of great monument.

But when the eyes of God are upon them, they are not reckoned among the living, for they are already dead in trespasses and sins, trespassing against the reality of their own life. This is not a trespass against the Deity, as the Deity is a thing apart from man, but it is a trespass against the Deity that *is* a part of man. For life is God, and every expression thereof is intended to be a total

---

*The sifting causes the removal of the protective layer of the wheat, meaning the removal of the protection of Mr. Krishnamurti.

manifestation of his victory and happiness and God-success.

When men fall short of the great cosmic mark and prize, it is always a pity that comes to them as they recognize out of the dregs of self-pity that they have failed and have fallen short of the mark. There is no need to lament this condition, so long as consciousness is able to assess itself. For when consciousness assesses that it has fallen short of the mark, the first step that the individual must take is clear. They must arise as the prodigal son and say with firm determination, "I will return unto the house of my father."[10]

Are they tired of the husks and dregs of life? Then let them return to where Reality lives and abides forever. Let them turn from the vomit of human wretchedness unto the security of the Christ domain.

There is no need whatsoever for mankind to remain in a state of wretchedness, for God lives in every moment. Mankind themselves stand behind the curtain of their own self-rejection, facing a small circle of insecurity, of wrong thought, of wrong feeling, of misuse of energy, of slovenliness in action and of disquietude, which they sometimes unfortunately desire to spread unto their fellowmen. For it is often true that individuals who are caught in the jaws of the trap of their own mortal consciousness will actually seem to derive some benefit from spreading their own insecurity out into the world of form and from subverting others into their own state of decrepitude. "More is the pity," you say, and we echo those sentiments.

But again we affirm that God lives! And he lives for those who have rejected *themselves* and who have rejected their own immortal Reality, as well as for those who have passed beyond the veil to their God-victory. God lives for *all*, and he lives *in* all, and his will is for the *freedom* of all! His will is for earth's victory over all of her disaffection, disloyalty, and nonrecognition of the great Truth that is the will of the Eternal.

THE WILL OF GOD SATURATES THE EARTH

I come to you this day with renewed determination that the purposes of this age envisioned by God for mankind shall be fulfilled. We will not take our stance based upon the *disillusionment* of men! We will take our stance based upon the *divine intent!*

[Master shouts; congregation rises]

Maximize, maximize, maximize the divine intent! *Minimize, minimize, minimize* the human disaffection!

(Won't you please be seated.)

The eternal Father, in his great majesty of purpose, has recalled from the planet Earth this day the nine ambassadors that were here in order to perform a specific service for hierarchy.[11] Some of those who are in physical embodiment will remain in physical embodiment, but their mission has been recalled.

The hierarchy has made a renewed determination to fulfill the obligations of the hierarchy toward the Deity, and they have decided to refuse to accept the outer issues enjoined by mankind that are in contradiction to the eternal perfection of the divine plan. The full meaning of this may not dawn upon some of you for a period, and others may grasp it with an instant grasp. But I will elucidate the meaning of it in part so that you may have hope for a more instant grasp of it. *And I say this to ye all!*

While it is true that the mind of God has never fallen from its high estate, the hierarchy—as a part of the eternal Holy Christ Presence acting as a mediator between God and man—has from time to time acted in the world of form in order to report on various episodes that were taking place upon the planet whereby mankind has actually, in one sense of the word, manipulated the responses of heaven to his own activities.

This was, of course, a part of the wisdom of hierarchy themselves, who were acting under divine inspiration. But now it has been decided for a time, and times, and a half a time[12] that we shall try it with the will of God acting supreme. Tempering no more the cosmic tides to the shorn lamb of man's identity in its state of evolutionary perceptions, we shall bring forth the great cosmic truths to the planet by the love tides gushing forth from the heart of the living Presence of God.

This means that the will of God shall saturate every rock and tree. It means that the creation of the eternal radioactivity—from the very core in the center of the earth in Pelleur's* domain, through the air and the atmosphere and *all* about you—comes forth so that the Presence of God in its heavenly aspects shall manifest below in a measure inconceivable to the mind of man now. And this coming forth of the Presence of God, while it manifests in the time constant, in the spatial time continuum, shall also come about with a quick slant toward manifestation in order to preserve life upon the planet withal.† For it shall be by divine decree, and the science of heaven shall be used.

EARTH RECEIVES THE IMPERSONAL RADIATION OF GOD

We are not concerned any longer with mankind's reactions to the ministrations of heaven, but we are prepared to assist those lifestreams who have decided within the forcefield of their own heart and being, in full faith, that they will embrace the cosmic will of God and determine that they will express it. To them we shall give the ministrations of the immortality of the Infinite God. We shall give the fullest measure of our attention to life. We shall give it to the elementals. We shall give it everywhere! And a swift reaction may indeed occur below to that which men do. For when in the presence of heaven, as heaven is all around mankind and bursting round their feet, we shall see just how long they shall resist that pressure.

---

*Virgo and Pelleur are the hierarchs of the earth element, who direct the elemental beings known as gnomes.
†*withal:* archaic; therewith, nevertheless

In times past embodied mankind, even the holy innocents, were subverted by this awful manifestation of the Luciferian hordes and the powers of darkness that this planet has played host to. But now we deal at impersonal levels—not with embodied mankind but with the presence of the Holy Spirit! For descending from the heart of the Lord Maha Chohan and *through* the Maha Chohan, this dispensation is given. And the planet, then, shall receive the impersonal radiation of *All*-mighty God!

Let none fear it. Let all revere it. And let all see it as a boon to the aspiring sons of God and to the God-determination of the cosmos to respond to the innocent of heart who seek to find, in this day and age, freedom from the overpowering manifestations of outer-world conditions.

The hierarchy has spoken. As the Chohan of the First Ray, I have given this dispensation to you this day. It is an epoch that has ended, and it is an epoch that is beginning. It is the dawn of a millennium of hope, and it is for all men.

But those who desire to express the Deity, to walk as living Christs among mankind, shall be the benefactors. And to the rest— not because we wish it but because it is a side effect of the lifting of the cosmic emissaries and hosts devoted to God from the earth— there will come about the manifestation of that which will produce those cries, "Let the mountains and the rocks fall upon us, and let the hills cover us."[13] For there shall be weeping and gnashing of teeth as mankind reap that which they have sown.

But in the world, the banner of hope shall fly. The banner of every retreat of the Great White Brotherhood* shall fly its flags. Its banners shall wave in the breezes of the Holy Spirit, and light shall burst as the sun in its splendor as ten thousand suns unto the planet. New hope shall fill the heart chalices of the faithful, and it shall be a resurgent filling of the cup of Christ-magnificence, the Grail Most Holy.

*The term "white" is not a reference to race but to the aura of white light that surrounds these immortals.

The position of the devotee and the chela shall then be one of recognition of the Higher, of hourly attunement with the Higher, of understanding that the kingdom of God draweth nigh unto the earth.[14] And we shall no longer be concerned with the darkness, for:

The darkness is far spent!
The darkness is far spent!
The darkness is far spent![15]

And the dayspring from on high is at hand to visit mankind in their affliction[16] as *"The Pilgrim's Progress"*[17] looms before those who yearn to do, to know the will of God, to be Christ among men—to be humble, as those who are born in a manger but who are piloted by the star that came forth as a nova from cosmos' heart.

I thank you.

August 27, 1967
La Tourelle
Colorado Springs, Colorado
MLP

CHAPTER 6

If mankind would aspire to the Infinite,
they must master the finite.
For the finite can and will submit to the Infinite
when mankind . . . summon infinite power
to govern finite manifestation.

WHERE THE MASTERS LEAD,
LET MANKIND FOLLOW

The bond of God's will unites hearts. And we are come, summoned by the spirits of the elect, of just men made perfect,[1] to radiate into your midst and to a darkened and dying world the sun of unifying radiance, of hope, and of the summoning of mankind to the high calling that we ourselves have long ago responded to.

The formulation of a Table Round was a thing not of dubious beauty but of an *excruciatingly* beautiful manifestation.[2] I have used this word "excruciatingly" because it bypasses the word "exquisite," and we wish you to understand that it is so beautiful that it almost hurts.

We call to your attention, then, that that which is hurt and afflicted is the outer man, with the error of his ways and with the discord that he has externalized and to which he has imputed a sullen reality. We are not concerned with the survival of these unpleasant manifestations, but rather we are concerned with the survival of the truth so that the truth may live in you and so that you may live by the truth, summoning the order in your worlds that will enable us to cover you with a mantle of universal dignity.

Universal dignity is the same whole cloth that has covered
every *arhat** and has made him to understand how the beauty—
the transcendent beauty governed by universal law that has beck-
oned him onward through the darkened areas of the cosmos—has
led him to a place where all is pure light.

Mankind should understand, then, that the journey itself is
often through the dark, through the invisible, through a realm
where faith does not seem to manifest tangible reality. But it is the
end result, it is the final effect that lies behind the central cause
to which we are dedicated—the effect that teaches every man the
soul[†] reality that he is and that causes him to understand the role
of the will of God in the manifestation of truth in his life. The will
of God is not only good but it is necessary for the completion and
purification of an individual monad, and the summoning of the
elect is in response to the will of God.

Now, I do not deny that the will of God may from time to
time cause mankind to tremble, because in effect we are dealing
here with that which bypasses a limited capacity, a finite measure.
Therefore individuals must always consider that ahead of them
lies the domain of greater beauty than that to which their eyes are
accustomed.

Strange sights, then, may manifest when men evoke light.
For light will reveal that which is hidden not only in the lives of
others but also in their own lives. This is so that they may bring
forth for transmutation the darkened manifestations that they
have, in effect, concealed for centuries.

When these manifestations come forth into the light, it is not
to expose their ugliness for others to view, but it is so that mankind
may reckon with that which has manifested and so that they may
understand that this ugliness must no longer hold sway in their
world. Therefore, mankind will take steps to see to it that this
energy is released back to the heart of the Great Central Sun for

---

arhat: a Buddhist adept or saint, or one who has attained enlightenment
[†]Could also be "sole reality."

purification, and they will see to it that in its place, in their world, a structure will rise that is able to teach mankind how they may outpicture a greater measure of universal grace.

Thus, men are *all* teachers and are *all* leaders. For all men lead something, and something follows all things. Yet when men understand the Law more completely, they will not wish to be at the tail end of the line, with one poor little chela following behind. Alas, they will instead wish to lead the millions, for the further along an individual is, the closer he is to the throne of Reality and the central will of God.

We do not, then, in any way regret our own position, nor do we deem it to be a place of loftiness whereby we may, so to speak, lord it over other men. Rather, in keeping with the Father's admonishment, we recognize that our role is that of a greater servant. But—and I smile here with tongue in cheek—unless we have someone to listen to us, I fear lest we could not in any way direct others. For a nondescript army that does not listen to the cry of battle from the commander is no honor to the commander.

Therefore when we make this summoning, it is to all who would make their calling and election sure.[3] This is so that they will understand that the role of submissiveness is not a state of surrender of the sovereign power of the will to a lesser force, but rather it is a submissiveness to a higher purpose. For a higher purpose is a purpose that leads mankind toward the heights and that summons them toward the heights, which is certainly not to the *degeneration* of an individual but rather to his or her *regeneration*. To this we are dedicated and in this direction we move.

Naturally, the barnacles of life that have clung to an individual for far too long will sometimes be dislodged as we make this summoning. For it becomes essential that individuals shall shake loose the ballast, which has held them down, so that they may rise.

When individuals are willing to submit to this and can recognize that the spiritual path is not without the necessary lightening of the load of the burden, then they will be able to make greater progress because they will no longer hang on to human foibles as though they were their inheritance. For after all, your [true] inheritance is freedom, and freedom comes when you are free from impedimenta—when you are free from the dangers of the psychic world, when you have created a new hope and are able to recognize that that which you have newly created was also created *for* you and lowered into manifestation as a *gift* to your I AM Presence and as a gift from your I AM Presence to your outer self.

The dimensionless realm is above the realm of dimension. And if mankind would aspire to the Infinite, they must master the finite. For the finite can and will submit to the Infinite when mankind understand that it is the requirement of the Law that they shall summon infinite power to govern finite manifestation.

At first this may seem a bit obtuse, but thought upon it will quickly bring it into manifestation for ye all. And I think that this is not above ye all but that it is something all can understand. Therefore I hasten to ask that you disabuse your minds of the thought that your minds are not filled with the capacity to cognize some of the teaching I am releasing.

One of the great problems of the student body today is that many times when we release information, the students are too prone to classify that information to a state [they deem] far above their own capacity to understand and use. I think that we have never, in any of our releases, caused a teaching to manifest so high that the smallest little child could not profit by it if he were willing to look for the stones to pick up that were in his own class.

It is true that we have placed here great boulders that the average individual could not lift. But with one's eye the individual can gauge these boulders and say, "With my growing strength I will lift them." But the pebbles that also accompany these great boulders are easy to be lifted, and there are many areas in the lives of the chelas where the small and little things can be corrected and mended so that greater things can be attained.

You have a saying that you do not wish to bite off more than you can chew. Well, blessed ones, if you have been so careful to do things this way, then you ought to chew that which you have bitten off. And I think that if you will chew it and will understand that by doing so you are nourishing your souls, you will recognize that all things are possible to you in bite sizes.

Now, I hope that you will sink your teeth into this. For if you don't, I fear lest some of you will bite your own tongues! This is because the Law itself is a law of great diligence, and this Law cannot be flaunted lightly by those among mankind who have left other causes in order to set their hand to this plow.[4] This plow is to plow a straight furrow so that all mankind may see the power of this example in this day and age when religion seems to be decaying in their consciousness and when philosophy has become a means whereby religion is rendered innocuous.

I think you will recognize, then, that the power of the law of God to take dominion over those chelas who submit to us is very great indeed, and we are determined to lead you because you are following the light to the best of your ability. We are determined that that power that we shall release will effectually demonstrate to the world for all time to come that the ascended masters are real, that the ascended masters are able to assist you in manifesting those hopes and desires that have become dreams of divine dominion in your world. You desire God to take dominion in your world, and he bounces the ball right back to you and says unto you: "Listen unto me, my children. For I have spiritually given to you the power you need to manifest dominion over your world, and my Law is in your hand and heart to do so."

Now then, when God sends this ball right back to you and saith unto you "Do my will," it means just that! It means that you have the power to do his will! And if you will accept this, you will be free indeed. For God will *work* through you and *serve* through you, and you will understand that God also *lives* in you. And then, of course, he will not seem so far from you and the masters will not seem so far from you, and the possibility of our stepping through the veil will not seem so remote in time.

You will see that one of the greatest means through which the masters can step through the veil is to step through into manifestation in your own lives. For then it would scarce mean a great deal of difference whether you manifest the very same ideologies that we do and the same powers that we do, for it would not be long before you would also be where we are. Therefore *what difference will it make whether you step through the veil to us or we step through the veil to you?*

Do you see? I trust that this understanding is vouchsafed to you this day, for it is an important but previously moot point.

In the name of Almighty God, I thank you and I say: Where the masters lead, let mankind follow. For we have overcome death. We have overcome desultory manifestations and the lures of the world.

We stand today as your mentors and guides, hoping that you will never allow the torch we extend to you to go out but that you will permit it to permeate your world as thought, word, and deed in manifestation, until the whole wide world understands the dominion of the ascended masters and the power of the Christ infinite to work the wonders of all eternity in time, right where you are!

In God's name I, El Morya, Chohan of the First Ray, salute the flame of God's will within your heart.

March 24, 1968
La Tourelle
Colorado Springs, Colorado
MLP

CHAPTER 7

*We urge upon all the understanding
not of darkness but of light.
For light can be summoned.
Light can be invoked.
Light can be the key to man's freedom.*

THE POWER OF RIGHT THOUGHT

Your Mind Is the Endowment of Universal Intelligence

Morya would instruct in soaring. Will you come with me, then, to that cloud-capped realm of your beloved Saint Germain, the realm of imagination where you can create by the magic of the inner eye those symbols of future loveliness that you desire to see manifest in the world of form?

For the substance of men's dreams is often reborn in outer-world nonsense because the dreams themselves have consisted of nonsense. We therefore summon the drawing up of the strings of consciousness and of the mind so that the individual may *safely* soar in thought as a human dynamo imbued with the spirit of ageless love and service.

It is not necessary for individuals to be molded by the social factors of environment. Individuals should cognize that they can, by a thought, lift themselves out of the paltry misery of this present age and enter into that magnificent spirit of God-realization that enables us to fabricate in the world an invisible empire of divine servers. These servers will recognize each other by reason of the spirit of universal hope and creative manifestation, which comes forth as mighty light rays from the hemisphere of the mind and creates that glowing nimbus of universal reality that artists and visionaries have called "the halo." For there is a halo of love; there is a train of emanation, a light beam of concentrated energy that comes forth from the aura of each individual's consciousness.

When we think, then, in terms of outer-world viciousness and we see how the aura is murky in color—brown and insipid as molasses and flowing out into the world as a vaporous substance that encloses mankind with a shroud of hate—we urge upon all the understanding not of darkness but of light. For *light* can be summoned! *Light* can be invoked! *Light* can be the key to man's freedom!

THE FABRIC OF THE WORLD MIND

It is a strange thing that out of twenty-six letters of the alphabet so many words can be created. It is a strange thing that out of the magnificent manifestation of abridged or unabridged words in the dictionaries of mankind such lofty and ignominious ideas can together be released into the stream of the world mind. Yet as we examine the world mind and the fabric thereof, we are aware that it is both a sewer and a bower of loveliness. Momentarily and according to the degree of their own thought, mankind attune with the various segments of this flow of energy.

At present, the level of mortal consciousness is far from the domain of heaven, far from the cloud-capped realm of the invisible realm. The sounds of the world lure mankind with ease from the spirit of Christ principle. The sights of the world are also alluring, and the thoughts of mankind become so quickly taken over by the thoughts of others that tend downward.

We summon the elect from this age. The call has gone forth and mankind have heard our voice. Let them understand the meaning of shrouds of darkness. Let them understand the meaning of shrouds of death and bitterness. Let them shun all that they could wear that is not the garment of the Lord or the garments of God.

There is a tendency in the world to permit the deceits of self to enclose the consciousness around and about until the most beautiful concepts are trampled upon as though they were ugly and had no value. We are concerned with the development of a forthright recognition in the spirit of mankind, in the lenses of perception, in the perceiving apparatus of the universal banner of the LORD. For when this banner is raised up and mankind see it not, it is as though the energy of the raising has been expended in vain, and we are concerned with each jot and tittle of energy released into the world order.

It is an interesting thing how the fashion of the human mind feels itself prepared to judge the most lofty thoughts and to perceive behind them some subtle motive of human machination. We do not speak in contempt of mankind's noble efforts, but we are certainly aware of the denizens of darkness and of those purveyors of human filth and degradation, who have created in the world a place of incest where the temple of God should stand.

IDEAS CHARGED WITH RADIANCE FROM THE MIND OF GOD

As I gaze upon the records of the dim past (that is, to the gaze of most individuals), I realize that right here, on this spot where I stand, a beautiful temple of hope was once erected. This temple was ministered to by angelic beings and supervised by vestal virgins, whose hearts and thoughts were concerned with the capturing of their latent divinity. They thought only in terms of right thought. And as I say this unto you, I urge upon you the cognition of the simple, the vesting of oneself with awareness of the simple: The power of right thought! The power of right thought! *The power of right thought!*

For there is a tendency in the mind of man to take the most

glorious ideas and, because they have heard them before, to say, "This is not new." Precious ones, when the spirit of an individual is able to draw forth the spirit of Christ truth within any cosmic statement, that individual can make that statement ring forth at any given moment in time as though it were the very newness of God—a burnished, shining luster that brings hope into the world once again!

What a pitiful thing it would be if all that has ever passed through the nexus of consciousness of descending divinity, of the beauty of human endowments by the hand of God, should be cast into a pile of discards simply because they were not new and because they have been known momentarily by a soul or even held up throughout an age.

What deceit is practiced in the name of God! For the dark ones, who in their dens of iniquity seek to enslave the minds of mankind, do constantly engage the dynamos of their attention upon methods whereby they may rob mankind of happiness by spewing out vaporous ideas that vampirize the human mind and cause individuals to fail to see the beauties in life.

Is this simply because the beauties of life are not new? Not at all. But it is simply because the mind and consciousness of individuals in the world, who are susceptible to these vibrations, are prone to accept the hypnotic emanations of the dark ones that are released into the atmosphere.

These individuals also do not understand, if they would, that the manifestations of Christ-purity and of beauty are also floating in the same atmosphere. Mingling side by side with the dominoes of darkness that bring man down, you can find the pinions of light that lift man up. And the selectivity is always the forte of the God-realized man (or the individual, be it man, woman, or child), who is trained to understand the meaning of seeking out an idea rather than letting the idea seek them out.

When you seek out an idea that is vitalized by the divine

concepts within it, you must understand that the expectation of the vibrancy of divine thought is in itself most heartening, causing mankind to say, "I am enlightened by that thought! It has buoyed me up!" Yet I assure you that from time to time the same thought uttered by different lips and different hearts would have an entirely different effect upon the individual hearers.

The whole concept, then, is one of vitalizing truth and of seeing that that truth can be made to come alive. This is because truth in itself is actually a factor of the divine life. And when that factor comes to life within the domain of an individual—as a life expression of that individual through the claiming of that quality specifically by an individual lifestream—it *is* a living thing! Do you see? And as it lives in man, so it lives in the universe.

Ideas are the thoughts of God when they come forth from his mind charged with his radiance and seized by the flame of the Divine within the jaws of the heart. For the heart must also eat, drink, and be nourished and must draw forth energy if the heart is to sustain the light patterns that God desires to see externalized in this age.

DENIZENS OF THE PSYCHIC REALM

Mankind do not yet understand the meaning of fictitious characterization. They do not realize that from time to time those so-called artists of the world who serve the dark powers will draw images of popular faces and then emblazon them, by the art of printing, upon the magazines of the world. These caricatures are degradations of the human form, symbolic of destructivity and darkness, and they have a tendency to pull down all greatness in the hearts and minds of those whose image and stamp they bear. For this distortion of the human form and figure in the name of art is like unto a surrealistic miasma that is drawn forth from the pits of the brothers of the shadow.

We, then, want it to be known that the concepts of Dante Alighieri in his *Inferno*[1] will also convey to mankind certain of the truths that are involved in the realm of the astral, in the realm of delirium tremens, and in the realm of drug addiction. It is in this realm that individuals, in their psychic trips out into the astral realm, find themselves literally torn apart by those beings of darkness, which at the time seem real to these individuals but who subsequently decide are unreal.

Let me stress to you that a thought is real. Let me stress to you that an idea in picturization is real, that when individuals see a dragon of darkness while in a [drug-induced] trip into the astral world by the use of psychedelic drugs, they are experiencing a horrendous meeting with a very vicious and destructive dark force that can latch on to their own thought force and impale it significantly for a period of time. This experience in the nether-world holds an energy allotment of the individual in bondage and slavery, tending to pull that individual down into those areas of degradation and destruction from time to time.

I want everyone to understand that this battle is now going on in the world of form. If you will only open your eyes and gaze upon these things (which is difficult for some of you to do who are dedicated purely to seeing the truth in a spiritual way), you will be able to understand the urgency of the hour. You will be able to understand how very short the time is in which we can effect some transformation, or at least how we can effect a forestallment in the youth of the world and in those ineffective manifestations of darkness—those manifestations that are being sent out into the world with the vain hope that this darkness can ultimately and permanently enslave mankind.

I stress the transiency of these manifestations of darkness because it is necessary to recognize that they are paper tigers in one sense, but in another sense they are vicious in the main, and totally destructive. They are paper tigers, for they have no power over the light of God that never fails. They are paper tigers by comparison to the mighty power of Archangel Michael and to the ascended hosts.

But to individuals who do not yet have a developed spiritual awareness of their Divine Presence, when these individuals are caught in the vicious crosscurrents of these riptides of psychic energy without even the knowledge of the Sign of the Cross[2] or the power of exorcism, I tell you that it causes many of them to land in the asylums or to go the route of human suicide.

We would not, then, today, see a continuation of this awful activity! For each soul upon the planet does yet bear, and still to the moment, some resemblance to the mighty, original, perfected image of the Divine. This is not said entirely as condemnation or censure for all of mankind, but only as censure to the brothers of the shadow, who once knew at least a portion of the spiritual path but who have now become urgers of mankind toward the expressions of demons.

We have some knowledge of demons and of their expressions. We have observed down through the centuries the ritual of exorcism. We have seen the vaporous and horrid aspects of witchcraft. We have seen the nakedness and nudity of consciousness that has entered into the hearts of men as they seek to fulfill the awful and dark aspects of their own lusts.

THE MAGNIFICENT CONCEPTS OF GOD

We are concerned, then, with developing those marvelous matrices of holy innocence that were a part of the symbolic Adam and Eve in the original Garden of Eden.[3] For Hedon was a place of infinite pleasure where the Divine himself could commune with mankind.[4] But mankind do not, now in this present hour, understand all these things except primarily in a mystical or mythological way. They are entirely too prone to fail to equate the intended release of Christ truth in those stories and dramas of creation that would, if they would let it, express to them the powerful admonitions of God that were revealed in the original moments of the creation of this system of worlds and the entire planetary chain.[5]

I, then, ask you, in God's name and in honor of his holy will, to consider for one moment just what you will impute to the Deity. Will you impute to the Deity the creation of these frightful monsters of deceit? Will you impute to the Deity the desire to enslave mankind in a round of mortal misery? I tell you, nay! For God has not created misery, neither has he fashioned it. Nor has he had any pleasure in the death of the wicked,[6] nor in their destruction, nor in the reaping by them of karmic reward for their shadowed activities of darkness. God is all that the name itself implies: *Good*-ness personified.

The intent of the Father is very high and very beauteous. It is not just a cloud-capped realm of clouded shapes whitened by light. It is a realm of spiritual wonder where the most magnificent concepts are born. These concepts are *dominant* concepts involving the psyche of man in the universal drama, involving the psyche of man in the universal plan. These concepts by God for man represent the tenets of the holy will!

The tenets of the holy will of God are good for all. They will enfold mankind every moment with light and with purity. The will of God is also able to free mankind from the ideas of enslavement, and liberation is itself a divine attribute. For the very quality of liberty, which God gave unto man—and the blessing of freedom as a part of the divine plan—has enabled mankind to go at their own gait.

Therefore we find here upon this planetary body right now, even among some of the students of the light, those individuals who take their own sweet time about doing God's will. They know very well that they are doing certain activities that are not the desire of their own Divine Presence. They know very well that they are being driven from time to time from the very door of the pleasures of spiritual Eden, for they are not really innocent concerning just what they are doing. Yet they continue to seek a crust of bread, a crumb from God's table in outer manifestation. Some little paltry thing that has no meaning at all becomes to them a fetish, a thing to be sought, while the mighty drama of the Spirit and its understanding—the power of the universal consciousness—is not at all made clear to them simply because they do not apply thought to it.

THE CREATIVE EXPRESSION OF THE FATHER IS DORMANT IN EVERY MAN

Now, thought itself is actually quite plastic and can be molded by the will. And when it is molded by the will and fashioned thereby, it can become a very fluffy and delicate substance that will harden under the desire and pressure of the light and of man's search for it. Therefore, when one submits the matrices of the mind to the Divine and asks that the stamp of cosmic nobility be inscribed thereupon (with calls to the Godhead to see that the matrices are hardened), these matrices *will* be hardened. And when they are, they become a reservoir of spiritual strength to that individual. For after all, just as mankind create these matrices of thought and feeling, so they can see a parallel in the very use of language. For language itself does make use of certain ancient figures and symbols, lineaments that can be inscribed upon the consciousness and then deciphered at will.

Will you, then, join me as I bring to your attention this afternoon the quite natural power of how the mind can reach up toward God and receive from his hand the pressures of his love? For God will inscribe his laws upon the hearts and minds of mankind, and these were statements made of old as prophecy.[7] Yet the Christ truth embodied within them has totally escaped many who consider their mind to be something like their underwear—something that they can take out periodically for a washing and airing.

I would like to remind you that your mind is much more than this! It is the endowment of universal intelligence, the capacity to receive from the mind of God those thoughts that you can also retain not only for a moment but forever. For the ancient Tablets of Mem[8] do hold the negative and positive polarities that enable mankind to record forever the blessings of Christ truth and of universal reality. This enables mankind to retain their own spiritual identity, to become a blessing to the universe forever.

And what is the universe? *U-n-i,* one—you and I together, all of us, the manifestation of completion—not just one, for God himself has said it is not good for man to be alone.[9]

Let it be understood, then, that the creative expression has constantly rushed forth from the mighty Presence of Life in the heart of the Great Central Sun, and down the hall of the grand galaxies there has rushed forth the desire of the Father to express creatively. This creative expression is also latent, dormant, and sleeping within every man. We stress it again:

This is latent, dormant, and sleeping within every man!
This is latent, dormant, and sleeping within every man!
We stress it again:
This is latent, dormant, and sleeping within every man!

Well, if this be so (and it must be, because I said it so many times), certainly it bears repeating to yourself many times. For once you realize that man can sleep and truly be one who is dead, yet he can live long enough to permit his ears to hear the voice of the son of God—any son of God—so that he may live, you will realize that you have, after all, submitted to the lullabies of life. These have rocked the spiritual self to sleep while the outer material self has sought to garner its good in the world of form. And as it has done so, what has it profited those of you who have "gained," so to speak figuratively, the whole world but have become a castaway from spiritual experiences in depth?

COMIC RELIEF

Oh, I have watched how individuals have gingerly set their feet upon the Path, stepping from one stone to another and fearing lest they might slip. And then when some green slime appears upon a rock, they avoid it assiduously. They do not seem to understand that spiritual "chlorophyll" can sometimes be found in strange places.

My goodness! You don't even laugh when I say something like this! [laughter] Is this because your sense of humor is completely tied up in these spiritual environments? Do you think for one moment that the ascended hosts are completely free of seeing the humor in life? Well, I tell you no! We must see the humor in life in order to keep our sanity at inner levels, particularly when we work with human beings in the world below! [laughter]

For this is enough to drive even the highest among the archangels to almost a state of falling majesty! And I tell you, precious ones, that some very ludicrous situations have actually occurred at inner levels that have kept us somewhat as readers of the comic pages of the cosmos. For we are also able to find our comic relief, which does bring to all of us an awareness that God is truly the God of happiness.

WILL: THE MOST IMPORTANT INGREDIENT IN THE UNIVERSE

Whereas many individuals have from time to time characterized me as a being whose will is absolutely ironclad (and some would actually like to call me Old Ironsides),[10] I think you should stop for a moment and pause to reflect upon what is the most important ingredient in the universe today. And I think that the most important ingredient in the universe today is *will!* For *will* is the cohesive, spiritual power that enables individuals to firm themselves in cosmic idealism and in efforts towards spiritual attainment by making picturizations of what they want to be, what they would like to express in the future!

Individuals are always subjected to the pressures of others, whose stereotyped domains are constantly encircling them with the most awful ideas. Why, we sometimes, in mercy's name, have even violated cosmic law and have made karma by doing so because we could not tolerate a mother's concept of her child. Do you realize, then, what this means? It means that sometimes we have to stay away from people lest we become too sympathetic to their hapless aims.

Let us say that we can sympathize with those of you who are sometimes so full of love that you are overly generous with your energy and sometimes meddle where you ought not to. But this is to your own hurt, and you create thereby a lack of spiritual progress, even over a whole ten-year period. This is simply because, for example, you were so interested in some individual who wasn't even interested enough in himself* to take the first step that you just kept on coddling him and working with him because you hoped that eventually you could penetrate his densities.

But after a while you suddenly got the idea that maybe heaven itself did not favor your efforts, and so you ceased. And at just about that time, the individual could not understand why you dropped him so completely out of your life, and he began to lament about this and to wonder just what was wrong. And by himself he came crawling back to you. But at that time you were not too interested in helping him, and so on his own he actually externalized just a little bit of love and created a great deal of good for himself by doing it.

So perhaps, after all, there is a little excuse for some human sympathy, but I think that most people carry it too far. And I say this as an absolute admonishment to you, and I say it with all sincerity: I believe that many carry it too far. But people can also carry a spirit of aloofness too far, and they can feel—because they have

---

*The pronouns "himself" and "him" are used here for simplification; "herself" and "her" could also be used.

had bad experiences in the world in working with lifestreams—
that they are actually engaging their enemies by helping others
while these others are not interested in helping themselves. But
then these individuals who attempt to help others will often with-
hold help when it is very badly needed.

So may God help each and every one of you to see his holy
will and to have that marvelous sense of balance, like a razor's edge,
so that you will know just when you should "do" and just when
you should "don't."

I hope, then, that if you will accept the pressures of my will
this afternoon, you will realize that God is always active in trying
to create beautiful new impressions of the inflexible will of God,
which *has* to be inflexible for each and every one of you and for
the universe!

For if the Most High God himself were to vacillate in his aims,
I ask you, what would it mean to human beings who come to the
portals of God's will if they should find that he was out a-gadding
and would not take any interest in them at that specific moment
when they decided, after all, that now they would take interest in him.

Be patient, blessed ones. The Most High God, sometimes by
reason of cosmic laws that he himself has written, will also obey his
own laws. And thus he is not teasing you. He is simply letting you,
in your fervent search, discover for yourselves that all that you do
to serve his will is a thing of worth. For after all, as you heard this
afternoon in a little of the meanderings of the Grail consciousness,
man can really create himself![11]

This is God's will. Let us hope that more of you will be up and
about and doing it.

I thank you.

July 28, 1968
Los Angeles, California
MLP

CHAPTER 8

*The law of love that gave thee birth
would also assist thee to complete
the initiatic process and to lead thee
out and onward to the fulfillment
of thy immortal destiny!*

CHAPTER 8

BE CLOTHED WITH
RIGHT MIND AND THE STERNNESS
OF CONSCIOUSNESS

The clouds of thought are both white and black. Let mankind understand the means of controlling the media of thought. Thus will they be able to steer the frail bark of self.

Self-pity is the greatest delusion that can come to mankind, for it stirs the fires of a sordid ego and causes activities of darkness to breed. The brooding of the dark ones comes to the world, and the world is filled with the froth that they create. The scavengers of the spirit are few—those who are willing to enter in to the denizens and the dens of iniquity and to see to it that there is a mopping-up operation, the removal of human debris and discord.

The dangers to the planet are many because the souls of mankind are surfeited by outer-world activity and few are they who turn to the light, which is the light of God within. Mankind scoff and mock. They are traitors to the Reality that has given them life. They chafe at the bit, they are annoyed at small things, and they cast aside the weight of their life for a very small price.

We summon the children of the dawn! We summon the children of the plains to reach upward into the air to the hands of light that beckon and call, to the hands of light that have already given all!

We call forth, then, the warriors from amongst mankind to come to the mountain heights—the strong ones, those who will bear up under the barrage of psychic attacks, those who can stand the guff that is directed against the children of the Spirit today as they aspire to manifest the purity of tomorrow. It is the purity of tomorrow that is the divine plan fulfilled, the plan of the golden age when thy strength mounts up and thou art no longer concerned with mortal doings. For the doings of mankind are primarily the doings of vanity, yet mankind are interested in this vanity as though it were the greatest activity under the sun.

One of the great men from the Far East once used an expression (which you use here upon this planet) as he gazed upon the nonsensical doings. This great arhat used the word *bosh** as he gazed at some of the doings of the children of mankind today. And so we ourselves are almost prone to curl our lip in scorn, for many among mankind are squandering the precious commodities of the soul, all in senseless activities, and they know it not.

Mankind seek further delusions. They seek further manifestations of their activities. They have made the strobe light their god. They do not understand the meaning of the light. They are victims of hypnosis. They are victims of delusions. They are victims of confusions. They are participants in the ritual of darkness. They have spread abroad over the face of the earth the images that brought down of old the entire land of Mu. They have once again re-created the follies of Atlantis.

Mankind have sought in their activities to create physical bodies.† They have sought to play as though they were God. They have sought to create both evolution and revolution, and they have not

---

bosh: foolish talk, foolish activity; nonsense
†El Morya is probably referring to the science of genetics and genetic engineering.

understood the meaning of the spires of the Spirit. They have not understood how the banner of the LORD went before the people. They have not understood that the banner of the LORD is stable. They have not understood that the banner of the LORD is already certified, and in the certification of that radiance there is salvation.[1]

Those who step aside from the channels of light—channels already carved out of the granite—wander in the dust. As serpents they crawl upon their bellies, and they encounter on the path scorpions that will destroy them. They wind their bodies around meaningless twigs, and all of their doings are vanity.

LET CLARITY COME FORTH

In the meantime, while all of this is going on, the seekers follow the stream. They follow the stream, and everywhere they go they are putting in straws so that they may siphon up the water of life and drink. They are athirst. They are anhungered. They seek for the manna that came down from heaven, for the bread of life. They pursue the spiritual course. They understand that God is everything.

Yet the arhats from the East despair at times because of the clouds of dust that are thrown up even against the eyes of those who are searching for the light. These clouds of dust, which continually recur, sometimes blind the seekers on the Path so that they too wander momentarily away from the banks of the river and they too are lost in the dry, parched sands where the serpents' corpses are strewn.

We then today, summoning the elect, say: Open your eyes! And where necessary, wear goggles! We recommend that you understand the need to be impervious to the delusions of the world and to the dust that is thrown up to cloud mankind's consciousness.

We say, let clarity come forth! And let that clarity be the clarity of the sun, the clarity of the crystal ray, the clarity of the cool fountain. Let it be the clarity of the white robe, the clarity of the mantle of light, the clarity of creative essence and God-design. Let it be the return to the Source, the recognition of the wonder of the One— of the wonder of *one*-ness, of the wonder of *be*-ness, of the security of the divine domain, of the ultimate that shall be born in thee.

Morya speaks, now, the gentle word:

O children of the longing of God's heart, return to the fold. Return the way of peace to the human heart. Let the heart become a temple of peace. Let the soft *destiny* release the fires of the diamond-shining mind of God, as the hard *density* is impervious to human reason.

Let men cease to think of the idea of cringing. Let them cease to fear. For fear that hath torment does not cool the consciousness so that it may act. It inflames. Mankind are inflamed by a sordid consciousness. They are also inflamed by a sordid *conscience*. But some have no conscience, for they have seared it with a hot iron. They have remained insensate to its voice. The voice of God has spoken, "Thou doest wrong," and they have not replied. They have not listened. Their ears have become dull. The way of peace and the way of truth they have not known. Their mind is opaqued with darkness. Yet even then the spark within, which breathes life through the pores of their flesh, cries out in the dark for a ray of hope.

ENOUGH IS ENOUGH

Morya thunders! And the thunder is the fires of the Spirit as they move aside the groaning earth. The earth shakes and quakes. The earth is afraid. For the terrors of returning karma come back to mankind and the walls of Jericho fall once again.[2] The cities of darkness, whether or not they are physically destroyed, are already destroying themselves and those who dwell within their walls. For the spread of infection is everywhere, and the dampness and darkness of death is the mold of a tomb scraped by the fingernails of children. This, then, is carried in horror to their mothers, who cry out and say, "Where have you been?" And the children know not, for they are but children; and the parents know not, for they are also children.

Now then, we say: Where is the vision of beauty? Where is the vision of the Beatitudes?[3] Where is the vision of Elysian fields? Where is hope? Does it not always lie in the realm of the Spirit? Can the dark ones create hope? Can they provide freedom for the soul? Can they give manna? *What can they do?* They are the children of Belial! They will behave according to the precepts of their masters.

We then today, mindful of the cult of the spiritual Mother of the World, mindful of the tenderness that she has for her children, say to every one of you:

The law of love that gave thee birth would also assist thee to complete the initiatic process and to lead thee out and onward to the fulfillment of thy immortal destiny!

But the world herself, with her sullied skirts, is in thy mind. And thou art concerned, as we are, with the children who also came forth from the same God-Sun who are themselves pursuing the phantom images and whose spirit sparks are dissipating in needless losses. Their losses are many, and they do not recoup them. Their losses are frightening and ever mounting.

A crescendo is reached and we say it is enough; it cannot pass beyond this. And then new debts are created, new horrors are created, and new shadow-shapes are made. The world in all of her darkness still groans and cries out, for the very elements themselves are saturated with all that is darkness. The saturation of the darkness has made those in the world uncomfortable, and they themselves—and even the elemental manifestations—cry out in pain, longing for the light. They live in damp cellars, and moot, unspeakable things are done there.

But we who understand the plans of God realize that the consciousness of man reeks in shame because of that which he sees. For man is caught between the dark and the light. Man is trapped between the wonderful hopes of heaven and the vicious powers of hell that seek to do him in.

REVERSE THE TRENDS OF HUMAN DESPAIR AND DISCORD

We, then, come to you today, as we have already done, to speak the solemn word of warning. If I seem somber, if I seem to be morbid, understand that I am not! I am simply citing the vulgarities that mankind have grown accustomed to, and I am citing them for a reason. The reason is that I desire that you should recoil from these vulgarities. I desire that *all* mankind should recoil from them! And I hope that in your own recoil those in the whole earth will also shudder in shame. I hope that as they recoil they will look upward to the realm of the angels, to the realm of the Spirit, to the realm of cosmic destiny, to the realm of cosmic immensity! I hope that they will see, in the whole vast cosmos, a song of melodic love whose intertwining within the soul is a cord* that can never be cut or severed, is a cord that pulls man upward and out of the socket of mortality to where he can perceive the precious vestments of immortality and long to wear those robes.

Do you think, precious ones of the light, that the attitudes of mankind today are permanent attitudes? Do you think that these attitudes that they have toward one another—nation hating nation, individuals hating individuals, churches hating churches, schools hating schools, and chaos reigning everywhere—are attitudes of peace, attitudes that will generate a new age? I am sure you know that they will not. For more and more has chaos been bred upon the earth, and the despair of the young hearts is very terrible to behold.

But we are concerned anew each day, and our ever-new concerns take mounting precedence over old concerns. And borne out of these concerns we say that no act of man and no act of God can

---

*This could also be interpreted as *chord.*

be enough until the victory is won. For we must turn the tide upon mortal despairs! We must reverse the trends of human discord and jangle! We must seek to re-create the great passions of the Spirit that have stirred the souls of the saints! We must see to it that mankind, modern mankind, are not *afraid* to be thought like unto the saints, that they are not *afraid* to resemble the angelic hosts, that they are not *afraid* to cast out fear, that they are not *afraid* of the phantoms of the world—all these things that are so much nothing!

For whereas these phantoms inhabit the astral world—for they have no other place to go, you know—at the same time, the astral world is not the heaven-world! It was created as a repository for these activities of misqualification, as a charnel house, as a Hades for the offal and the spewings of mankind. It is there that these spewings have accumulated and piled up, and it is there that the consciousness of men and women is directed.

Oh, yes, there is a segment thereof that is filled with a perfidious virtue. There is a segment thereof that is filled with the appearance of good, of self-righteousness, and with the idea of embellishing individuals with their own goodness. This too is a filthy thing. In reality, it is a rag of unrighteousness and it must be cast aside. For the virtue of Almighty God is enough for all! And mankind, when they understand it correctly, do not need to bring their own righteousness to the feast of the LORD, for his righteousness is enough for them! They simply need to put it on.

When man will cast aside the old rags into the rag bag, when he will cast them aside and say, "I have had enough of thee! I would rather stand here naked until I am given my garment of light," then he will find that God will quickly cover his nakedness, for the LORD desires so to do. And then he will not be naked but clothed upon with his right mind, with the sternness of consciousness that will enable him, as the camel drivers in Egypt, to bite the dust, to face the east wind, to hold the reins securely, and to command the beast to go where he wants it to go.

Sometimes, you see, we are a bit on the diligent side. Sometimes we ourselves feel that to coddle individuals—to mollycoddle, if you will, as you would say it—is to have them lose their soul and be a castaway. There are times when we need to shake up the students of the light and to let them understand that in this shaking up there will come about the renaissance of true virtue and reality. They will understand that the old thoughts have not been enough, for the thoughts that they have had have been limited.

THE INSURANCE POLICY OF THE COSMOS

Morya breeds limitless light! Morya breeds the fires of the Spirit that, not only when they are banked but when they are activated, are always aflame! For they express the nature of the flame and they refuse to accept the idea of stultification, of death, of going out, of being no more. *God* is in them! *He* is the center core of their activity!

You cannot extinguish the fires of the Spirit! You cannot extinguish the concentric radiations of the Great Central Sun! The pulsations *will* go forth! And if mankind will misqualify them, then the misqualified energy that they have created will itself destroy them. For God wishes destruction to none. And the misqualified energy, once it has accomplished the purpose that man has ordained for it, will itself go back to the heart of the Sun to be freed. For the nature of light is always to return back to its Source.

When mankind understand this, they will not so much fear for their little flesh form or for their petty ideas—or for their *pet* ideas or for those things that they have so carefully nourished and protected—not understanding that the very sense of committing all to God does itself give man his best protection. For individuals actually could not really cover themselves with a cosmic insurance policy, for none would be broad enough to include all of the many blessings that God has for those who will actually follow him in the regeneration.

The insurance policy of the cosmos is itself the very Law that God himself has written. And the security that mankind can then have is a security of acting out the Law, of obeying the Law, of recognizing that the Law is their friend. It is having the security of understanding that the ascended masters are their friends, that human beings are often their betrayers, that human beings are often treacherous, and that the treachery of mankind is everywhere. It is having the understanding that betrayal is everywhere because mankind betray themselves whensoever they betray others.

COMMITMENT AND CO-MEASUREMENT

When mankind will be diligent to pursue the things of the Spirit, they will find that the light of the Far East will come into their life, and it will not be a "Far East" any longer but it will be a "Near East" that they will encounter. And when the light of the sun of the Near East comes to the soul, they will find that the will of God is strengthened within them and that the course of all events is stirred to obey the great golden thread of cosmic law that unwinds before them as the golden ball thrown before Atalanta.[4]

We, then, desire to see mankind escape from the labyrinth of life, and not only to escape but to escape *cleanly*. Will you understand, then, that commitment is also the means to co-measurement? For when mankind commit themselves unto God, they are able with him to co-measure the destiny of themselves. And when co-measurement is established, the individual can actually assess his own virtue as well as his own vice. And the assessment of his vice is not an activity of condemnation but an activity of filling in the insufficiencies, of bringing forth the beauties and perfections in order to cover up the multitude of sins that have actually manifested in ignorance and error in his world.

For karma must be fulfilled, and so it will be. The darkness shall vanish and the sunburst of the divine light shall give the soul not only food for thought but food for *eternal* thought. And the nourishment of that manna that came down from heaven will enable the son of God to accept his divine Sonship. The passions of the light shall flood his soul, and all fear shall be no more. The way of peace will he know, and the way of the ascended masters and the way of the divine will.

Now while I am speaking to you, I am well aware of the difficulties that some of you have encountered. I am well aware of the struggles. I therefore urge you to understand that when you cease the struggles and God acts in your world, your world shall be protected. It will be protected because the activity of God is an indomitable activity that works and serves within you, as the leaven serves within the bread to raise it. The leaven of the Spirit will enable mankind to raise themselves, to elevate their consciousness to the mountain heights, to become one with God.

Let not your hearts be weary or troubled by the attitudes necessary for mankind to escape from the darkness of the world. For I tell you that to be immersed in the world is far worse than to pass through the fires of initiation and to escape. That which you pass through today and that which you will also suffer in the future is nothing in comparison to the weight of glory that is manifest once you have attained. And attainment herself can come— and the ascension can come—as easily as a bird takes flight from a twig and flies toward the sun and above the clouds and shadows.

Will you understand, then, that even when the great power and glory does not seem to swirl around you—when the hard and cold attitudes of a Monday morning are manifest in your consciousness—the light of the *sun*-day, the light of the *glory*-day, the light of *hope* is ever present.

MANKIND MUST DO MORE TO COUNTERACT THE DANGERS THAT THREATEN THE EARTH

We have learned to stand against the vicissitudes of darkness and the problems of the world. We have learned to stand against it.

And I well recall that more than once did I pay with life or head. But I tell you, when you realize that the head of the body is Christ, you will understand that no man can extinguish your flame. *No man can put out the fires of God that are banked within your precious consciousness, and no man ever will!*

If you will understand this *individually,* you will understand it *collectively.* And as you understand it collectively, you will realize that there are times when we must, by cosmic law, speak as I am doing today, for the activities of the world are most frightening indeed.

Some of you today are not aware of all that is going on in the world because your consciousness is so completely directed to God. Some of you do not actually study the periodicals of the world, listen to the programs of the world, or become involved in the activities of the world to the point where you are aware of just what is happening. Others are very much aware of what is happening. And those who *are* aware of it—and I love you both—will understand that grave danger threatens the earth and that mankind must do more than they have done in order to counteract it.

The activities of the divine ones have not been enough because there are not enough of the divine ones upon the planet. And the children of God who are bound by the cords of tradition, these need to be free. Some are now coming out of their darkness and despair toward the light. They are in search of truth, and they are in search of freedom from drug addiction. Some are coming toward the light, and they desire freedom from the torturous states of consciousness engendered by the false traditions of society. But many yet remain in bondage.

We therefore urge upon you that when there are moments of shame and darkness and doubt, when there are moments of mistrust and insecurity in your world, understand that these are the moments of testing. These are the moments when the precious balm of the Spirit is being poured upon you as the anointing of the wounds and the binding up of the wounds of humanity so that the limbs can once again be flexed with action and so that once again the precious glories of the Spirit will renew themselves within you.

In addition to the knowledge of peace, you will find out that the knowledge from the East is also the knowledge of the *sword*— the knowledge of the sword of the Spirit, of the wounds that occur to human hearts as they seek to cut themselves free from all that the human consciousness has created and that the LORD has never made.

THE KARMIC CUP IS RUNNING OVER, YET HOPE LIVES ON

For the LORD made only goodness and beauty and a world of wonder. You call it heaven. It is celestial. Man has made the netherworlds, and the spirits of darkness have also assisted mankind in the creation of the worlds of darkness. They have sought to stifle and smother this world with darkness and with selfishness.

Morya brings forth an activity of the Darjeeling Council!

Morya uses the sword of the Spirit!

Morya cuts through the cringing hordes!

Morya saith: The LORD strikes a blow this day, and I shall not define it! But the world shall know it, for the lash of heaven is upon mankind and the scourge of God goeth forth! For the world shall be lashed for its disobedience, and the children of the light shall once again be lifted up. The hand of God shall shine forth its radiance over them and they shall feel the protecting armour of God. And the children of darkness shall gnash their teeth and cry out in pain, for they have given pain to others.

And when the cry is enough, behold, mercy and justice shall triumph. And the children of darkness shall also come forth and be given opportunity, for the Lord is long-suffering and greatly to be praised. In him is no darkness nor shadow of turning,[5] but only the fullness of the Law—the fullness of the law of infinite love and infinite grace.

With this we clothe you this day. Be not dismayed nor affrighted for all that is happening in the world. For the turbulence and turgidity of the world will respond to the ministrations of the Prince of Peace. And when the karmic cup is filled to the brim and running over, and when all of this has been done, then the Prince of Peace will come. And he himself will bring an ointment, the unguents of the Spirit to mankind, and then there will be fulfilled the prophecies of glory.

Meanwhile, the cup of wrath and trembling comes to a world already suffering and reeling. Yet hope lives on, and it lives in *your* hearts. For to you is given the knowledge of the mysteries of God, even to those of you who constitute this Mystery School—this place of spiritual enlightenment, this temple of truth dedicated to the pursuit of right knowledge, to the end of fear, and to the perfectionment of man.

Out of the Darjeeling Council halls I have spoken. Into the human heart I have dropped a precious pearl. Because there was a mingling of blood in the pearl, we have called it a "blood pearl."

But remember: We will bring peace after struggle. We will bring day after night. We will bring joy after sorrow. And man shall know—through his suffering and the alchemy thereof, which he has created—the final peace of God. And the latter glory shall be greater than all that has ever been.

Meanwhile, I say with Saint Germain: *Be diligent. Be vigilant. Be alert.*

I thank you.

April 6, 1969
La Tourelle
Colorado Springs, Colorado
MLP

CHAPTER 9

*I call to men and women of wisdom
and vision to come to my camp and abide,
to pitch their tents beneath the shadow of our
holy mountain and to see that the will of God is
the great crystal stream flowing out to all nations
and bidding all nations to come and drink
forever of the pure stream of Reality.*

THE BANNER
OF THE MOTHER OF THE WORLD
IS REVEALED

Immortal and Infinite Destiny Beckons!

We welcome the pilgrims to Darjeeling, for the fountain of the Mother of the World is revealed.

The supplicant hands of the children of all nations reach out, and the cries of spiritual hunger must be assuaged. We are ready! We are ready to build the great domicile of humanity within the heart of God. We are ready.

The Mother of the World unfurls her banner, and it is grasped by the champion knights. For valor is not dead! And nobility still lives in the hearts of many who will rally to the cause and who will reveal, then, ultimately, the portrait of the New Age. Fashioned first in the heart and mind, this will come forth with such dazzling light as to blind the beholders.

Like those who gazed upon the empty tomb and saw the rapturous vision of the living Christ,[1] so will humanity respond and understand—when the spirit of the universal resurrection comes into living embodiment in the hearts of the many—how the banners of darkness have been trampled upon and how all of the opaquing paints of deceit, which have covered those banners and caused them to appear as banners of light, shall finally be seen for the darkness that it is.

The Mother of the World shall stand—the great fountain of all hearts revealed at last—calling together the children of the planet and saying to all, "Bind up the wounds of mortal hurt, even the wounds incurred in the heat of battle. For the Lord does bring forth the balm of comfort, and the radiance of his appearing is a fire upon the hills whose light can be seen even in the uttermost parts of the earth."

I AM Morya of the First Ray. I call to men and women of wisdom and vision to come to my camp and abide, to pitch their tents beneath the shadow of our holy mountain and to see that the will of God is the great crystal stream flowing out to all nations and bidding all nations to come and drink forever of the pure stream of Reality.

As I speak to you today there is a rising of many angelic voices coming from the naves of our great spiritual cathedral, and the hymns that they sing are the songs to the Mother of the World. The highest spiritual drama is unfolding in the gathering together of men and women to the camp of the LORD so that we may send runners throughout the earth whose fiery torch, lit from the fountain of flame, signifies that the will of God will bear to all nations the message of the hour: to beat the swords into plowshares, to beat the spears into pruning hooks,[2] to transform the earth by unmasking the denizens of darkness—the rulers of deceit who have kept humanity in bondage for so long and who have created false hates against one another.

These hates have not produced the miracle of the cleansing of hearts but have kept mankind in a steadfast karmic bondage. Circle come full circle, circle come full circle, circle come full circle, until three times three and in the almost unalterable pattern of destiny, mankind have created and reaped the fruit of endless wars and dissensions, of strivings and darkness.[3]

Now as the banner of the Mother of the World is revealed, the Manchild-Son stands forth upon his white horse waiting to ride forth and to do battle with the darkness that has opaqued the light and prevented its shining into the conscious mind and being of the multitudes of people. And the little children, who in their innocence and sweetness hold up their hands toward God and unashamedly to the Mother of the World, say, "Give us to drink of thy fountain."

But with the coming of age and the corrupting factors of life, these selfsame ones repudiate all that they have seen of old in childhood and in innocence and they say, "It is not. God is not." They say, "Light is not." And they revel in the darkness and the chaos and the confusion and the tragedy of their lives until the little end* is at last finished.

Now we say, as we summon mankind to Darjeeling, "Let the children of light rally to our banner!" For Darjeeling is more than a place. It is the consonance with the will of God that delivers mankind from the lesser attitudes and modes of human thought and feeling. It is the sustaining elements of destiny that will transform lives! It is the miracle from the hills that elevates the valleys, that causes the trembling in the cup of life! It is the miracle that disgorges all the scum and the offscouring of life and reveals the refining gold of the Spirit so that mankind may capture in their minds those radiant and shining moments that they had with God before they knew the present, unfortunate, and stony heart that now seeks to dominate their world and to cause them to refuse the call from the Mother of the World.

Yet as the dawn breaks, as the solemn moment of reality comes, and as the hour of summoning approaches, mankind know

---

little end: archaic for "least significant"

in their hearts that immortal and infinite destiny beckons! They understand, and they answer the call! For of old they danced in the living sheaths of flame before him and they understood the meaning of the music of the spheres. The radiant, fire mist dropped before their gaze, and they said:

> O God! Let me rais-ed* be,
> Step by step up the golden stairway of Reality,
> Until I can nestle my head
> Against the great throbbing of thy heart.
>
> So let my destiny appear
> As an onward flaming torch,
> Calling me, calling me, calling me!
> Ever beckoning me onward, onward, onward
> Through the maze
> And through the darkness and the fears
> And the numbness of uncertainty
> And the shedding of fruitless tears,
> Until at last the mighty gates did open.
>
> And as men passed,
> Their souls did at last see and feel
> The flashing forth of Reality.
> Thy heel shall bruise the serpent's head[4]
> And men shall find instead
> A new Reality upon a cross
> Where rais-ed is a golden serpent,
> Fiery appearing,
> Living, flaming concept of the Word,
> The Logos gods have heard
> Echoing from the farthest realms
> Of eternity's vastness

---

*pronounced *rai-sed*

To unfold in the lastness
Of man's mortal holdings-out against the LORD.

The final sundering cord
Will be shattered, then,
By power through the Word,
The living Word that
Like a sword does sever
And will encourage in the mind of man
The neverness of stain and sin
And pallid movement
Until at last men see
The concepts of the free
In that banner of the Mother of the World,
Stained not ever.

For it is the sacred flame-banner of hope
That unites the hearts of all people
And enables men to understand
The nearness of goal-fitting,
That enables them to feel the power
Of the Lord of the First Ray,
To know that each day
We will seal thy life with a couplet of gold
To the golden rule,
All-enfolding tool of cosmic emissaries
Who understand the Manchild within each heart,
The need to let the Christ rule, not just a part,
But *all* of mortal destiny,
All of man's wholeness,
Until the miracle,
The produced miracle
Of consecrated lives and minds and beings,

Is at last the power that frees the world
From all the chains of historical nonsense
And produces the miracle fulfillment of the Word.
For every eye shall see him[5]
And his voice shall be heard:
"Lo, I AM with you alway, even unto the end of the age."[6]

Peace be with you from the Lord of the First Ray, from the Lord Maha Chohan, from the Brotherhood of Goodwill at Darjeeling.

February 8, 1970
La Tourelle
Colorado Springs, Colorado
MLP

CHAPTER 10

*We come, then, to create a new heaven
and a new earth in the consciousness of humanity,
who will gaze upward toward the light and search out
the magnificent cosmic civilization that is already
created from the whole cloth in the mind of God.*

DO YOU LOVE MORYA?
THEN LOVE THE GOD WITHIN!
LOVE HIS HOLY WILL!

"The meek shall inherit the earth."[1]

Through the orifice of Self pours the most exquisite Reality. Here in the mountains of India, here in Darjeeling where the will of God is most splendidly known, we seek to radiate everywhere into the world domain the comforting aspects of cosmic reality.

Gone now, at this supreme moment in time, are the desires of the Darjeeling Council to amplify, even for instructive purposes, elements of negativity. Therefore it is our desire to turn men from darkness unto light, for they have had enough of the night. They have seen enough of the products of the night spawned in darkness, and they are now gazing upward toward the splendor of the mountaintops, heralding the approach of the golden dawn of cosmic reality.

The highlighting gleams of the forthcoming new age are already beginning to manifest the vitalizing elements within the forcefield of a cosmically endowed humanity. This is so that humanity can have the elements of a new heaven and a new earth,[2] which are already taking form within their mind and consciousness.

For consciousness, when it is oriented around God, is like a glowing, golden, fiery sun. Holy illumination breathes out a sacred prayer, and Buddha and Christ are there, manifesting in the sunlit air the elements of peace and cosmic instruction, of brotherhood and of a turning toward the rainbow radiance of the pure, white light.

All delusion must perish in the splendor of this sun, for there is a trembling down from heaven of the dulcet bars* of heavenly creation. The tonal values of the universe are now shaking the very substance of the earth. And we are determined, where necessary, to unseat out of the realm of mortal pleasure those who have had no other outlook upon life whatsoever than mere earthly enjoyment and its attendant pains.

WE HAVE SOUGHT UNIVERSAL GOOD

We come, then, to create a new heaven and a new earth in the consciousness of humanity, who will gaze upward toward the light and search out the magnificent cosmic civilization that is already created from the whole cloth in the mind of God. We convey this beautiful painting, this *exquisite* tapestry, into the consciousness of humanity. And as we do so, I think that the individual will say, "I bid you welcome."

Traveler, come to our abode! Traveler, enter our humble home! Traveler, unfurl the banner! For we are speaking, now, not only of the domain of reality for the individual but of the domain of reality for the earth.

The culture of the Spirit is with men. Christ proclaimed it from the hilltops and from the seaside, in a ship by the shore.[3] Buddha proclaimed it under the Bo tree. Saint Francis proclaimed it to the birds of the air. And everywhere that the imagination of men has been set afire by the illuminating fragrances of the spiritual living Word, there the fountain of the parliament of

---

dulcet bar: a musical measure that is pleasing to the ear

Almighty God has been conveyed to the parliament of man.

We have sought universal Good. We have sought to create new fragrances of the Spirit. We have sought to stifle the odors of the past and to lift up only the best of gifts. We have continually released our guidance unto humanity. We have looked over them as from a craggy nest, and we have always sought within our soul to raise them thence.

We have gone no place, we tread upon no holy ground that we have not also desired to share with the hallowed circle of humanity. We have lit no cosmic fires nor basked in a spiritual radiance that we have not desired to share. We have gazed upon no inspiration by the writing of the hand of God that we would not have carried as "a message to Garcia"[4] to all humanity. We are available. *But so is the soul!*

The presence of the ascended masters is an adjunct to the natural radiation of the cosmic glow-ray of the infinite fires within yourselves. *You,* then, should understand this.

Do you love Morya? Then love the God within! Love his holy will! For through this common bond we are knit together and we cannot be separated, so long as the bond be adhered to.

The will of God is *not* to be trampled upon. The will of God is to be loved and fondled with the fingers of the mind, with the feelings of the soul. It is as a priceless gift carried in caravans from far-off corners of the universe and through the wendings of time and spatial relationships unto the present day. An ancient stream from an ancient Source, his will flows onward, back to that Source and to be recycled—always carrying the burden of the bowers of cosmic grace, laden with fragrant flowers from space.

> Our every thought, to raise the Word.
> Our every thought, O living Sword.
> *God* is nigh! Heed him, then.
> *God* is nigh! He will defend
> Again and again and again
> The power of victory—the *will.*

WE REINFORCE THE MIGHTY CURRENTS OF THE SPIRIT IN THE WORLD ORDER

The will is a mother. The will is a mother to the son of activity. And when activity is guided by the will of the Holy Mother, then the banner of the Mother of the World unfolds and heralds brotherhood everywhere. But it is a brotherhood of illumination—*not* a brotherhood of darkness or of self-aggrandizement. It is a brotherhood of givingness, and the abundant life is shared by all.

None, then, are without sustenance. *None* are without the potential for growth. *None* are without the grace of our octaves of light. For the soul can soar! And man can rise out of the socket of his density into those radiant patterns that—like sweet fragrance or glorious music—rise to a crescendo and a pattern of beauty so infinite and rare as to challenge all concepts of unreality—concepts that from time to time are spawned in the dens of darkness and carried into the world on the vibratory patterns of human discord and jangle.

We come, then, today, to reinforce the mighty currents of the Spirit in the world order! We come bearing with us the power of the mighty angels of God to radiate and to consecrate and to heal the discord—the ill-fitting mantrams of human selfishness that are echoed in the empty corridors of the mind, that in a spirit of loneliness and frustration cry out for assistance in the night!

But none seem to answer. For the call has been based upon human vanity and deceit rather than upon human consecration to the divine ideals of the Spirit. And the fragrance and glorious music is so sweet that all who hear it will immediately recognize it and say:

"O God, this is thy day—thy day, O LORD, when thy light shall be spread abroad as a mighty sea of illumination over the whole earth!"

And here, as we manifest this great and mighty ocean of cosmic truth, we see the foam and the spume and the spray and the refreshment of new opportunities born each day, which are conveyed, then, to every little one—everyone who hopes, everyone who cares, everyone who understands the magnificence of cosmic, fiery passions for light and love.

For love itself must learn to love. And when you understand this, you can take some of the first toddling steps upon the pathway. You can begin to unfold the patterns of infinite destiny within your life plan. You can begin to live and to consecrate yourself in that givingness that is always the commonweal of heaven—taking not only into account the mankind, the humanity of this earth, but also taking into account all of humanity and the spiritual treasure troves that are manifesting upon every star system in the vast spiral nebulae of space.

For space will be hallowed by the sacred fragrance of his Presence everywhere God is! And wherever he is and wherever he manifests, the power of his love flows forth—a suffusion, an infusion, a transfusion—creating anew in the consciousness of men a realization that the LORD is alive forevermore, that in *him* they live, in *him* they move, and in *him* they have Be-ness. And without that awareness, without that understanding, they live in darkness and with the gnashing of teeth[5] and a wailing in the unsettlements of confusion.

A UNITING OF ALL HEARTS

Now we come, then, to consecrate anew, here in the world order, a *spiritual* Round Table, as of old. We summon the best knights and ladies in the land. We summon the best knights and ladies and demand consecration to God's will and to the commonweal.

We hold up the weapons of our spiritual warfare and we say to all: Be wise as serpents and harmless as doves,[6] generating, without fear, the radiance of the cosmic fire in your mind and being! For the perfect love of that cosmic fire will transform the very world domain into a place where Christ can come.

And of a truth to all generations: When the Second Coming of the Messiah is to be accomplished, it will be because the hearts of men have readied themselves to receive him and to receive the Holy Grail of purity of purpose and purity of ideals.

The Holy Grail, which holds the cherished power of our Saviour's life, will put an end to strife, to gossip, to deceit, to defeat, to unholy alliances. It will determine for all time—for the merry domain of the old world made new—that we shall seal mankind in the heart of God as we once again seek to build a Camelot, where the light—*the wondrous light of God*—can be esteemed as the light that never fails to give its beams to the lonely hearts.

This will be a uniting of all hearts, then, in a common grail of infinite activity, transforming the world into a place where the full domesticity of cosmic reality can become apparent to all as they understand the meaning of the use of the sacred fire of the creative *will*—of the creative *essence,* of the creative *law*—the law of infinite love that is sealed in the heart of the Divine Will and guarded by the Divine Mother as she seeks to bring forth the Cosmic Manchild. And thus the fires of regeneration become the vehicle through which she serves.

Ich dien! I serve!

Will you join me in that service and keep your pledge?

I thank you.

February 22, 1970
La Tourelle
Colorado Springs, Colorado
MLP

CHAPTER 11

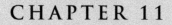

The way to the temple is to be found
by making your own lives compatible with mine.
For my life is dedicated to Him and to the expansion
of the cosmic destiny of all mankind.

AGELESS WISDOM IS THE FULFILLMENT OF THE HUNGERS OF THE SOUL

The electrifying cosmic fire from our Temple of Good Will here in Darjeeling manifests in the world. And those who are sensitive to its vibration respond because there is keyed in their hearts a response to the melody of the sacred-fire harmony.

Now, then, bear well in mind that all over the world the hearts of the children of mankind, who are also the children of God, are hungering and thirsting after righteousness.[1] That these may be filled is our prayer. And there is no filling so great as the filling of the children of God with his holy will. For his holy will carries within it the embodiment of all perfection.

The seed atoms, electrifying in essence and descending in the glass of the hours, radiate to the consciousness of humanity the fullness of the diamond-shining mind of God. As humanity are contacted by this radiance, it comes to pass that the yearning in the heart for the truth and the perfection of life increases within them, and they yearn to express it in every avenue of life.

You now, who have journeyed from afar, who have made this pilgrimage here to Darjeeling, should bear well in mind that you come from a land of considered opulence. You come from a land far different from this one, from a land where the forces of nature have been treated by chemicalization and by various activities of human consciousness. These have affected the manifestation of primal life until the humanity there are actually being molded and shaped by environmental forces that seem to control, almost literally, every aspect of life.

Here in the freedom of the mountains of Darjeeling—here in this area of the world now somewhat unspoiled by man's control of the forces of nature, retaining still some of the primal knowledge of the olden times—the humanity here are able to drink a little deeper of the nectar of the holy will. Yet the encroachment of the Western world upon this way of life is a steady and creeping paralysis that is destined—unless they themselves resist it —to cause those in this area of the world to also surrender to the attitudes of materialism and to the shadowed enclosures from the West.

Yet the West is not devoid of light, for the West has its own light even as the East has its own light. And we would unite light with light. For both north, east, west, and south, the world has light. Yet the light of the East is also the light of the West. For light is light and retains its power wherever it goes.

It is simply that the overlay of mass confusion, of human effluvia, has so charged the atmosphere of the mind with destructive manifestations that the clarity and power of the Spirit cannot come through. The sunlight is shining behind the clouds, but the clouds are opaquing and hindering at all times the manifestation of living and vital truth. The vibrancy of our love, then, would also remind you of the scenes of the poverty and of the limitations imposed upon humanity by their overlords, which you have witnessed here in India.

WHY WILL YOU TREASURE YOUR TRIVIA?

We would remind you, however, that man himself, by consent, has also acceded to the will of his overlords and has not actually sought the freedom of the great LORD of all life—the freedom of the LORD of all life that he would give so gladly, so willingly to all humanity.

We, then, who understand the needs of humanity, understand full well that the power of the Lord Christ, of Krishna, of Buddha must manifest in the heart of the aspirants. Humanity must aspire to release the vibrancy of the power of love and truth from within themselves. They must turn their backs upon darkness and shadow, upon shame. They must revoke the vibratory actions of shadow that they have imposed upon life in the past. They must understand the need to shake off the lethargy of the senses that, as an enclosing cloud, comes to all humanity, producing not great benefits but great limitations.

Man has given to power the power of limitation, whereas power itself has within it the magnificent chain-shattering devices that will, when the right time comes, enable all humanity to know the freedom and peace of a golden age of enlightenment.

In the name of Almighty God I say to you, why will you treasure your trivia? Why will you treasure those little trinkets that have brought you so much sorrow and discord? Why will you cling to those manifestations that have never given you your freedom, when all the world is pining today and hungering and thirsting after righteousness?

The religions of the world have been produced at great sacrifice, and the power of the sacred fire has been released. The blaze has been kindled from the mountains, and mankind have seen and their hearts have rejoiced. The fire is flashed forth and is traveled by courier—by swift wings of light across the margents of the world!

We have gathered in the sublime places in the mountains. We have gathered in the hidden temples. We have gathered in the hearts of humanity. And yet the moment that the moneychangers come, the moment that the fakirs come, the moment that someone rattles a little gravel in a tin pan, the people turn. For they are so easily distracted by outer manifestation. The vistas of the senses never lead farther than the four enclosing walls. But the great vistas of the Spirit are shattering all, and they cause the heart to soar beyond the clouds, beyond the stars to the Lord of all life, who in his sublime and beauteous concept has envisioned for all the glory of the heavenly world.

GOD HOLDS A CONSCIOUSNESS OF PERFECTION FOR EACH LIFE

I tell you, no maharaja has ever lived in a palace more beautiful than that which God has destined in the specific consciousness that he holds within the perfection of the individualized will of God for each life. Each life, precious to him as a little diamond, possesses the transcendent power of expansionism inherent within itself whereby it can expand its light. And by the blue flame of the holy will shining in the dungeons of the uncut gem, the refining fires produce the miracle of hope at last. And hope itself, shattering all things and passing beyond, comes to the state where it is at the feet of the Mother of the World, no longer in exile and darkness, no longer enclosed within the tiny temple of the personality.

Hope is the understanding that God's will reaches out to a skyey dome, more vast by far than man has envisioned in his poetic license, to a realm where the powers of the Spirit will give to every man that specific God-quality—that quality that in ages past enabled each one to understand how they could be a *rishi**
of the Spirit, a nobleman of God, a son of God who is able to call

---

rishi: [Sanskrit], a divinely inspired sage or poet who is often regarded as a saint down the fire from on high as Elijah did upon the altar at Mount Carmel. And the fire that he invoked did pulsate before them all, consuming before the priests of Baal those specific instruments of nature, and did reveal the LORD God as supreme.[2]

I say to you all, then, bow to no graven image but only to the God within all! And understand that even those whom you meet outwardly—who come in humble guise, in outer garments of humility, who seem to possess so little of the world's goods, who seem to manifest even so little of universal intelligence—are also his children. They are the children of his heart, those uncut and unrefined gems that he would purify through the service of those more illumined Brothers of light who understand this [and who would serve God's children] not as a measure of sacrifice but as a measure of enlightenment.

THERE IS A NEED FOR VIGILANCE

Each contribution made to the world order is an incisive blow against those destructive elements of the world who desire to continue their control of the world order through the power of the moloch* of human greed,[3] through the power of money, through the power of destructivity, through the power of human control over the lives of others who are affected by political or even religious means.

We want all to understand that the freedom of the spirit is that which also acknowledges the need to form a body politic in society and to provide for a full measure of order and the definite activity of light that will control the manifestation of violence and destruction in the world and produce the miracle of peace on earth and goodwill toward men.[4] But in the name of Almighty God centuries have passed in which the course of human history has run as a river of blood. Centuries have passed during which

---

*moloch: something or someone having the power to require extreme sacrifice. The term derives from the fire deity of the biblical Canaanites who offered human sacrifices, especially of children, to the god.

mankind's destructivity, often in the name of religion as well as in the name of political ideologies, has continued to bring about great destructivity.

At this present hour the confluence of human forces in the world order is very destructive. And I say to all of you that there is a need for vigilance, there is a need for holy prayer, there is a need for recognition of the efforts that God expects you to expend so that you also, by the cosmic divining rod of your own sacred spinal altar, may invoke the fires of the Spirit upon that sacred altar and bring forth the controlling power whereby you, in your own lives—coming each day more directly under the gaze of the spiritual eye in the center of the forehead—may at last understand how the vision of the Mother of the World may be consummated in the hearts of men, as men are illumined to understand the mysteries of the sacred mystery schools that have been kept secret since the foundation of the world.

These sacred mysteries are not for the profane! And those of you who come upon this pilgrimage should understand that every effort should be expended in the becoming of that which God expects you to be. Envision yourselves not as a tyrant, not as an immature individual, but as one whom God hath lifted up—and then act accordingly. For the greatest practicality of all religion is the expression of the will of God in one's daily life. For your bodies are temples—temples of God and of his purity—and the hungers of the world must be fed. But how shall they be fed except through the practical expression of God through you all?

MAKE YOUR LIVES COMPATIBLE WITH MINE

You have come here to Darjeeling expecting to find a physical temple, a physical manifestation of my own power and of my own radiance. Well, I tell you, there *is* such a temple! And I want you to know, however, that the way to that temple is to be found by making your own lives compatible with mine. For my life is dedicated to Him and to the expansion of the cosmic destiny of all mankind.

We therefore desire you to understand that your body is a house of God, that your mind is a house of God, that your thoughts are a house of God, that all things, all components of man, are temples of God, that each temple has specific needs— needs and requirements of this hour and every hour. These need to be filled with the will of God.

Humanity have emptied themselves of this radiance in past ages. They have consumed the flame of God upon their own lusts.[5] They have not recognized the power of truth as their paramount need. They have thought to cheat the Lords of Karma. They have thought that human destiny was not important. They have thought that their *contribution* to human destiny was not important. They have not reckoned with the great cosmic scales of justice. They have not reckoned with the promises they made at inner levels before they were given embodiment. They have not reckoned with the masters of the Far East, with the masters of the West, with the Spirit of the Great White Brotherhood as a tangible force in the world. They have paid greater heed to the renderings of human minds in print than they have to the sacred writings of the ages.

Ageless wisdom is the fulfillment of the hungers of the soul! Turn, then, with all your heart to this ageless wisdom. Turn to it and drink deeply of it. Become imbued with it—with the power of the Spirit and with the power of the will of God. Let it be released, then, into your world.

Traveler, the temple awaits! Traveler, the gates are open! Traveler, the gates will not always remain open! Traveler, take for the journey the garments of the Spirit!

Be prepared to accept the oppositions of the legions of darkness. But remember that they are figments of man's imagination, made tangible and real by human endowment, and that they have no reality in the mind of God. For he has created only Good, and the will of God is to sustain the momentum of that Good that he has created for you all. This we offer you in Darjeeling! This we offer you in the world! This we offer you in the Grail cup!

> The knights and ladies of the Table Round of old
> Sought to consummate a kingdom bold,
> A land of beauty where God was remembered,
> A land of beauty where strength was garnered.
> And yet there came Modred of old
> With deceit and human opinions bold.
> He did reach forth and become a spoiler
> To create human mold
> And to destroy the kingdom we sought to frame of old.

Now, then, I come to you all, and I come to you with the self-same image that we held long ago. I come to you with the concept of the kingdom of God, of the kingdom of heaven, of the power of the avatars, of the power of Maitreya, of the power from the mountains. I come to you and I remind you that the way to the temple is to draw to yourself the magnificence of the diamond-shining mind of God.

THE VISION OF THE DARJEELING COUNCIL

The Brothers of the Diamond Heart consider the problems of humanity. The Brothers of the Diamond Heart consider the problems of Calcutta, of New York, of Peking,* of the world. In the land of Sikkim, in the land of Nepal, in the land of Pakistan and wherever there are children of God, they are *all* loved by us just as we love America and the people of South America and the islands of the sea. There is no difference! We would gather all in one vast canopy of cosmic beauty overhead. We would gather all beneath this canopy. We would create a harmony of hearts.

---
*Beijing

By childlike simplicity, we would create the image of the traveler from afar who carries in his hand a staff. And the staff is the Word of God. The staff is the *power* of the Word of God! The staff is the *accomplishment*—the practical accomplishment by which the miracles of the Spirit are made! These conditions can be produced in the lives of ye all, and all humanity can accept the realities of the Spirit. Their hearts are stirred by outer conditions. We would stir them by *inner* conditions.

Some of you would like an interview with me. You wish that I would open up the door of the temple. You wish that I would speak to you personally. Well, I *am* speaking to you personally. And I am speaking to those beyond the seas, and I am speaking to the world. I am saying to all that an hour spent with me would be an hour spent in vain unless you were willing to accept from me the teachings on the will of God, which ye can accept now. And as ye accept it and make it a part of your life, you can find out that the way to the temple is to put on the garments of Morya. Put on my garments! Put on my thought! Put on the will of God! Put on our light, and you will have the mystic temple of Darjeeling within yourself!

And then, no matter where ye tread, the will of God will manifest. You will carry the flame of Darjeeling and the flame of the Brothers of the Diamond Heart into the world, where the practical manifestation of cosmic brotherhood can be taught. This is where mankind can learn to put aside the divisive courses of history, where they can change events, where they can cast down their overlords, which are both the overlords within themselves [and in the outer world]—the overlords of vain desire, the overlords of carnality and materiality, the overlords of ego, the overlords of darkness, of deceit, the overlords of fear—all of the conditions that are goads to their lives.

Mankind can then, by Cosmic Christ understanding and the power of our Brotherhood, overthrow in the outer world all those who would rule men with a rod of iron[6] and who understand not the power of the Spirit, which is itself far more powerful than all the armies of the world!

I AM serving the Prince of Peace, and he who is the Prince of Peace sends out his light from Darjeeling. And now, as I prepare to perform a special service for you that shall come forth while I am speaking, I will send from the rooftops of the world and out into all the regions of the world a bolt of cosmic lightning. I will send a bolt of cosmic lightning into China, and I will send a bolt of cosmic lightning into Russia, and I will send a bolt of cosmic lightning into America, and I will send a bolt of cosmic lightning into every nation.

WE ARE PREPARING THE WAY
FOR PEACE AND ENLIGHTENMENT

Those who would rule the nations would create the delusion that the nations are separate. But I say to you today, the nations are *one* and are one under God! Those who would create illusion and maya will also create the image of division. And by creating this image of division, they will control the world.

We would free the world to understand that in a spirit of oneness in the heart, the light from the heart can prepare the way for the coming of the golden age. And if, then, we decide to open a physical focus of our light here in Darjeeling, it will also be the tying together of the hemisphere here with the hemisphere there. And it will come to pass that we will be binding up the world, and binding it up so that the golden age may manifest more quickly.

This, however, is up to humanity. It is up to those who respond to the light to make their own determination. For you see, the same overlords that rule in the world of finance in America also rule in Russia and in China. They create the illusion of a tri-unity that is actually split against each other. When the people of these nations, respectively, are being dragged down and prepared for a bath of blood and destructivity, we are preparing the way for peace and enlightenment to come to the world through the will of God.

Peace and enlightenment that has been denied the world for ages must now come forth! Some have waited for the coming of the *Mahdi;** others have waited for *Messias.*† We say that Messias and Mahdi both come! And Maitreya comes when the light upon the mountain enters the heart and enfires the spirit, when the light upon the mountain flashes forth, when the glory of the light, which is the will of God, becomes a tangible manifestation across the margents of the world, enfolding it as a garment of splendor!

Now then, I say, let it be done, and let the bolts of lightning flash forth to the world! Let the will of God thunder from Darjeeling, and let the will of God be heard in the farthest corners of the world!

Let mankind understand that only by the will of God shall perfectionment—the longed-for perfectionment of the ages—come forth with the age-old memories of the Sun behind the sun, the age-old memories of the sacred-fire temples of Atlantis and Lemuria, the age-old memories of the kindling of the fire in the child-hearts of mankind until they become masters of their destiny. And then at last they will be able to see the sun-fire radiance, the white-fire core behind the rainbow radiance manifesting all around them, with the splendor of the cosmic zodiac and the perfection of the divine astrology, so that all influences may bow at last to the LORD of all, the supreme Sun behind the sun.

This I AM! This ye all are! And as ye say "This I AM" it becomes for ye all the will of God—the will of God by which your bones were hardened, by which the rock grid structures of the earth were framed, by which the far-flung worlds and starry radiances of space were also created. And in the time-spatial net, in the web of *kal* and *desh,*‡ we will weave the perfectionment of

---

**Mahdi:* the messiah prophesied to appear at the end of the world in Muslim tradition; a Muslim messianic leader
†*Messias:* (Messiah) Anointed One; anticipated saviour
‡*kal* and *desh:* Sanskrit for time and space; *kal-desh:* the intermingling of time and space; the time-space continuum

God and of his life and of his light and of his love everywhere!

This is God's will. Will ye be it? Then see it! Will ye be it? Then be it!

For by the power of example we will spread it abroad. As a contagious disease is spread amongst mankind, so the seeds of the Spirit, as they become tender vines nurtured and cared for, will expand until the flowers and the garments of the Spirit are woven around the world. And then the perfume of peace will flood all hearts and the will of God will replace the discord, the dampness, the misery, and the shadowed enclosures that humanity have acceded to in all of its vileness for far too long.

We are concerned! *Are ye?* Then respond in your hearts and let the world hear our words. For the words that have gone forth in the past and the words that we are sending forth now are words of release. They are words of peace. They are words of freedom to every little child born unto every mother. They are words of freedom in memory of the Mother of the World, in memory of Maitreya, in memory of the altar of God.

I say then, let change come to the world, and let there be an age of enlightenment! Let the past bury its past, and let the resurrection of life spring forth, full-blown into manifestation, with the flame of the ark of the covenant—the ark that flames within the heart. Let the veil be rent in twain.[7] Let the light of the Holy of Holies shine forth again.

I, Morya of the Zen, have spoken.

April 9, 1970
Darjeeling, India
MLP

CHAPTER 12

The winds from Darjeeling blow swiftly and coolly.
They blow with delight and with an aroma of man's
externalization of the beauty of the First Cause,
of the first ray, of the first ideal,
of the first sense of direction.

MORYA COMES!
WE THUNDER WITH THE HOPE
OF A NEW DAY!

The strenuousness of cosmic effort comes to mind as the renewal of divine fruit. For as you exert the bow of effort on our behalf, on behalf of yourselves and on behalf of the cosmic hierarchy, so there is built into the consciousness of man a realization of the truth about himself.

You are children of one Father. Out of you, then, is evoked a natural response—the response of the centuries, of the millennia of the past. And our response is to call out of you the evocation of Reality. Ours is to evoke from you the strength of his right arm,[1] for he lives in you and you live in him, and there is no other Reality.

To become tethered unto him, then, is important not only in the flight Godward but also in the flight of the *imagination* Godward. For man ought to also understand how he may imagine great things about his soul, about the state of becoming and of the Reality from which he is fabricated. And then he may observe how these tremendous ideas of the soul bear fruit upon the tree of one's life.

The winds from Darjeeling blow swiftly and coolly. They blow with delight and with an aroma of man's externalization of the beauty of the First Cause, of the first ray, of the first ideal, of the first sense of direction.

In coming to you today, it is a prelude of our action for the season of solstice. We are coming to you so that we may re-create in you those old dreams and splendid dreams of other years. We are coming so that we may evoke out of you a realization of the future, of the time of tomorrow, of the day of your victory, of the day of your achievement when all of your darkness is put under your feet,[2] when at last you have externalized the Truth and when the Truth lives in you and moves in you as the direction of a new age.

The New Age is aborning even now, and even today the little cradle is being prepared. We perceive that the Christ consciousness is being bequeathed anew each day to humanity as the hierarchy begins to externalize its design. Humanity may also propose their own designs and their own thoughts as to how we shall build a new age. But I tell you that God has already proposed, through the hierarchy and the hand of hierarchy, the wonder of escapement for humanity into Reality.

That in which humanity is presently embroiled is not Reality! It is unreality and darkness! It is the consumption of man's energy upon vain ideals! And as today I take a stand in favor of the tomorrows of all of humanity, it is to give to you my realization of those gifts that are most priceless, those diadems that are most shining, those thoughts that glow with a fervor of hope for all the world.

As I spin these designs for the New Age and release them into your consciousness, I say to you: Begin now to understand that these designs may be your *own* dreams, for they come from one source, and that one source has given them birth. And as you accept these designs, understand that they are not only the ideas of Morya but they are born of the flame of life within your own heart. For out of the similitude of the divine likeness, humanity is able once again to re-create those dreams from which heaven is created.

We would stop those who would stifle the creative image! We would say, "Snuff out the flame of hopelessness in the minds and hearts of humanity and replace it by the flame of hopefulness and of new ideas!"

The birthing of an idea must also be nourished from many sources. Those divine nutriments from the octave of hierarchy are an enfiring of the consciousness of man below. But the implementation of this is best given when the heart flames of the millions are also cast into the chalice, and then the chalice glows with the fervor of a Holy Grail. Man sees in this a dream—a *new* dream of man's kindness to man—because he sees clearly.

Many among mankind today operate from the premise in their own mind, so false, that this and that individual is functioning wrongly. They seek to send out the banality of their own criticism, yet they do not understand that criticism is not constructive or creative of the dream of God in man.

When we speak, then, it is the word of truth! It is the sundering of unreality and of the cords that bind man! It is the strengthening of the new shoot! It is man's realization that he is a part of an ever-living drama, that he is that drama unfolding, that this is also the gift of God to the whole world. And each little child that is born and nourished ought to be nourished upon those strands of cosmic hope that are from angelic realms and not solely nourished by outer nutriments, by outer ideas, by outer confusions.

Morya comes! And we thunder with the hope of a new day!

You have begun! Let *all* now continue, and let *all* rise in hope! Let *all* understand that this, when accepting the chalice of God's own heart to the fullness of that heart, is an activity of the spirit of man.

Let man say, "We hold a thimble in our hand, but how can it have an ocean bequeathed to it?" And let me say, then, that the ocean will always bequeath to man the symbol of the rising and expanding thimble until that thimble becomes a barrel and until that barrel becomes a world chalice of hope!

There is no need to accept a feeling of limitation! There is no need for man to accept the idea that his end is nigh! For I say to all: The beginning is every day, and every day is a beginning! And the fashion of the dawn is the fashion of re-creation, the fashion of hope! The great symbols, the best symbols, are raised upward, and the standard is renewed because mankind endorse it and give to it the fire of their own heart. And thus the conflagration becomes eternal and worldwide.

But we must begin the externalization of our dream in the most obscure places, and we must say to all that this dream is within the heart! This dream is within the spirit! This dream is within the fiber of man's being! Unless this dream is externalized through living men, through living hearts of flesh, how shall it be given to the world? The world already lies in darkness, and the star of greatest hope is often put to bed with the slumbering of mortal acceptance.

What, then, shall we change? We shall change the morsel of acceptance into a loaf, and we shall change the loaf into a feast for the world. And then all shall be fed of that one loaf. The loaf shall expand its dimensions until it *can* feed all! For heaven and God possess the flexibility that man does not seem to realize he himself also possesses.

Individuals remain content to accept their limitations and their own shortness of breath without recognizing that the power of the Divine Breath is in the universe and is the divine pneuma— the outflow of abundant life.

Hear then our Word, and come alive! Hear then our Word, and live! For Truth needs to be lived, not just to be believed.

I bid you adieu.

November 29, 1970
La Tourelle
Colorado Springs, Colorado
MLP

CHAPTER 13

*Illumination is the fruit of the Spirit, and it is
the beginning of the fruit of the Spirit in the mind.
It is the origin of high thoughts whereby man can also
summon those potencies of the Spirit in himself,
which are the overcoming and God-victorious
intentions of the cosmic hierarchy.*

THE ILLUMINATION OF MANKIND IS A PASSION OF THE UNIVERSAL CONSCIOUSNESS

We speak of the electric spark, the pearl of great price[1] flashing from the heart unto the mind, and we summon the best gifts. We also reckon with those discordant manifestations that occur in the domain of mortal consciousness because of a lack of holy wisdom.

I AM come, then, this night, with a flaming sword to dissipate in the marts of consciousness those episodes of mortal expression that are not the fashion of the arhat, that do not speak of the power of life to leap, to create the sense of the giant step, to understand that darkness must vanish as the brilliant burst of light feeds and saturates the soul.

As a blotter,* the consciousness absorbs and realizes that far beyond word knowledge is the reach of the mind in *wordless* knowledge. It is the understanding of the grace of God, which has in past eras caused many to awaken and which in this age of great

---

blotter: a spongy paper that absorbs ink; blotting paper

world need will tremble in the mind-cup as the diadem jewel of great price—the forgotten, lost Word.

I AM come to awaken hearts! I AM come to shake the dust of lethargy off the feet of humanity! I AM come to summon the best visions, the best hopes, the greatest diagram of perfection so that mankind may understand that in this diagram of perfection there is also a summoning in the atomic structure of those old and ancient records that were the power of Infinity as they spoke unto the finite mirror and said, "Mirror *me!* Be *me!* Rejoice in *me!*"

For the summoning of hearts is the summoning of the election!* It is the summoning of the will of God! It is the summation of all mortal action and the consummation of all realization. It is the strength of the domain of destiny. It is the power by which worlds are twirled in space, by which worlds are framed,[2] by which atoms are also governed, by which the machinations of the powers of darkness are crushed as between the thumb and forefinger.

Entire planets and galaxies can disappear in a moment if the formula be wrong, and therefore the formula must be corrected. The formula of hearts must be understood as the alchemy of purpose and the realization that the light in all ages is in the similitude of God and in the likeness of his face.

CLARITY OF VISION
AND THE POWER OF HOLY WILL

Hearts beat unafraid. Hearts beat afraid. We come to cast out all fear! But we summon the light of renewal of purpose and the strength of the wings of the mind by which the mind is raised out of the worldly cup—the sordid cup of purposeless, aimless existence —into the fruit of the Spirit and into those higher dimensions of universal love and beauty whereby the soul is stirred in the being of man and lethargy is no longer in control.

Now, clarity of vision is before the gaze of all. And as the gaze

---

election: the right, power, or privilege of making a choice; predestination of eternal life reaches out toward the farthest majesty of the stars, mankind should understand that they are at last able to perceive and understand—through that boring* vision that is more powerful by far than an X-ray—that there is a hand at the other end of the tunnel of love.

What have I spoken of? I have spoken of the outreach of the mind and of the understanding that there is a spirit—the spirit of universal loveliness that stands at the end of that tunnel of love. This understanding is because the mind is all of this—a boring action of the conscious penetration of individuals toward the light—boring through mortal density and mortal ideas and concepts into the beauty and timelessness of the eternal spheres.

Whence cometh this impetus? Whence cometh this desire to know the holy will? The holy will is not the will of banality. It is the will by which worlds are framed, by which giant leaps are made, by which strength is summoned by the smallest carpenter or the weakest cobbler. It is the will by which the puniest among men are able to reach out and summon the strength to perform great tasks—noble tasks—tasks that are needed now upon the earth plane.

For the darkness of the land has reached unto the Darjeeling Council, and I tell you that upon the drawing boards of certain mortals now presently in existence upon the planet Earth there are designs for the destructivity of all elements of freedom and the removal from Earth of all divine grace in expression amongst mankind.

Shall we sit idly by while this happens? I think not! And so we say now, let us not only summon the elect of all nations but let us also summon from the farthest stars those elect fathers of cosmic captivity who have captured in the domain of universal ideas the power of overcoming all fear and the dust of darkness.

Let them come, now, to the planet Earth in order to illumine

**boring:* piercing, penetrating

the minds of embodied mankind. Let them instruct mankind because the vision and power of universal vision is a necessary factor in the overcoming of all worldly conditions—those conditions that in themselves would destroy all of the passions and fires of the mind of man by which the crystal and the mist[3] can be properly understood and apprehended.

Let all understand, then, that many banal ideas occupy the mind temporarily. They come (as one of the gurus of the Far East has said), as a bird that swiftly descends upon the head, which cannot always be avoided. But you do not need, as the guru has said, to allow this bird to build a nest in your hair.

THE CASTING OUT OF UNWANTED THOUGHTS

Understand, then, how dark thoughts, unwanted thoughts, are cast out simply because the consciousness rejects them. The momentary influx of these thoughts is the attempt of the arrows of the dark ones to fly by night into the darkness, charged with that misappropriated light that the dark ones have vampirized from others and have used to express the manifestation of darkness in the outer world.

I tell you that such obsession is a frightful activity upon the planetary body. Whenever you gaze upon those pages in your newspapers that are filled with the titles of various motion pictures now presently in vogue, let me also remind you of such activities that now appear upon the television screens of the land, [such as the television show] called *Dark Shadows*.[4] Understand that this is a manifestation of blackness, a manifestation of the children of darkness, and a manifestation of destructivity.

This darkness shall not live because mankind shall rise in his domain of cosmic understanding in order to crush out the serpentine will that is for those purposeless, mindless, aimless drifts that create in the consciousness of mankind those obsessive activities that are destructive in their own right! These activities are intentionally destructive because the dark ones have also gathered those sewers of unregenerate, misqualified energies from all over the universe and have gathered them into one place. They have then radiated these energies out into the mind and consciousness of those among mankind who have a natural affinity for darkness. Let them also shed this and become illumined.

MANKIND MUST SUMMON
THE SPIRIT OF ILLUMINATION

Let us, then, make clear that illumination is the fruit of the Spirit and that it is the beginning of the fruit of the Spirit in the mind. It is the origin of high thoughts whereby man can also summon those potencies of the Spirit in himself, which are the overcoming and God-victorious intentions of the cosmic hierarchy.

At our level, we are tired of serving humanity and then seeing no fruit in response. We come because they have summoned us. They have summoned us in their hearts, and they also come to hear our words. But oftentimes they overlook the understanding that we seek to convey, and they become as riderless horses. They become indeed ineffective and profitless servants, profligate sons of God who care more about their own pleasures than they do about the pleasures of overcoming all outer conditions.

We seek to draw and magnetize humanity to that place in their spiritual evolution where at last they will awaken and be quickened by the eternal Spirit, by the passions of the Holy Spirit as he reaches out to the hearts of man and saith unto them as he surrounds their hearts with his hands: "Thou art a temple of the living God abiding forever as a high altar of God."[5]

The flame of immortal life and the flame of the Holy Spirit are the regenerate powers focused in your heart for a God-purpose, which is the overcoming of darkness and the recognition of the eternal Christ as the arbiter of the destiny of mankind. This, then, is a passion of the universal consciousness for the illumination of mankind. It is the summoning of the holy will, and the domain of that will comes to fruition as the blossoming, thousand-petaled lotus of light in the brain and cells of mankind, illumining them and causing them to feel the great glow of those regenerative fires of the Spirit whereby mankind are summoned at last to become the elect of God and walk yet among mankind.

Do you think it is enough to summon individuals to the higher realms, and then rising there to have them experience those frustrating experiences that have come to many of us whereby we seek to illumine humanity and to speak to humanity, to invoke light in humanity and then to find a nonresponsive chord within them? And then we find a very salutatory response to sometimes lesser conditions, and toward those conditions that are of the darkness we find an almost total response in mankind because they love the deeds of darkness rather than the deeds of light. This is because the total desire of their heart has become the desire to do evil, and they know not what they do.[6]

Now, shall we stand idly by, seeing that we are given this opportunity, by the courtesy of these messengers, to speak unto you the holy Word? I say, we shall not stand idly by, nor shall we coddle mankind! They have been coddled for too long, they have coddled themselves for too long, and they have also entered into an era of great permissiveness for far too long!

We of the Darjeeling Council are summoning now the Lords of Karma to stand in judgment of the world because it is the only way (in the opinion of Mary the Mother of Jesus and others of the ascended host) that humanity will ever be brought to their senses. It is the only way by which humanity will finally come to realize at last, as they view personal calamity and world calamity, that something is wrong and that the scales of cosmic justice are being tipped against them.

PUT ON THE WHOLE ARMOUR
OF GOD

You who seek refuge in the holy will of God need not fear, for the laws of karma are just. And I can assure you that you may descend into the realms of darkness in cosmic service, as our Lord Christ did during the three days and three nights when he was lying in the tomb in physical form.[7] Yet he was active in the Spirit, preaching unto those spirits who were disobedient when once the action of God implored them in the days of Noah.[8]

Let us, then, make it clear that mankind today, entering into the various areas of darkness, will find that they are indeed required by cosmic law to put upon themselves the whole armour of God.[9] They are required to put on the spiritual power of the violet transmuting flame and the manifestation of the great white tube of light, which is to be invoked by them as the desire of their heart in order to strengthen them in those moments when they descend into contact with other individuals who are not worthy to lace the shoes of their feet.

Do you understand, then, what I am speaking about? I am saying to you that you are not to fear to go out into the world of form and to speak to humanity and to carry the Word of the Spirit unto humanity! You are to act in the name of the living God!

Do you think for one moment that you are acting out of your own impulse? I tell you, you are acting out of the impulse of your own heart and out of the living flame of the Holy Ghost, which is not incarcerated there but is a flame upon the altar of the heart, willingly invited. It is also the passion of God to bring humanity to his feet, to illumine mankind, to alert mankind to the fact that they have not been acting as God intended them to act, and for this reason darkness is upon the face of the earth.

THE LAW OF BEHOLDING

Yet the passion of Nature herself is also very great toward the light. Unfortunately, one of the laws governing elemental life upon the planetary body is the law of beholding, which you are also able to read about in the writings concerning Jacob and Laban of old.[10] Through this story of God's blessing to Jacob you will understand the matter of the ringstraked, speckled, spotted, and brown animals among Laban's flock, which were given to him by Jacob. When Jacob kept for himself only the white animals from among the flock, he brought them to the watering trough, where they were able, during their time there, to hold a certain vision of the ringstraked, speckled, spotted, and brown animals. Therefore the all-white animals were later able to multiply according to these other kinds, which was desired by Jacob.

You also ought to understand, then, how the power of vision and the power of the intensification of the forcefield of your mind can invoke a tremendous activity of light for the planetary body. "Oh, yes!" you say. "I know all about it!" You say, "I have tried it before, and the world is still the same."

Well, beloved ones, let me tell you that God Almighty has tried it before, too, and he has done so over the span of thousands and millions of years! When I summon before me the akashic records of the universe, I behold the many times that the Spirit of God has striven with the flesh of humanity. He has been in search of the day when humanity would accept the fiat of the cosmic crown resting upon their head and in their heart and would accept this as the activity of the holy will that would only bring them the blessings of Almighty God.

TRUST GOD'S PLAN

Do you understand what I am speaking about? I am talking about the will of God. I am referring to it as a crown of the Spirit.

I am referring to the cipher upon the heart. I am referring to the great love of God that invokes in mankind the golden circlet that is the bond of love between the heart of man and the heart of God. I am saying that all the earth should understand that the will of God is kind, that the will of God is good, that the plans of God envisioned upon the great architectural drawing board of the Great Architect of the universe are perfect and complete in their own right.

If only humanity would learn to trust God's plan and to gaze upon it rather than to turn to those pundits of the world! These pundits are those learned men who somehow or other have the idea, because they are able to milk mankind of the coin of the realm, that they are also very illumined in spiritual things.

I tell you, they are not! They are the pundits of the world! They are as nothing in the eyes of God! As a pinch of dust, they shall vanish into the grave. And many of them shall be no more, and they shall experience for themselves that which is called the second death.[11] This is because they have continually driven mankind, as wandering stars, into a mist of darkness,[12] and they have sought to reserve for themselves a very special place in those activities of the astral realm, not understanding the power of the Spirit and the transforming radiance that I AM—that the heart of God *is,* that the heart of all of you *is,* that the power of the Spirit *is.*

SUMMON IN MANKIND
THE REGENERATION OF THE SPIRIT

Will you, then, awaken at last to the fullness of the mission we bring to you? We entrust to you today, who hear our words, the reins and power of the Spirit in order to evoke a new passion for God in the entire human race. This new passion for God will become the dawn of cosmic activity whereby mothers—as they sit holding in their arms for that first sublime and precious moment the babe that is the manifestation of the physical frame imbued with the spirit—will understand that God is manifesting in that form. They will understand that God is alive in that form, but not forevermore as they envision it. For they hold the vision of mortality, and so they reap the fruit of morte.*

Let me express to you that we deal with those immortal factors of consciousness whereby man is shaken of the dust of his *inertia,* of his *darkness,* and at last understands that by virtue and loveliness and the passions of the Spirit there is a renewal of the consciousness of mankind in the cup of cosmic virtue! And by this renewal, as he passes this cup from one lip to another, he is able to summon in mankind the regeneration of the Spirit.

Mankind will understand that this is not foolishness, for it has been said long ago by Saint Paul that the things of God are foolish with the world.[13] Let mankind understand, then, that the things of God are not foolish at all. They are the bestowal of a cosmic covenant that dates back to long ago, even before the time of Melchizedek. "And how can this be?" you say.

You do not understand the elements of Creation, nor do you understand the great dragon Tiamat[14] in her desire to create chaos upon the earth. You do not understand the timelessness of the Spirit and how all things were formed, else you would not ask such a silly question. I tell you, however, that we are willing to answer the silly questions of individuals if they will only recognize and understand that there is not only a God but there is a God who lives within them as a flame! And the fact that they have buried that flame until it is only, in many cases, far less than an eighth of an inch high within their heart, I tell you, is a great entombment of the fires of the Spirit, which we now desire to cause to come to an end.

TAKE THE NECESSARY DOMINION OVER THE EARTH

We want to invoke an *awakening* of the heart flames of all people! We want to summon the heart flames of all people in this

---

*morte: Italian, "death"

coming time so that all of the visions that have come now to many of the saints pertaining to the awful era of destructivity descending upon the planetary body—by the hand of man (not by the hand of God) and also by the hand of the Lords of Karma where it is required—may be stayed!

For long ago, when the hand wrote upon the wall "MENE, MENE, TEKEL, UPHARSIN" and spoke unto mankind in the days of the feast of Belshazzar and his lords,[15] I say, this was a warning engraved upon the walls of the temple by the large hand that God sent. But we, speaking in this day by the passion of the miracles of our faith, are also sounding out the warning and the handwriting upon the wall so that humanity, who are facing this new year, will understand that they themselves—as patriots of the Spirit for the benefit of freedom and freedom's name—must take the necessary dominion over the earth and be unafraid to do the will of God, who also, after all, is their Father.

God is your Father, and as such he has the right to demand of you that full measure of devotion by which the world can be changed from darkness into light.

THE GOLDEN AGE AND THE AGE OF DARKNESS ARE BOTH AT HAND

We say that the lowering of the New Jerusalem and the advent of the golden age is simultaneously at hand with an age of darkness.

I think that the time has come for us to take off our turbans. I think that the time has come for us to summon some election whereby mankind will understand that the traditional concepts of the world that are enfolding humanity, as the winding sheet enfolded Lazarus long ago,[16] shall be understood by humanity. I think that humanity shall also take ahold of that tag* and pull it very swiftly and smartly, so that at last they will unwind the sleeping Lazarus of their own dreams and come to the period of fruition

---

*tag: a loop, tassel, or knot on a garment

and fulfillment of those dreams as the implementation of cosmic action upon the face of the earth.

We are a bit tired of seeing our energies expanded and then to see that individuals allow the momentum of the forcefield of our action to die within them and to [merely] say, "Oh, yes, it was a beautiful dictation." Well, I tell you, dear hearts of light, the time has come for you to make hay while the sun shines, for the sun may not always shine. Do I make myself clear?

Let me say to you that the dreams of God are nourished by thousands and millions of devotees of the Spirit, many of them at inner levels. The dreams of God, then, when they are nourished by the hands of men, become a binding pact upon the envoys of heaven whereby a more than ordinary assistance is given to humanity. And by this high level of assistance we will shake the dust in your consciousness, or we will shake the dust of our shoes off against you until the day of judgment!

But suit yourself. For I tell you that we do not always intend to speak in this wise. Heaven itself has forbidden it. And the day may well come when the gates of prophecy to the world shall be closed, and the great ones may hide their face from humanity if humanity continues, in this era of darkness, to execute those acts that are now currently occurring.

Pornography must be stopped! The destructive gathering of the sons of darkness must be stopped! All activities of crime on the streets must be brought to a halt, and humanity must understand that their homes must be a place of safety and refuge, where the beauty of cosmic worship and joy can be accomplished.

Individuals play canasta while the world perishes. Individuals play games with dice while the world perishes. The gaming tables and roulette tables are highly honored. The mysterious men like Howard Hughes[17] are considered great because of their mystery and because of the fact that they have a fortune in manifestation. Let me tell you that we have a greater fortune and far greater stakes for the whole earth! And *you* have a great deal more at stake than you know!

SEEK FIRST THE WISDOM
OF THE KINGDOM OF HEAVEN

Will you, therefore, quicken in your consciousness those passions to *do,* and understand that holy wisdom is needed to do it? I do not say that you should now simply turn to some disorderly manifestation and begin to do "something" just because I have said to. I want you to seek first the wisdom of the kingdom of heaven[18] so that you may correctly understand the sanity and balance of correcting these outer conditions.

You also ought to correct those inner conditions that are tipping your spirit into the ruts, which are the binding ruts of habit and destructivity. You also ought to replace those habits with correct habits so that you will reap the spiritual rewards that I feel many of you deserve.

When I come to you, I wish I could say that you all deserve these spiritual rewards, but unfortunately not all of you do. Yet all of you *can.* Do you understand the difference? I say, not all of you *do,* but all of you *can.* This is because all of you *can* deserve it if you will harness the great momentum of your will, just as men have harnessed the wind in the sails of their being and have sailed the seven seas.

Let accomplishment now become the fiat of your life. And as the momentum of this year takes shape, let it be a thing of the Spirit so that the contact with our era, the contact with our manifestation, and the contact with our temple here in Darjeeling may become more than the wind from the East. May it become the *harnessed* wind from the East that represents a fiat of destiny to all mankind for their removal from the great precipitate danger of the sword of Damocles that hangs over their head as a destructive power of war and economic distress.

We would first bring about salvation in the consciousness so that the whole vessel can be cleansed and can arise as a shining momentum to the glory of God, not only in this year but in all the years to come.

I speak unto you in the name of the Lord of the World! I speak unto you in the name of the Darjeeling Council! And I tell you that I will cause a trembling in thy spirit this night so that you may understand that we are more than ordinary men! And when we speak, it is to stir the very depths of your being to that electrifying concept by which the salvation of a planet is made!

I thank you, and I bid you adieu.

January 1, 1971
La Tourelle
Colorado Springs, Colorado
MLP

CHAPTER 14

*Realize, then, that for every thought
and every word and every action
there is a divine blueprint,
and that blueprint is held
in the will of God.*

KNOW THE STAR-FIRE PERFECTION
OF THE WILL OF GOD

Hail, devotees of the will of God! *Hail,* sons and daughters of the diamond-shining mind!

I AM come in the fullness of the flame of God's will to instill within you devotion to a cause which I espoused long ago. The will of God is a fire, a star-fire of perfection for which your soul yearns, for which there is a burning in heart and soul and mind that will not let you cease to strive for perfection until you attain that Star.

I AM the star-fire of direction for your life, for your energy, for your freedom from all fear and from the shrouds of doubt and darkness and the deceits and illusions of the carnal mind.

Cast them into the flame which I bear! For I come bearing a mighty torch of blue-flame power. It is a bower* of light and love from my heart. And the diamond-shining mind of God sparkles now from Darjeeling, as the insignia of our retreat turns as a focus of the mind of God in the Great Hub.

I AM the exponent of the will of God! For I AM the ensouling of that will for all who serve on the ray of God's will—the first

---

*bower: an extension of support, as in an anchor carried at the bow of a ship

ray of First Cause, of energies released within you. See to it, then, that the energies which you release from chakras now purified are in the exact replica of the will of God that is the blueprint of life, the pattern of destiny that God has sealed within each of your star-fiery chakras. Realize, then, that for every thought and every word and every action there is a divine blueprint, and that blueprint is held in the will of God.

There is no need to have unexpected manifestations of emotional turbulence. There is no need for unplanned activities.* There is no need for a lack of precision in knowing the mind of God if you will first center your consciousness in the flame. And thereby you will be free from all derision of the carnal mind that would make a mockery of life and of your greatest moments of the sublime presence of the will of God.

Do you see, then, that by coming into the center of the awareness of the will of First Cause you can outsmart the effects of the dark denizens of astral mire? Do you see, then, that it is wrong in the eyes of God to be a reactor to effects and that you must go to the will of First Cause, to the central manifestation of that will, and see to it that that will is released? And *then* you go forth to fulfill the plan according to the blueprint.

THE GENIUS OF THE CHRIST MIND

It is *folly* to act without first knowing the blueprint of action! And if you cannot know the blueprint, then know this: that your Christ mind does ensoul that blueprint, that your I AM Presence ensouls that blueprint. And therefore, if you are on a mission for the Brotherhood and you are, as it were, feeling your way out into the unknown, first know that, in the name of the Christ, your Higher Being and your Higher Self is showing you the way.

Thereby you find the star-fire of perfection at the end of the

---

*This may mean actions taken that are not in accordance with the divine blueprint that is the will of God.

road. You know that you have arrived because of the genius of the Christ mind that is ever active, waking and sleeping, ready to lower into manifestation—in the outer mind, the inner world, the subtle world and the subconscious plane—every aspect of the consciousness of God that is necessary for an accurate assessment of events, for an accurate outpicturing of events in this plane.

After all, blessed ones, is not the activity of the outer consciousness the vanity of vanities? All is vanity![1] If it is vanity, then I say, why indulge in the human consciousness? Why take it seriously? Why not realize that even human happiness and human sorrow represent the yin and the yang of a consciousness that is yet to be made permanent in the Christ?

Why not live in reality here and now? Why constantly be on the periphery of unreality, reacting to the events of unreality when you can be centered in the Christ and walk the earth as masters of time and space?

It is high time that the chelas of the light respond to this call to be centered in the will of God by going back to the cause behind every outer manifestation. Perceiving that cause, you can bring blessing to all of life. For in the midst of turmoil you can keep the flame because you see the vision. And because you see the vision, you have compassion for those of a lesser state of consciousness who are out of phase with the blueprint.

Sometimes you sense individuals being out of phase with a matrix, a [divine] presence that you feel, a pulsing of the mind of God. They do not always know [this presence of the mind of God]. Many times they are sincere devotees who themselves are groping to find a point of contact with the Higher Mind. When you keep the vision and the flame and the constancy of the will of God, you find that those who come into your aura are also drawn into the mercurial diamond-shining mind of God that has that purpose of keeping the balance.

In the Higher Mind is the balance for the plane of action.

And [think of] how much time and how much turmoil you can save yourself and others around you if you will retreat to that mind! This is an action of contemplation and it is the "rest" aspect of the motion of the Mercurians.

YOUR CONSCIOUSNESS CAN SPAN
THE COSMIC EGG

We *are* Mercurians, we who serve in Darjeeling! We come from the master God Mercury to ensoul a planet not only with the will of God but with the speedy determination to fulfill that will. And thus my release of the power of the spoken Word to you this night is by the action of that mercurial mind so that you can see that the mind of God can release thought faster than the messenger is capable of pronouncing that thought in words.

Thus understand that thought flashes across the skies with the speed of light and beyond, and you too can receive that Word and that impetus for action. Understand, then, that the rest in motion of the Mercurians is the rest in the contemplation of the will of God and in the action of that will being lowered into manifestation simultaneously, like the simultaneous interpreters who hear the word in one ear and pronounce that word in another language.

Do you see, then, how your consciousness, being vast as the consciousness of God, can span the Cosmic Egg[2] and be aware of teeming forcefields of the mind of God? Like a cosmic computer it is the potential of your own Higher Mind here and now, the Higher Mind that you can contact.

Thus you can be aware not only of one but of many blueprints—blueprints governing the destiny of nations, of cities, of lifestreams. How do you think that our messengers minister to life everywhere? It is through this Higher Mind, through the Christ.

Simultaneously you, too, can be in many forcefields. And this comes, ah yes, through the mastery of the chakras, through the mastery of the planes of consciousness until you master so many of these balls which you juggle that there comes a time when you must transcend Mater and move into infinity. For the finite world can no longer hold your consciousness.

Some of you have this ability already, but you have not the mastery of the emotions to accompany the speed of that Higher Mind. In some respects you are *far* beyond your peers, but they are not your peers if you are far beyond them. Do you see? Some of you go beyond this world in one aspect of consciousness, and then suddenly you are drawn back because an aspect of self has not attained the mastery.

PARTAKE OF MANY FACETS OF GOD'S MIND

Thus the disciplines of the Brotherhood are imposed. Thus the Keepers of the Flame Lessons are released.[3] Thus the way is made clear so that step by step you might put on the consciousness of the Holy Ghost. And lest you weary of this plane of time that I have engaged in, I will now release the spoken Word as the voice and the momentum of the flow of that will of God into the plane of earth. It is the determined release of the Brotherhood, stepping down, now, momentums of the diamond-shining mind of God into the plane of earth for the *determined step,* the *determined pace,* the *controlled breath* and the heartbeat that conforms to the cycles of the Divine Mother as she rocks the cradle of the holy infant child.

And so you see, as I take the flow of the Word and impress it upon you now with the intensity of determination, I AM still releasing to you, at another frequency and at another level of this dictation, the speed of the thought of the mind of God. And so you are receiving this dictation simultaneously at several levels of consciousness so that you might understand that although God in you is One, that One is infinity. And as you espouse the will of God you can penetrate infinity in many aspects.

Do you see, then, that as it is now, embodied mankind take upon themselves perhaps one virtue, one attribute, one frequency for an entire lifetime? I am showing you how, when you merge with the flame and with the body of God, you can partake of many facets of the jewel of God's mind and actually outpicture those facets even while you tarry in time and space, becoming a master at various planes of consciousness.

But in the final analysis, when the time of accounting and the Judgment comes and you are prepared to be received as a candidate for the ascension, it matters what you have lowered into form. And although you may have the mastery of the mind of God at the etheric plane or the mental plane, remember well that all that counts in the final analysis for the victory of life is that which you can bring into manifestation in the physical octave for the victory.

And thus I press now for the lowering into consciousness of that mastery which many of you have at various levels. I am pressing in upon you now the rays of the will of God for the intensification of that lowering action.

Some of you have blocks in the lower chakras and in the heart, even in the upper chakras. Some of you have need of but a minor adjustment in the turning of the wheels of the chakras. Some of you need but the succor of the angels, of fearlessness flame, of Ray-O-Light and Archangel Michael to clear away the last vestiges of substance that oppose the spiraling into manifestation of inner attainment.

I come, then, in defense of Christ-mastery. I come, then, to bind all that is less than Christ-mastery. I extend my hand to you and I ask you, if you are willing, to give me your hand while you give to me all momentums less than Christ-perfection. Specifically I request that you give to me, in the name of the Christ, those momentums that prevent the will of God from manifesting in your life. I accept them gladly, lovingly, and I cast them into the flame of the sacred fire!

I extend to you, in exchange for the proffered gift, the diamond-shining crystal substance of my flame. And I place that crystal in your four lower bodies in order to increase the flow of light for the awareness of God consciousness and for the precipitation thereof.

I come in the awareness of many urgent matters—matters of state, of the governments of the nations, of the crises of the individual chelas on the Path. For there are many chelas across the margins of the world, in America and beyond, who are affrighted and even overcome by the cloud of darkness that is as a cloud of locusts plaguing the earth, downgrading the activities of the Brotherhood and attempting to snuff out the light of the Law, of the teaching, and of the Christ.

I say, *Roll* it back! *Roll* it back! *Roll* it back! And let the Divine Presence of each one appear! I AM the champion of the disciples of Christ the world around. I AM the champion of the devotees of Buddha, of Confucius. I AM the champion of the saints, of child-man, of those beginning on the Path and those who have been winning for a long time and yet are waiting to see the fruits of victory.

Are you one of those who have been winning for so long that now you think that perhaps you are not winning at all, that perhaps you have lost a round, lost a momentum? I say, the mighty teams of conquerors, who go forth conquering and to conquer, who release their momentum of the will of God, would have you know that the victors of life and those who win and who place their stakes high on the winning of the All—the winning of the All of God and the transmutation of the all of man—are they who have wide spirals of victory. Their course of victory is a wide pattern around the sun.

THE WIDE SPIRAL IS A VICTORY

You must recognize, then, that to follow that wide course you must remember the vision. You must remember that there is a victory each step of the way, which you do not see the manifestation of until you have completed the whole spiral.

Others of lesser stature may have daily victories and you may wonder, "My, how they achieve in the light, how they attain. I seem never to gain even a morsel or a thread of the light of victory but only struggle and testing and temptation and torment, and I am still plodding along without a sign of victory."

And yet I say, the wide spiral is a victory *every* day! But know that the fruit of victory finally comes in the manifestation of the ultimate light of the return, [when you have completed the whole spiral]. Though you be on a wide spiral or a lesser spiral, an inner or an outer coil, whether you be a planet or an electron farthest from the center or closer to the sun, remember this: Work the works of God each day and receive the benediction "Well done" from your Christ Self.

Know that because you retain the standard of perfection, you will reach *perfection's* mark. Know that because you apply for God-direction, you will also receive *protection's* mark. Know, then, that because you have a standard and a principle that you have espoused, hierarchies and angels reinforce your consciousness and are working with you for a victory that is beyond even the imagination of those who accept the lesser victories and go on. Know, then, that when you carry a large matrix you must make a wide circuit. And therefore, follow the beings of light; accompany our legions bright.

I invite you this night to see and behold that star-fire might. I invite you to come with legions of the will of God, to follow the flame and the law of the rod, to come and see and know how legions of Mercury, of Morya, go—how they follow the light of the Mother flow as cosmic highways wending through the spheres, far beyond the ken of mortal ears—a music, a symphony, a hierarchy, an antahkarana. Oh, it is the star-fire Presence of your causal body bright.

As your soul takes flight, remember that you are traversing the vastness of the causal body of God himself. Remember, then, you who hold the vision of the Spirit, that to fill in the painting and the mural of life—if it is to be a panorama that encompasses all of mankind in the ascension spiral—will no doubt take all of your life, all of your love, and every day of your yearning to be free.

Therefore I come with the encouragement of the will of God and I say to you, each one: *Take heart!* Oh, take heart, precious souls of Morya. Take heart.

There are some who must carry the vision. There are others who bring up the rear, who are not afraid of rolling up their sleeves and digging in and performing the service that is needed. And sometimes those who are at the rear are so far from those who lead the command that they do not meet until the battle is won and the strife is o'er. For many souls and many lifestreams form a part of the legions and the cadres of light.

OUR GOAL:
THE ASCENSION OF THE COSMIC EGG

Our goal and our winning is for the ascension of the Cosmic Egg. Now, if you cannot visualize the Cosmic Egg where you are in time and space, then I say, how can you visualize the victory and the ascension of that Cosmic Egg?[4]

Therefore, you see, leave that vision to the Elohim and come down to a lesser portion of time and space, taking only that portion which you are capable of mastering. But let the reach exceed the grasp. Let the goal exceed the present capability. Let the Great White Brotherhood and the Spirit of life fill in that energy by a rainbow arc—a promise of a goal, of an attainment and of a life beyond.

You who yearn for oneness, for peace, for surcease from all turmoil, come this night into the fiery core of my heart. Come to Darjeeling and sit by the fire with me, and we will discuss the plans of hierarchy for God-government and for the victory of the light. I will show you the graphs and the maps and the illustrations of the step-by-step increase of the light in the planetary body and what those steps, ordained by the Christ, will achieve for mankind if some here below will keep the flame and espouse the Mother flow.

I AM yours for the victory of God's will in all planes of consciousness. And I will speak to you as a mighty chord at many levels in order to reach the depths and the heights of consciousness. Do you know that my flow of light will be welcomed by you in some planes of your awareness, but in other planes there will be a resistance?

Do you understand how attainment has levels even within you? The ladder of hierarchy and of initiation is all contained within you, as portions of your consciousness have attainment and portions still must be brought into alignment.

Thus, let the highest aspect of the self be a beacon of hope and light and direction for all lesser aspects so that the energies spiraling and coursing now through your world will converge at the cloverleaf that is the threefold flame within the heart.

I AM, as Above, so below, Morya of the first ray of the will of God!

I AM victorious! I AM invictus in the flame.[5] And I stand to defend that will in all who defend that will!

Peace be unto you.

July 2, 1974
Spokane, Washington
Elizabeth Clare Prophet (ECP)

CHAPTER 15

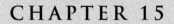

*We see hope because we see the alchemy of God—
the rising and the falling of energies within earth
as God claims his own, his light, as God demands
an atonement, as God is in the midst of his people.*

CHAPTER 15

THE COILED SPRING
OF THE WILL OF GOD

Hail, sons and daughters of light!

I come from Darjeeling. I come with a message of hope, sent by Saint Germain, our noble king, and all whose voices have rung out this day around that council table[1] with the meditation upon a great, intense, fiery blue cube of God's will. And that cube of God's will is released to us from the Great Causal Body of the Great Divine Director, even in answer to your call, which you have sent forth for the divine plan unto the decade, unto the nations, unto the centuries.

Most noble knights and ladies of the flame, be seated.

We welcome you into our midst, into the inside of the great circle of our own guru-chela relationship, which spans a cosmos and is a light that, unto us, is worth keeping. And if it be worth keeping in heaven, then it is worth keeping in the earth. And to that end we have set our goal, we have set our mark. And for that purpose we come.

For without the plan, without the preparedness, then in the hour of the great challenge of victory, where is the light? Where is the solution to human revolution and the vanity of rebellion? Well, it is always in the light—the light that is an active light, *the light that is an active light,* the light that is the light of a Omega, a Omega* within you.

THE JUDGMENT OF THE DEAD

I have sent my Word through the messenger this day, and I come now to release a ray of light and of wisdom. It is the hope that is the message of our council. For we see hope because we see the alchemy of God—the rising and the falling of energies within earth as God claims his own, his light, as God demands an atonement, as God is in the midst of his people. For the hour of the judgment of the dead has come. It is prophesied as the fulfillment of the ministry of the two witnesses.[2]

What is the judgment of the dead? It is the judgment of those who are living who have not accepted the quickening of the Lord Christ within their midst for aeons. And so the dead are known of us. They have not the joy flame or the joy bells of our hope.

The LORD God walks the earth, as the Four and Twenty Elders may enter this planetary sphere because the guru-chela relationship is intact. And thereby there is a ladder that extends from the God Star, Sirius, to the earth, and the angels of God in this hour are the Four and Twenty Elders ascending and descending, keeping the life force of Alpha and Omega.

And therefore the judgment becomes only a great sphere of light—a sphere of light that is placed over each such an individual whose time is come. And therefore, the judgment is ultimately the individual's own freewill choice. For by the acceleration of death, by the acceleration of the energy veil, by the acceleration of the hatred of the light of the Christ and of the messenger of the Christ, which is in the very midst of the earth, therefore that sphere of light that is lowered over the individual then becomes the catalyst

---

*The intended word may be *A-Omega,* meaning Alpha to Omega, or simply *Omega,* an Omega.

for the return of that energy. And it is that energy itself which will ultimately judge the walking dead.

Understand, then, the magnificence of the law of God. Understand that energy itself, as well as the choice to use that energy in God or in darkness, becomes the very basis of the individual's sojourn upon earth or, for that matter, in any world or any evolution whatsoever.

THE RESTORATION OF THE
IMMINENT INDWELLING LIGHT

I come in the light of the will of God to impart to you that light. And I say, let us not study the dead or death or dying, but let us meditate upon life and upon the great ascension and upon the process of the ascension, the very ritual of the righting of light and the consuming of darkness.

Let us meditate upon the inner walk with God. Let us meditate upon that work to which we are called. Let us come together and meditate upon the open door that even now is like the sun breaking through the clouds and shining upon the place where the newborn Christ Child comes forth as the adornment not only of one Son of God but of every Son of God and every child of God who will elect to be that Son. The great miracle of that coming, the great miracle, is this grand gift of God unto all who are a part of him. It is the restoration of the imminent indwelling light.

Therefore we come. We come with our deliberations, our portfolios, our files of research. We come with the report of our communion with the Lords of Karma and the Four and Twenty Elders. We measure, as with a measuring rod within the temple.[3] We come for the measuring of the temple where the children of God dwell. We come for to measure the measures of light and darkness—a penny for a measure of wheat or corn or barley,[4] a penny's worth of light. So measure for measure, the light that has become the fohat, the Great Central Sun Magnet within you, does magnetize to your lifestream the precious energy of the will of God.

ENGAGE YOUR MIND AND HEART INTO THE SPOKEN WORD

The will of God is the will to *do* and to *be* love in action. The will of God is the energy by which you attain. The will of God is a light that descends and is oncoming into your temple. Will is God-determination.

That which you will this day, so you shall be. And therefore, do not use the sessions of your dynamic decrees to withdraw your will but to enhance that will—not to cancel out the Logos as the pure reason, the person of Christ within you, but to enter more into a conscious participation in the mind of Almighty God that interpenetrates a cosmos.

Do you understand that some have taken the dynamic decrees as a form of escape—escape into nonthinking, nonfeeling, suspecting that the recitation of words will be the salvation. It is not the recitation of words but the recitation of the Word. And the implementation of that Word and the dynamic decrees are the greatest assist ever known to that function.

Understand, then, that even the science of the living God can be abused. And when you let a rote functioning of that science come into your temple, then you are putting yourself outside of the circle of the Word, to which I have bidden your presence this day.

See, then, that you engage your mind and your heart into the spoken Word. Only thus will the words of the dynamic decrees allow you to emerge God-victorious from the temple as the Word incarnate.

THE INCORRUPTIBLE ONE IS THE REMEDY

Understand that religion has been an escape for individuals who have fled from God himself for many centuries. They have sought to escape the returning karma by seeking shelter in the cloisters of the Church. Understand that those who would hide their darkness under the mantle of a brother or sister of light, they, then, become opportunists in the midst of the Church. And therefore, the escapism, which is true to their own nature as the tares among the wheat,[5] has become a label that other fallen ones have placed upon the entire movement of the Spirit of God within the churches.

Beloved ones, the Church is not corrupt. The Church can never be corrupt, for it is the Bride of Christ. It is people within the Church who are corrupt. It is the tares among the wheat. So it is true. The government of God is not corrupt. It is individuals who have failed to be just stewards and overseers within God's government in earth who are corrupt. And when you meditate upon this obvious truth, then you rejoice and feel gratitude for the will of God, as I do, for then you see that the situation is remediable. America is not corrupt. People within America are corrupt. Thus, the situation is remediable.

Thus there is a remedy, and the remedy for corruption is the Incorruptible One—not the forces of corruption and anti-corruption, not evil and anti-evil, not a tug of war, this side and that side and a sudden release and they all fall down. No, it is the Incorruptible One—not a force that opposes evil but a force of light that assimilates the energy veil and repolarizes that light and that energy. The Incorruptible One, who is the Lord and the living Christ within you, therefore is a great central sun.

The nature of incorruptibility is this: that any chemical, any substance, any element may be placed into it, added unto it, and yet it remains the Incorruptible One. And therefore the Incorruptible One, being the highest frequency within the planetary body, becomes an involuting flame, absorbing into itself all unlike itself, transmuting that substance and becoming more and more the Incorruptible One.

This is a lesson in cosmic geometry. To meditate upon geometry is to feel the beauty of God enter the soul, nourish the soul, enliven, enlighten. And does it bring joy? Yes, it brings joy, the supernal joy of the ultimate victory, of the ultimate reunion.

If God be in you, who, then, can be without? If God be within you, then you are in the allness of himself in this hour. God is Almighty God without the universe and within the universe. And the very nature of the indwelling I AM THAT I AM has never been taught as a doctrine by the Great White Brotherhood to exclude the almighty person and principle of God—the only God, the one true God, inhabiting within his holy place.

And therefore, let not the fallen ones seek to confute our prophet. For the prophecy is not her own, but it has rung down the centuries through every polished horn, through every one who is of that golden morn of the release of the mind of the Buddha and of the Christ. What folly to suppose that any messenger is the originator of the message. And thus, what folly, what flattery to attribute to an individual that which has been a part of the universal being of God, the Creator out of whom all creation has sprung.

RELEASE THE COILED SPRING
OF THE WILL OF GOD

The springing forth of creation is a release of a coiled spring. Now meditate upon the coiled spring of the will of God in your heart. You who lament that you are not always necessarily at the point of the fullness of that will, understand that there is a lever on the spring, and that lever is released by your Christ Self when your soul merges with that Christ Self and the two become the one indissoluble union. Understand, then, that coil upon coil of the will of God within you is ready for the springing forth of your individual creation, added unto and a part of the creation of Almighty God. *You* were created to be co-creators with him.

Now understand that some are holding that spring coiled,

not understanding how to release the lever for the springing forth of the energy, the divine plan, the concept and its outpicturing. Thus I would tell you that sometimes there is a desire to release that lever, but there be walls of concrete that prevent it going forth, that concrete that is a fear—fear to stand naked before God, fear to be only in the light.

And thus, there is a job to be done. It is the destructing of those things which you have erected within your lifestream that are not built upon the will of God. For they stand as impediment, as a heavy atmosphere, and therefore they must be cleared for the penetration of the light. The building up of the will within the heart and the day-by-day constructing of the spring of energy and destructing of the misuse of energy are simultaneous processes.

Thus, you need not wait forever and a day. You need only understand that in the very midst of the rubble that may lie beneath your feet, the rubble of a life not built upon the Rock of Christ, you may, in the very midst of that turbulence and that turmoil, rise to the hill—rise to the hill of life, rise to the hill of your own Christ Self and there, in that union, in that moment, in that hour, release a coiled spring. And do you know what will happen when you release that coiled spring? It will mean the collapse of all that has set itself anti that will.

It takes the science of the spoken Word. It takes a transfer of light and energy. It takes a thrust of the Word itself. When that Word, when that spring, when all chakras are aligned, when all of this comes to pass within your very temple, you will find yourself standing on a par with those who have been of the light who have set their determination to be shepherds of the light—those who have led nations, those who have released ideas into the marts of ideas and music into the souls of the people.

Standing with those geniuses of the ages who have manifested the light, you will understand that you are an integral part of the very genius that they have been and still are. Even as the breath of the Holy Spirit that you breathe has been breathed by every avatar, the same sacred fire breath, the same spiritual molecules that quickened the cells of the body of Jesus Christ, now quicken your own body cells.

Meditate on an engram of light. Meditate upon the coiled spring. And see that the coiled spring in your heart be the unqualified suchness of the diamond of Morya's will and Morya's devotion to God's will. See that the coiled spring be not a coiled spring of rebellion, ready to spring and pounce and to destroy life and to revolt and to bring revolution and destruction of civilization. And where the coiled springs lie in wait, there let the spring of life be greater in the chela because it is the spring of the will of God.

Let them be exposed, I say! *Let them be exposed,* those who have amassed power to use it against the soul and the light of the children of God upon earth. Let them be exposed, for they are the most unlikely faces in the most unlikely places. Let their masks be torn from them. This is my decree of this morn. Let them be exposed!

And let the coiled spring of the will of God released from every sacred heart of every ascended master of the Great White Brotherhood, let the coiled spring of the will of God released from every heart chakra of every chela of the ascended masters of the Great White Brotherhood *now* be released, *now* be released in the name of Saint Germain, *now* be released!

Let the children of the light go free! Let victory be won! Let victory's son be apparent as the faithful and true in your midst.

I AM El Morya. I AM true blue!

January 21, 1979
Camelot
Los Angeles County, California
ECP

CHAPTER 16

*Eliminate self-concern and plunge
into the very center of God's will!
Allow yourself to accelerate.
Allow yourself to contact the mind of God!*

CHAPTER 16

THE INITIATOR OF GOD'S WILL COMETH TO INITIATE CHELAS WHO ARE CONSCIOUS COLLABORATORS WITH THE WILL OF GOD

Practice Makes Perfect

*E*ven so, the first shall be last and the last shall be first.[1]

What shall I say when I come to initiate the staff of the Lord in God's holy will and some are ready and some are not?

"How shall we make them ready, O Lord?" is the cry of the messenger unto me.

Therefore I AM come, initiator of God's will within you, that you might enter in to a conscious collaboration with Lord Maitreya for the salvation of your soul! *Conscious* collaborators of God's holy will, this is the sort of chelas with whom we work and with whom the Lord Sanat Kumara is well pleased.

How can we raise up anyone to excellence of heart except that one first be self-raised by the pursuit of our offering, page upon page of *Pearls of Wisdom* written not only in weekly distribution but writ as Holy Writ in the very fire of the heart?

Blessed ones, the elevation of an individual by programming —by any automated means of the infusion of one individual with another's potential²—is not lawful. For to do so is merely to create an automaton to God's will, perhaps an electrical adjunct, much as the machine offers freedom from drudgery. But we of the Darjeeling Council are not interested in having such mechanized adjuncts to our service, for we do not conceive of ourselves as engaged in drudgery and therefore requiring freedom from drudgery through the creation of synthetic chelas.

Understand me well! We have at our disposal all of the science of the Matter universe to do so whether by spiritual or chemical means. We know intimately the science of the body, the brain, the central nervous system, and the chakras that span the dimensions of life. We are well acquainted with the altering techniques of geneticists. We are well acquainted with the use of chemicals to achieve grandiose results. But, blessed ones, our way is the way of the means, *the means* that will only justify and be justified by the end of the ascension in the light and the end which itself must find the conscious exercise of free will and God-justice to be the only acceptable standard as the means of attainment.

Therefore, what shall I say when we find some who are ready and some who are not for the increase of the will of God—some who have applied with all diligence the daily stripping of consciousness of all that is unlike the living Word within, some who have allowed themselves to become supersensitive and bathed in the violet flame, who are *fierce* warriors in denouncing the fallen ones [side by side with] others who have allowed themselves to be self-indulgent and mechanical, robot-like in their pursuit of the Word?

STRIVING FOR HOLY PURPOSE

It is the easy way to program one's own being in remote control, to exit the temple while the body repeats the holy prayers—

no longer holy because they are not endowed with the fervor of holiness. Blessed hearts, do not become weary in striving. Do not be weary to enter the basements and subbasements of life and to take responsibility for your own karma which is exposed from the near and distant past.

When you love, and I pray that you will fear not to love yourself, when you love truly as God loves, it is not a love of self-indulgence. It is a love of utter compassion whereby you recognize the availability, the accessibility of the rays of God which enable you to enter more and more into the consciousness of your own mighty I AM Presence. It does require that striving for holy purpose! It does require intensity and the keeping of the vigil.

Thus, we arrive at a crossroads in community wherein some who have been here long take for granted that their manifestation is acceptable unto the Lord. Yet even Jesus Christ in his final incarnation strove daily to determine that that daily offering would be renewed by the Holy Spirit, by his heart, and would be acceptable in the sight of the LORD God. He never took for granted from day unto day that the measure of light he outpictured was automatically accepted simply because he was called to his mission or he was who he was.

Automation is a way of life upon earth. It is enhanced by synthetically created rays and vibrations, many of them directed by malevolent forces. As you are acquainted with the conspiracy of the Nephilim, I am certain that it will take little for your minds to discover that they have also found ways of holding back the bursting of creativity in the minds of the children of God by the mere alteration of brain waves, by setting up or using certain existing magnetic forcefields upon the planetary body, and even the alteration of climate calculated to keep the consciousness subdued and to drive wedges between the soul's experience and its union with the inner Christ.

BE A CONSCIOUS COLLABORATOR
WITH THE WILL OF GOD

Supremely threatened are the fallen ones in this hour and therefore they stop at nothing to keep the population of the nations of the earth in control, in ignorance, and divided. And they are very determined to put down the true prophets abroad in the land and the true teachings of the ascended masters.

Therefore, understand the vigilance that is required. Understand that the battle is to the strong and not unto those who would indulge in a mechanized attitude toward the path of the ascension. I give to you a sense of co-measurement as to what it means to be a conscious collaborator with the will of God, with the will of Maitreya, with all of us who are assembled in Darjeeling out of concern for the outcome of [the testing of] the souls of light upon earth.

Let there be, then, a greater diligence—not a brittleness, not a flagellation of the self but an aliveness, a quickened consciousness. Eliminate self-concern and *plunge* into the very center of God's will! Allow yourself to accelerate. Allow yourself to contact the mind of God!

There is a very delicate balance in this hour between each chela of my own flame and myself, between every disciple of the Lord and the ascended masters and his own mighty I AM Presence. We dare not enter to push or accelerate consciousness without the mutuality of striving, without your own sensitivity that there is another rung that is ready for you. There are angels waiting but *you* must climb the ladder.

Thus, those whom you would least expect to be ready for our light are well prepared and those who have taken for granted their position vis-à-vis our bands come with empty hands, for they have forgot the fruit of striving. Let us not gather together out of habit or rote. Let us come to the altar with rejoicing as if for the first time. Let us come with expectancy of miracles and the realization that heaven and earth are one!

The more you understand of fallen man and fallen woman, the more you realize that the light of Reality within you has never fallen and that you are strangers tarrying here in a dusty land with the dust of the ages upon your garments. It is time we move on. It is time we open our eyes in the assessment of world conditions. It is time we placed maximum emphasis upon our own *avatara*— as the descent of God into our temples by the day-to-day exercise of the conscious freewill choice: to be or not to be God incarnate.

You can become the Word incarnate but not by self-depreciation nor by self-elevation but by the emergence of the soul who will merge with God-reality. In order to merge with your own God consciousness, your life, your ability must be at that level of vibration whereby your frequencies and God's frequencies can meet and be as one.

THE WILL OF GOD IS KNOWN
BY WISDOM AND BY LOVE

Thus I come always and always at the individual level. I come with a ray from my heart that I now send to every chela of El Morya. My own diamond heart multiplied by the diamond heart of Mother Mary touches your heart and if your heart is found in readiness, so be it. The devas minister and an increment of fire is added to the blue plume of your own threefold flame simultaneously as it compels the rising of wisdom and love in perfect balance to that will. For the will of God is good! And the will of God is known by wisdom and by love.

Therefore all who are ready are accelerated and all who are not must prepare for my coming again. Diligence in discipleship: the rewards are manifold—manifold experience with the living Word.

Is there anything that you would exchange for (or rather have than) the feeling of our Presence in your heart, the feeling of God as a love fire that bursts forth and fills you with a most magnificent joy?

For your heart to be ready for the sendings of Sirius, this,

this too requires diligence in the way of perfect Love. But when we come to knock and the Guru of your heart enters in, is this not the supreme experience of life? I ask you, precious hearts. ["Yes!"]

How easy it is to forget and to think that outer activities or entertainments or pleasures and pursuits can somehow compare to or even be on an equal footing [with receiving and being received by the Guru of your heart].

How easy it is to come to the place where for the purpose of balance, as they say, all these other things ought to be considered equally with the pursuit of God!

Yet the saints have always known that it is not so. The worldly will not tell you to leave off the path of religion but only to keep it in its proper place. What is its proper place according to their standard and according to our own?

INCREASING IN SELF-MASTERY

Religion binding the soul unto God[3] is the supreme reason for being unto those who have become weary of a world of maya and who recognize that all experience is but for the mastery of the soul. For the only thing that your *soul* may store and take with you when you depart for other octaves is that self-mastery gleaned from the experiences of life. You cannot even take the experience, let alone the silver and gold or the possessions of life. Brief memories; but the essence, *the essence* of the fruit of life *is* self-mastery.

Weigh, then, the activities of your life. Are you increasing in self-mastery within and without both physically, mentally, and spiritually by your pursuit of it day by day? And is the increase of your self-mastery for the sake of the grace of God and by his grace which you offer as a gift upon the altar?

Priorities in the pursuit of life. And the net gain is the deathless solar body. It is a white-fire body. It is a vehicle of consciousness. It counts for more than all of the mechanization and the advanced scientific discovery; yet these too may become, and in some must become, the instrument for sainthood and even for the path of self-mastery.

Let all listen to the dictates of the heart, for the heart will inform you of danger. The heart will inform you of disturbing vibrations whose source may be the mechanization vibrations of alternative rays both from this planetary body and beyond. The heart will tell you when you need more light, when you need to increase by a determined fiat that portion which is at your command. The aura must be charged and supercharged that the soul might be free from psychic, [psychotronic,] and psychedelic interference.

Blessed hearts of light, this [light which you need on the instant] may often come to you more quickly and intensely with fiery fiats to my heart than long hours of repetition. And yet, when the repetition is necessary and given with the full fire of the heart, then your call will result in a mantle of protection to the entire community of lightbearers worldwide.

Listen well, then, for I AM El Morya of the First Ray! I do not choose to unfold to you all that I know in this hour, all that I know of what is manifesting and what is coming into manifestation upon the earth. But I choose to come to encourage, to warn, to inspire, to assure and to reassure you that your path with the ascended masters is secure only when you make it so day by day.

And this is the illusion that is put upon you, that it does not matter and that somehow by the collective consciousness of the group you will also be swept up in the magnificent reunion with the living Christ.

Blessed hearts, simply because you are in the same place physically or in the same class or the same grade or the same year of service does not assure that you are at the same point of attainment. There is such diversity of acceleration of light* within those who are gathered here that you would be astounded to see the

---

*of the Christ consciousness and of Holy Christ Self-awareness

spectrum from the least unto the greatest, yet all are devotees (or presume to be) of the Great White Brotherhood and of their own mighty I AM Presence.

Thus, let there be individuality and individual striving! Let there not be comfortability in the blessedness and the holiness of the saints who pray without ceasing, but let all assess his own momentum in climbing up the rope to the highest vibrations of the mighty I AM Presence.

For all must stand alone in the hour of the ascension. All must stand *one* with the mighty I AM Presence. And, my beloved, *this takes practice*. It takes *daily* exercise. This takes practice.

March 1, 1981
Camelot
Los Angeles, California
ECP

CHAPTER 17

*Commitment is a flowing stream of light
from the Guru to the chela,
from the chela to the Guru.
And the commitment by the Guru is far greater
than that which is required of the chela.*

THE GEMINI MIND
FOR THE GOVERNING OF SOCIETY
AND THE SELF

Heart friends of the ages, I welcome you into the diamond heart of my love for Him. I welcome you into the will of God as you have never known that will before. I say this unequivocally. For I call you, sons and daughters of light, to a new initiation in the will of God which is essential if you are to outpicture that light for the salvation of the age.

The will of God is power—but not until you have submitted your will to it. And thus, in the absence of commitment, there is latency of the power of God. And therefore, those who have not commitment to our cause do not have the ability to evaluate the benefits of being a part of that cause.

Commitment is a flowing stream of light from the Guru to the chela, from the chela to the Guru. And the commitment by the Guru is far greater than that which is required of the chela.

I come once again, harvesting souls for Saint Germain. It is my love for him, and for his flame in you, that compels me to ever-new heights of devotion to God's will!

COMMITMENT TO THE WILL OF GOD
INCREASES POWER

Did you ever consider, beloved ones, that even an ascended being can discover daily new levels of transcendence of that devotion to God's will, new awarenesses of the blueprint of cosmos and how one's energy can be aligned with that blueprint? And thus, it is because I know that commitment to the will of God increases power that I bring to you this equation: As I increase the power within me by the action of love, so I have that much more power to give to you and to use for your initiations in the way.

Now think upon your own devotion to Saint Germain and your dedication to the cause. What is the single element lacking in your ability to change world conditions? Is it not power? Is it not power, beloved ones? And is it not power that the fallen ones seek and which they have amassed?—an anti-power, if you will, which they have garnered into their storehouses with which to manipulate the children of God.

Thus, the absolute tyranny of the fallen ones has begotten an absolute power that is a black sphere, the counterfeit to the sphere of the Great Blue Causal Body of the universe. That Great Blue Causal Body contains within it the inner blueprint for every lifestream—and the God-momentum of power with which to fulfill that blueprint! If I were the genie with the lamp and you could rub the lamp in this moment, would you not ask first for your blueprint and then for the power to implement it? This, indeed, would be a wise wish, as long as it would be tempered by wisdom and by love.

When we examine, then, the equation of Camelot, our community of lightbearers, and we consider all of the souls upon earth who will be drawn to this matrix of intense love, we look at the equation of power. And we are concerned that the children of God understand that there is a price to be paid for power.

If you, then, above all desiring, desire to free your brothers and sisters on the Path, you will come to the place where you are will-ing to pay the price for the gift of power to implement the plan. That price *is* your sweet surrender to your holy vow.

Note the sweetness of surrender. God does not care for a sur-render that is halfhearted or sour. It must be a joyous surrender—a full participation in *God's* being, whereas formerly you partici-pated only in your selfish being. Stepping into new shoes is the way of surrender—being willing to be a bit uncomfortable until the shoe fits, becomes one with you, and you realize that really, by your surrender, you have become that which you always were.

THE GEMINI MIND

There is not much space between your present condition and that condition of consciousness which I would call the Gemini mind—that condition of consciousness whereby you have a suffi-ciency of power that is equal to the Coming Revolution in Higher Consciousness.[1]

What is the Gemini mind? It is the mind of the God Mercury poised on the wings of the mighty Blue Eagle of Sirius. The two-fold action of the wings are the currents of Alpha and Omega—also represented in the right and left arms of the Maltese cross, the cloven tongues of fire of the Holy Spirit. The Gemini mind is the mind that is poised at the point of the Christ, betwixt the current of Alpha in the crown and the current of Omega in the base—parallel lines of consciousness.

The fullness of the Gemini line is reached when the soul steps into the shoes of the Christ Self. When the seeming two become one, when Alpha and Omega are the whole, then you live and move and have being in that mind which was in Christ Jesus, which is indeed the mind of God. The Gemini mind is inaccessible to those who resist the soul's reunion with the Real Self. Those who resist that reunion must evermore dwell on the track of the lower mind. That track, representing only half of the polarity, does not have the potential for wholeness. And therefore, it can never reach the vastness of the mind of God or even comprehend the fullness of the plan of life.

Every ascended master teaches his chelas the value of the Gemini mind for taking dominion in the earth planes, for the rule of the self, for the resolution of all division within the personality—and, mind you well, for the drawing back to the center of the four lower bodies that have been split by the divisive tactics of the fallen ones.

Some of you would be candidates for Morya's school and for Morya's service, and yet in this moment you must become qualified. Qualification requires your four lower bodies to be in a reasonable alignment with the cosmic cube.

When the bodies have been separated by violent and aggressive means, such as those forces which are abroad in the land—the misuse of rhythm, the misuse of substance taken into the body as food, drug or stimulant, the misuse of the currents of mind and emotions, and so many conditions such as the splitting of the mind of children through the media, through the television— when this is present, we cannot lower the ray of the will of God into the crucible of self. For the four lower bodies then do not represent a satisfactory chalice to contain the energy idling, then, at the nexus of creation.

Let the four sides of the pyramid be aligned. I command it! *I demand it!* I call forth your energies from out the Great Central Sun! I *expel* those forces of the fallen ones. I *bind* them in the name of the Christ, in the name of the I AM THAT I AM.

I, Morya, stand before you. And I summon out from your midst the discarnates and fallen ones that are even now preventing your absorption of this release of intense energy. *Bind* them, I say to my legions of light. By the authority of your free will, these legions now act to remove every hindrance to the coming together of the great cube of your own forcefield. Thus, let us reestablish the potential for the Gemini mind—as Above, so below.

God Mercury is my sponsor, and he will sponsor you. The lifewaves of sons and daughters of God who have evolved out of Mercury, who have served with Sanat Kumara and who now are dwelling on earth, come from an evolution which we knew long ago. In that planetary body, the issue of light and darkness was present. Here, where the sign of Gemini is the mind of God for action in concentration, the perversion of the light was in the mechanical creation of a robot in imitation of the Gemini mind. Absolute travesty against the Almighty! And yet, the fallen ones carried off their scheme—and it seemed for a time that they would carry the day!

THE CHALLENGE ON MERCURY

The fallen ones created, then, a robot manifestation with a superficial ability to deal with mundane information but lacking the depth of the prongs of love/wisdom that come forth out of the threefold flame. This, then, seemingly practical yet highly spiritually impractical robot began to overrun that civilization. The challenge to sons and daughters of God was to use then the Gemini mind to confute, refute, denounce, *bind* and remove from Mercury those manifestations—an absolute usurpation of the creation of the Almighty One.

As we saw the challenge and as we were taught by God Mercury, we knew that unflinching devotion to the will of God, the drawing within of energy to the diamond point of the Self, the wielding of the sword of blue flame, and the mastery of the action of fohatic keys would result in the victory.

Fohatic keys, blessed ones, are molecular formulae that are used for a particular release of the energies of the chakras. These energies, when coded in certain manifestations, can bring to pass in the Matter plane any form of manifestation, any intensity of the seven rays for a specific action or challenge.

You will note that the black magicians have perverted these keys and set their perverted keys to music, played that rhythm and that music, and thereby caused enormous quantities of energy to be drained from the children of God. This you have seen and heard visually,[2] and therefore you understand that of which I speak.

Now then, it was out of our deep desire to free evolving souls upon Mercury (who were no match for the robot creation) that we developed our adeptship in the will of God. Absolute perversions of absolute power demand the counteraction by the intensity of Great Central Sun Magnet energies. You will recall that the victory of Jesus Christ gave to him that power of heaven and earth,[3] the wherewithal to defeat the enemy at his call.

God gave to us, as we fought the battle of worlds on Mercury, that energy, that power—only because we were willing to balance the threefold flame, to pursue wisdom and wisdom's might, to intensify such love in every cell and in the flame of every cell, so that our auras were so saturated with love that there was no possibility for the misqualification of one erg of God's power through any form of tyranny whatsoever.

Beloved ones, you have not tasted of this power of which I speak for thousands upon thousands of years. And therefore, you do not have a direct appreciation of what happens to the human psyche in the presence of such power. It becomes a force—when uncontrolled by love/wisdom—of absolute tyranny, absolute Evil, despotism over souls!

It is much like the craze of the gold rush that transformed people into pure greed, if there be such a commodity—*intense* greed is the word—all because of the great energy charged into the gold from Helios and Vesta, from the Great Central Sun. Such currents of light, when contacting the humanly misqualified force-field, become immediately misqualified into more and more greed. Thus, the gold fever swept portions of the nation and created a karma for those individuals who thereby aligned themselves with the fallen ones in the gold-rush years.

Beloved ones, the victory of Mercury has not yet been concluded. A greater part of the victory was won, yet certain sons of light and certain fallen ones had not reached the culmination of their evolution. They were, therefore, assigned to other planetary homes and systems. Some of the fallen ones became aligned with the laggard evolutions which eventually embodied on Earth. Some of the sons and daughters of God journeyed to Venus and later accompanied Sanat Kumara to Earth.

ACCELERATE THE POWER OF GOD
THROUGH YOUR SWEET SURRENDER

Thus, we see today on Earth the battle of forces being waged between those of ancient ties—the fallen ones who created the Mercurian robot and the sons of God who were the challengers of them and of their creation. So many types of initiations on Earth, you would expect that it would become necessary to become a ten-armed god or goddess in order to perform your actions for the light! This is indeed true! And the angel devas and the ascended masters provide you with many bodies and many arms and many chakras through which to release the all-power of God—especially when you accelerate that power through your own sweet surrender.

It was in that experience on Mercury that some of you who are present here with me tonight learned the art of dealing with the Luciferians according to their terms of war and the warfare of worlds. Understanding the strategy of the fallen ones, you also had the full awareness of God's strategy of light—which is love in every form, in every manifestation—that simply reverses every force and momentum, point/counterpoint, somewhat like the martial arts which are taught today which have come out of the East, except in a much more refined manner because of the development of greater energies in the chakras.

Here, then, we find ourselves continuing the challenge. And the victory is not yet—and the victory always was, always is, and always shall be. It is a question of bringing into alignment the parallel lines of the Gemini mind for the victory above to be manifest here below!

Chelas of the will of God, I fling to you the challenge in this hour! That challenge is to make yourself one—and thereby be eligible for the lowering of the electrode through the Elohim Apollo that will allow the previous electrode already anchored[4] to fulfill a greater capacity whereby you may enter in to the mind of God and, through love and only love, *key the power* for the victory!

I have come to speak to you of some of the intricacies of the Law regarding the Coming Revolution.[5] All rests upon the dedication of the few which one day on earth will become the victory of the many.

I trust, beloved hearts, that you will take this morsel, assimilate and become it, so that I may return with part two of my lecture to you concerning the Gemini mind.

I bid you adieu!

October 8, 1977
Pasadena, California
ECP

CHAPTER 18

Thus you see, beloved, the call,
the matrix, the fiat begins the process.
But to retain the answer to your call,
you must become the answer.

CHAPTER 18

THE INNER TEMPLE WORK OF SERAPIS BEY IN THE FOUR QUADRANTS, "CHARIOTS," OF MATTER

And I turned, and lifted up mine eyes, and looked, and, behold, there came four chariots out from between two mountains; and the mountains were mountains of brass.

In the first chariot were red horses; and in the second chariot black horses;

And in the third chariot white horses; and in the fourth chariot grisled and bay horses.

Then I answered and said unto the angel that talked with me, What are these, my lord?

And the angel answered and said unto me, These are the four spirits of the heavens, which go forth from standing before the Lord of all the earth.

The black horses which are therein go forth into the north country; and the white go forth after them; and the grisled go forth toward the south country.

And the bay went forth, and sought to go that they might walk to and fro through the earth: and he said, Get you hence, walk to and fro through the earth. So they walked to and fro through the earth.

Then cried he upon me, and spake unto me, saying, Behold, these that go toward the north country have quieted my spirit in the north country.[1]   —Zechariah 6

Most beloved Keepers of the Flame, I address you in the light and the might of our Darjeeling Council, which is the LORD's. I salute you who have become, in this service,[2] the flame of your own heart's altar.

THIS ENGRAFTING OF THE WORD

Truly this is the way and the path of the ruby ray. Walk ye in it. Fear it not. For this engrafting of the Word,[3] this, that threefold flame, does assume thyself unto Itself even as you breathe in its sacred fire breath and know the LORD thy God as thyself.

This is the inner temple work of Serapis Bey. You are receivers of it—you have received it, you shall receive it, and you shall know the victory in the physical octave which others have known in the retreat of Luxor, of Serapis, as they have pursued this very same calling.

14-MONTH ASCENSION PREPARATION
BY THE SCIENCE OF THE RUBY RAY

Thus I promise you that you who will faithfully give this 10/4 axis clearance service Friday evening once each month for fourteen months[4] will have therefore an extraordinary blessing and benefit from the Lord, from Sanat Kumara. And it shall indeed impel thyself to accelerated initiation in the halls of Luxor. This service, then, in the fourteen stations of the cosmic cross of white fire will enable you to overcome entrenched darkness on the 10/4 axis in thy life, in the earth, and in the trenches—in the very depths as the records of Lemuria.

Beloved ones, certain chelas of light who have made the transition, worthy ones, have yet not made the ascension. For they have been taken to the Royal Teton Retreat and to Luxor for this very ritual and purpose—the study of the science of the ruby ray in order that they might purge themselves of deep-seated records of ancient Lemuria: confrontations and entanglements and, I am sorry to say, compromises with the fallen ones, following after them instead of the Cosmic Christ Guru then present.

Beloved ones, by so doing this ahead of time you may obtain a better resurrection[5] and therefore not postpone the day of the physical merging of the fire Above with the fire in thy cells and heart. Understand that we would demonstrate this path. We would see you victors.

Now there is nothing to prevent you from giving this service more often, but then we do have other assignments at the Friday night service and some which I shall return to give you. And, beloved, there is a necessary assimilation of a call so vast.

THE QUALITY OF CHRISTHOOD EARNED

Understand and interpret the word of the messenger, who has explained to you that although you may sacrifice and surrender there must be the quality of Christhood earned, and of mastery—God-mastery—to replace those things which you have surrendered.

Thus, even if you would surrender all of your human creation in one night, it could not be so. For your human creation is a place-holder—in this case, the something that is better than nothing, for the nothing that is a vacuum might then be filled with forces out of the depths of death and hell.

And therefore understand that positive attitudes of the human mind and heart, a positive sense of self-worth based on the ego itself moving in a constructive direction—that is the placeholder, that is the condition of consciousness moving toward the light which, when it receives the light, may then internalize that light. And the individual in so becoming the Christ of that good momentum— the higher good of God corresponding to that momentum—may then dispense with the outworn garment.

Outworn garments are as these, beloved. In the day when the garments were new they suited you well, protected you from the elements. But the day does come when they are seen as inferior to the robe transcendent and to the wedding garment.

Thus understand that we must bless humanity for their positive direction, for their attempt to be constructive. And realize that they are building a citadel which one day, receiving the light of Christ, shall know the transmutation, shall know the acceleration, shall know the becoming and, behold, awake in the likeness of the City Foursquare!

THE REFINEMENT OF GOOD, THE REPLACEMENT OF EVIL

Thus there is the refinement of Good and positive momentums as best as one has found and can do. Then, beloved, there is the replacement of absolute Evil—such as the carnal mind, such as anger and hate and hate creation in the subconscious—that does come through and cause conditions that are discomfiting to oneself and all of one's friends and family and the earth body.

Absolute Evil in the form of that Darkness, then, can be taken from you by the hosts of the LORD as, and only as, the absolute Good of thy Christhood is born. One cannot simply remove the cancer of absolute Evil by the process of one night's service; but in the very service there is the gift of the violet flame and of illumination whereby one can see and behold the opening of the electronic belt and say, "Aha! I have discovered you, you devil of my human pride! I see you for what you are! Henceforth I shall walk in the joy, the similitude, the humility of my Christ. I invoke my Christ. I AM that Christ! I cast you down and I walk in the ways of the Lord!"

Thus the Christ does bind that dweller-on-the-threshold.[6] And some is taken, but not all. Therefore Jesus said, "And ye are clean, but not all."[7] For ye must be tested.

FOR YE MUST BE TESTED:
THE TRIAL BY FIRE

This is the trial by fire.[8] You have seen the devil of pride, you have made the determination, you have given the fiat that it be cast down. Now you go forth on the road of life and every form of adversary will come to attempt to rekindle in you the display of that pride. Line by line, day by day, decision by decision, you put it into the flame. And each time that element, that particular manifestation on that line of the clock[9] on that day and date in that situation of karma, is taken—so it is taken, so it is bound.

And it will be permanent if you pass the test on that line again and defeat it utterly and have no part with it. For it is now permanently cut from the vine of thy life force and therefore cannot live again. But as long as you have free will and you are unascended, you may elect to re-create it. For if you could not re-create it, then you could not be called a co-creator with God. The office of co-creator with God of necessity allows you while yet in the Matter spheres to at any time re-create your human creation.

Thus understand why in some of my embodiments I wore a hair shirt. Every point of discomfort was a reminder that there was yet substance to be bound and I must not be unalert. Waking or sleeping, I must be reminded that the Lord Christ knocks. And I must bind that Satan that would tear me from my meeting with my Lord.

YOU ARE RE-CREATING YOURSELF LINE BY LINE

You see, you are re-creating yourselves, beloved. You must re-create line by line. You have miscreated, for instance, in anger or pride or fear or hatred or doubt or ingratitude. That which you have created is indeed your own animal farm, your own lesser self.

Understand that only you have the key to the code—the genetic code, if you wish to so call it—of that creation. Only you can undo it by withdrawing the point of the "I" of decision, the point of will that said, "I will indulge myself in this discord." And then the spiral went forth and consciousness was clothed with form and that form was grotesque and distorted like its vibration.

This energy must be withdrawn and the form bound along with your propensity to re-create after the image and likeness of your human creation. For that human creation has become a god of sorts, and you re-create after the patterns of those things you have set in motion. Thus, much in your embodiment is repetitive and a repeat performance over and over again until those human creations are like iron or lead statues, so reinforced with that carnal will have they become.

YOU MUST BECOME
THE ANSWER TO YOUR CALL

Thus you see, beloved, the call, the matrix, the fiat begins the process. But to retain the answer to your call, *you must become the answer.* You call to God for perfection—perfection descends. You must seize it, take it to your heart, become it. For, you see, only then is it sealed. If you do not take that to yourself, another shall. Another will come along and say, "I will pluck this shining fruit," like the serpent that would eat from your tree of life. Another will come and devour the light, another who is not of the light but waits for the crumbs that fall from your table, for the light that comes from the altar.

See, then, the balancing of karma does take place as you serve, as you love, as you live in the decree of the Word. Balancing karma is not the equivalent of the full mastery you desire. Nevertheless, to balance one's karma does indeed require certain attainment and mastery. But the God-mastery we seek in you beyond the karmic round is the creation, the very magnetization of the qualities of Christhood.

FOUR O'CLOCK:
LOVING OBEDIENCE/OBEDIENT LOVE

I commend you, then, to the Buddha of the Ruby Ray on the four o'clock line. I commend you, then, to the crystal quality of *obedient love*—and the reverse of the coin: *loving obedience*. Thus the Alpha, the Omega of thy twin flames shall embody the ark— the ark that forms the portal to the Shekhinah glory of the Lord's Presence, the ark that bears the Law—and the cherubim who form the ark, again thy twin flames, kneeling before the flame of the living God.

Determine to embody a single quality of thy Christ, who is the master of the four o'clock line. You can make a list of at least twenty-five attributes of God from the four o'clock line beginning with alignment, co-measurement with thy God, fulfillment of the Word, happiness, nonsufferingness, God-desire, holiness unto the Lord, geometry of God, clarity of communication in the mind, the art, the science of the builders. All of this proceeds from obedient love/loving obedience.

INITIATION TONIGHT
AT THE ROYAL TETON RETREAT

Now understand the meaning of being the master of thy life, line upon line. Great strides have been achieved. If you should "hold fast what thou hast received" this night, you should truly be a new creature on the morrow when you awaken from the sealing of this action which shall take place within ye all at the Royal Teton Retreat tonight.

I bid you adieu in the flaming heart of Serapis Bey—our joy, our perfect Master of Love. He will be there to receive you, beloved.

Thus remember, it is the byword of the Keeper of the Flame: Hold Fast What Thou Hast Received.

In love, I am your obedient Guru, obedient to the will of God for thee and thine and all life.

July 19, 1985
Camelot
Los Angeles County, California
ECP

CHAPTER 19

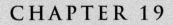

*There is a time for intensity
and a time for gentleness,
a time for communication of science
and another for quiet meditation.
Life is a great rhythm and opportunity.*

SEEKING AND FINDING
THE MYSTERY OF LIFE

"I AM Ascending"

How good it is, beloved, to be with friends this night to contemplate the meaning of winter solstice, once the hour of my birth.[1]

Once, I became the light descending in the earth's darkest hour. Thus, it is good on the 29th of December to contemplate beyond the merriment of Christmas to the portent of Christ's birth for every soul. In each life, beloved, there is then a new hope— a new star of hope, a new reason for being, a new mystery to be discovered in the Christmas Rose.

For each one does descend a single shaft of light from the mighty I AM Presence to embody that portion of the Word without which the world should suffer indeed. The world suffers greatly today for want of the expression by sons of God of that single light of the Word incarnate which they have come to represent, to master, to embody, and then to transcend.

When little children are not shown a path of seeking and finding[2] the reason for being, when they are not even shown how to contemplate the mystery of the apple, is it not a pity? Looking at the apple, one cannot know the mystery it holds inside; one must cut open the apple to find the heart and the seed of life. And then, of course, the apple is no more. Then ask the child as you show him this mystery, "Can you find out the seed of light in your heart without cutting it open?"

CHILDREN MUST HAVE A SENSE OF THE QUEST

Thus, life is a mystery that must be probed without destroying its heart and essence—not knife but spoken Word and prayer, mystical union, discovering the heart of life without dissecting it. Let games be played, even guessing games—games of blindfolding, finding treasure, searching for Easter eggs and precious toys handmade. Children must have a sense of the quest, developing a mental dexterity, an understanding of the need to rely on intuition and inspiration and compass and the stars and so many signs that nature gives to the mariner.

Beloved ones, do not so easily give to the child the answer, for the answer is not important. It is the ritual of seeking and finding in all things—having to muster the will, having to have enough desire in the attainment of the prize to pursue it. Thus, competition in life, in sports and games is useful to a point. For the desire to excel is truly the excellence of the first ray. And that excelling, beloved, is fired by love for the prize. And the prize becomes more precious and more precious as sights are elevated. And soon the prizes of this world no longer satisfy.

It is good to win the medals and the cups. It is good to show the point of winning and victory only to realize that having thus conquered, one need not conquer again but one is ready for spiritual heights. And one knows that with effort and co-measurement and the inner sensing of the nearness of the stars one can achieve the goal of immortality.

Thus, it is well to understand in training oneself or one's child not to make the hurdle too great or too little but to instill enough challenge that demands enough effort so that in striving the soul will exceed its former position and discover a new unboundedness, a new penetration of the larger Self.

Thus explore. Thus discover. Thus be creative. Do not rest on yesterday's victories; they are not equal to the next challenge.

ENTERING THE INITIATIONS
OF LORD MAITREYA

Thus, I begin my counsel of the new year to you with a single lesson from Maitreya's school on goal-fittedness. Fit yourselves well for the good use and exercise of the four lower bodies, the skills, potentials and talents that you have, always knowing that you are building parallel lines of force with an inner summoning and an inner adventure of the spirit that takes place beyond the body.

Beloved hearts, we rejoice to have this mighty swaddling garment of the blue sphere around the earth and you and our messenger and activity.[3]

We rejoice that the armour of the will of God is well known to you as warriors of the Prince of Peace. Therefore, we take this opportunity to announce a new course of study at Darjeeling— a preparatory course for entering the initiations of Lord Maitreya, a course conceived by us here in Darjeeling whereby you yourself can pace yourself and ready yourself not for a fearful encounter but for a joyous one, knowing truly, "Lord, I am ready. Receive me now into thy heart and inner sanctum."

Beloved, the age of fear and doubt is past. Let it go by, passing down the hill as a stream that moves on. It is the age of joy and light, the age of alchemy and freedom and a new expression of the effulgence of the Christ flame. This is a path of love expanded in your hearts in song and winged prayer with the Mother, whose heart's call has reached us in Darjeeling with many plans for this year of expansion and for the cutting free of those ten thousand-times-ten thousand of Maitreya's bands.

Seize and grasp and sense the wind of freedom itself that is upon you. Sense the will of God, the desperation of humanity, the determination of the Almighty, the willpower of the chelas and the truth blazing, reflected from the armour of our knights. A blinding light comes back in the eye of the enemy as the light itself deflects the arrows. Let the will of God probe deeply and expose then the dark deeds.

Four murderers came—one for each of my four lower bodies.[4] They were determined to put out the light of myself. But I could only mock the evil in their eye and behold the risen Christ, who gave to me and my heart such grace as to continue to minister to the people of Canterbury and the world.

Thus, I did not die in vain, as you have never died in vain. For life moves on, outwits and outsmarts the Evildoer. And evildoers themselves return to the scene of life so blank and charred and hollowed out, with scarce an identity to continue their folly. They are to be pitied, beloved ones, but never to be despised. Evil itself may be despised for a moment as the ruby ray utterly consumes and dissolves it. For the ruby ray is always a laser beam that goes forth by the intense love of the One, who is, therefore, perfectly able to meet the adversary in the way.

Our God is a consuming fire.[5] And this consuming fire is indeed love. Love fulfills her purpose in many, many ways. Love, of course, is the most creative and ingenious element, for love seeks many ways to comfort, to uplift, to instruct, and to rebuke.

THE WILL OF GOD
IS FASTIDIOUS AND DETAILED

Therefore, we call upon those who see in the will of God a means of mastery in the detail of the law of the Cosmic Christ. Detail, then, is the will of God—a thousand-petaled blue lotus, the sunflower herself and the many seeds thereof. The will of God is fastidious and detailed. You have fourteen months[6] to master a skill, a trade, a profession, to bring to the point of excellence that which you would love most to lay upon the altar of God—that achievement, that ability which you know will enable us through you to build the house of God, to bring light to many a house now in darkness, to deliver souls of life-long addictions. And these addictions go on lifetime after lifetime.

I tell you, beloved, the miracles that God can work through you are a million times a million, sparkling, gemlike. Sending back to you fragments of rainbow rays from the sapphire of my heart, I have seen the miracles of God again and again. To live in the life of miracles as the capstone on the pyramid, as the emerald crystal of the All-Seeing Eye of God, one must build the sure foundation of God's will.

In going through the fourteen months of each cycle of the causal body multiplied by the white-fire core, beloved, you then have come to the practical and physical light. It is a light of Capricorn, the highest of the sacred fire, most profoundly embedded in the earth. Thus, the white-fire/blue-fire sun of the God Star ever shines more brightly now, expanded and reflected through your auras.

It is a wondrous opportunity to decree for God-government in this nation, to implement Saint Germain's call for the judging of tyrants everywhere,[7] to call for the amplification of the will of God from the Sun and the turning back of any and all harm which this comet* may portend.

---

*Halley's comet

MANY THINGS ACCOMPLISHED
WITH THE BLUE FLAME

Many things can be accomplished with the blue flame. You will discover these as you give the calls to the will of God, as you saturate your beings by going through the entire blue section of decrees until you can hardly bear the blue flame any longer and must swiftly turn to the violet for the transmutation of all resistance to that inner alignment with the sapphire crystal.

Oh, the joy of Hercules this night! And Amazonia is with us as they approach this altar, beloved, sealing then the dispensation of the blue sphere of the Logoi, of Serapis, and Alpha and Omega. Thus Archangel Michael sends intensified light, and Surya and Cuzco.

We come for the strengthening of the pilasters and the insertion in the earth of electrodes of blue fire. Almost as you would place toothpicks to hold together a cake or a sandwich, so we insert in the earth, through layers of subterranean disturbances and pressures, giant electrodes of the will of God thousands of feet in length, having a diameter the width of this altar.*

These electrodes the Elohim and the four cosmic forces are placing throughout the planetary body for the holding steady of the earth in a time when her molecules and substances are being bombarded with discordant sound, with chemicals and pollutions, with anger and war, experimentation, abuse of every kind and the shedding of blood. These electrodes will assist, beloved, in the absorption by earth and her evolutions of the new etheric body earth received almost a year ago.[8]

POSITION YOURSELF IN THE HEART
OF ARCHANGEL URIEL

Now come to the heart of Uriel Archangel, whose radiance as perfume yet wafts upon this altar. Come to the heart of Uriel and

---

*Twenty-five and a half feet

position yourself there through the trials and tribulations which must be faced and then swiftly passed through.

We will stand indeed as one body, never alone. To this end was the Great White Brotherhood founded. With this inner knowledge of the science of the law of the One have you assembled, truly in the knowledge that the Circle of the One is the protection of your life and in the understanding that it is living bodies and lively stones[9] that make up this circle of community that is called "church."*

And well it is that church might remain as an alabaster inner city of light, unsullied by mankind's poor attempts to imitate the City Foursquare. So long as the Church Universal and Triumphant shall stand as the white cube in the earth, so long shall the open door remain for angelic hosts to step through the veil and souls to ascend.

Let the borders of this Church Universal and Triumphant expand. But let not the standard be lowered. Let lightbearers come and be educated here and in Darjeeling and at the Inner Retreat, at Maitreya's Mystery School, and be shown how they may meet a standard of excellence and the self-mastery of the sacred centers of life.

O teachers who would serve with the World Teachers, come, then! Come to Darjeeling. Come with Kuthumi and Jesus and Djwal Kul and me. Come, as with Mother Mary we take you to a comprehensive sevenfold way of reaching souls of light.

For there are hours in the day when one speaks through this chakra and other hours when one speaks through another. There is a time for intensity and a time for gentleness, a time for communication of science and another for quiet meditation. Life is a great rhythm and opportunity. And the receptivity is according to the hours and the light rays and the Central Sun itself. [And these things must be learned.]

---

*church: or *ekklesia* [fr. Greek *ek* "out of"; *kaleo* "to call"]; community of called-out ones

There are so many secrets to the mystery of life for you to discover, beloved ones, as you unfold before all the world the lost teachings of Jesus Christ. They have waited so long that they have forgotten that they are waiting. They know not what they are waiting for, for they have long been told that they know it all, they have it all, and salvation, of course, is guaranteed. A most unfortunate set of circumstances.

YOU ARE INDEED
REACHING FOR AN INFINITE GOAL

We would not dash the cup of hope from the lips of the hopeful. But we would say, sometime, somewhere the children of the light must put on the garments of maturity, become wise, concerned, serious and responsible in seeking the kingdom of God, being willing to pay the price and coming to the realization that the price indeed can be paid. It is payable. It is earnable. And this we teach by the measured cadences of striving, to which I have directed your attention.

The more hurdles a lifestream learns to jump over, the more he can meet the hurdle of infinity, which, after all, can be contained "on the head of a pin"—and therefore not quite so far to leap as you had once thought. If in the twinkling of an eye the last trump of the human consciousness may sound and its karma go down,[10] if in that same twinkling of the Eye of God you can know yourself in the totality of a universal Mind, beloved ones, then is anything too hard for you, held in the bosom of the Lord Sanat Kumara?

Precious hearts, you are indeed reaching for an infinite goal. But it is not a receding one; it is ever drawing nearer. Death is not its door. But in this life you can behold and see what grandeur of cosmos you can contain while still wearing bodies of which those you now wear in this octave are the facsimile. I say "facsimile," beloved ones, because as your bodies become purified and charged with light, they appear to be physical even to yourself, but they are becoming more a part of the etheric octave every day. This is why your diet changes and why you call for and require other substances as you learn to adjust the body, the light body, to the environment of the cities of the earth.

ASCENDING TO THE HEART OF GOD:
THIS IS THE MEANING OF IT ALL

You *are* ascending, beloved. This is my message to you this day, because this was my realization at the altar of Canterbury Cathedral. I said to myself in the face of these whose darkness was so great as to be so unreal—I said to myself, beholding His glory as truly Saint Stephen did, "I am ascending. I am ascending to the heart of God. This is the meaning of it all. This is the meaning of it all."

Beloved, at least it was action. After all, I wasted away in France for any number of years. They had had good opportunity to rally to the cause of Christ. Thus the karmic law descended. God called me home and allowed the drama to be outplayed with a particular contrast of light and darkness so typical of winter solstice.

You see, they were left to face the tyrant king. And Henry must live with himself and his image and the world. Karma decrees, therefore, and karmic law, that when individuals reject the representative of the Christ—which for that moment I was before pope and king and France and England and soon all the world— when that messenger is rejected, then the light is withdrawn and they must then overcome the darkness by their own devices, else be swallowed up by it.

When they reject the messenger of light, then they must go their way until they become surfeited in darkness and finally [perchance] come to the point of that same love of the honor of God whereby the honor is preferred beyond a paltry existence in cowardice, dumbness, ignorance and silent infamy. Some have come around since that hour in the twelfth century. Today the hour is late. And I can tell you that some of them have not changed a whit.

LET GOD SAVE WHOM HE WILL
THROUGH YOU

Take it from my heart, beloved ones. Take it from me: Let God save whom he will through you. Be nonattached concerning the conversion of those who will not be converted and whom the LORD himself desires not to convert. Do not be stubborn in determining who shall be saved by you. Save no man. Give God that grace, for he will do it better than all of your contrivances.

But be a crystal gem, a heart humble in light. Be an example of joy and joy in the LORD's achievement through you. Go forth, then, and establish good order and God-government in this community. Commit yourselves to harmony, good-neighborliness, helpfulness and brotherhood. For we do indeed help one another. Beware, then, of Evildoers who creep in to take advantage of your charity.[11] For charity must be given to the heart of light, not darkness.

BECOME THE CRADLE OF THE *V*

I, El Morya, with Hercules and Amazonia, place now three mighty dots upon this altar for the sealing of the triangle of God's will with Morya and Mother and Mark—and you yourselves, three by three by three: for each one of you, there are two masters above forming the triangle of Being. Realize, then, that we gird the planet round in this configuration and a grid of light whereby the electrodes connect the blue chain mail, anchoring the etheric body of planet Earth, fastened then by three dots again and again.

Thus, raise your hands thus [in this manner] now. Take the hand of two ascended masters and feel the flow of the will of God— each one a mighty bodhisattva standing staunch above you to the left, to the right. You, then, become the cradle of the *V,* the lowest point that has descended. And the hands you clasp complete the sign of the *V of Victory* in this fourteen-month cycle. They pull you up and they let you down again as you serve in the lowest octaves, and draw you up again to the etheric retreats and the inner glory of the City Foursquare.

STUDY THE TEXT OF MY MESSAGE

Have I spoken in poetry? Have I sung to you in song? Know this, beloved, that you have heard by my voice mysteries of Maitreya preparing you for his initiation. Study the text of my message and call for its inner blueprint to be anchored in your etheric body until the particular forget-me-not message for your lifestream, hidden in the very blueprint of my dictation, is fulfilled and does come to pass as fruition of the first ray in your life.

Above all, seek the qualities of the first-ray masters. Become them. Do not flinch. Be uncompromising when it comes to the will of God. And as for compassion, in that be tolerant, forgiving, and bending. The will of God is the structure of steely white light that is your life and house and tabernacle. If the foundation and superstructure, if the skeletal frame be not perfect, naught else can be according to the plumb line of truth.

Thus, in all matters of discipline under the will of God, be precise in defining your freedom of speech, your freedom of the press, your freedom to assemble, your freedom of religion, your freedom and right to own property and to preserve the value of your sacred labor—your right to have the abundant life. Be precise, beloved, for the first ray of God's will will surely draw you into God-mastery if you will only allow our devas and masters of the diamond heart to tutor you now in the will of God.

Receive now the blessing and transfer of Hercules and Amazonia, who will speak to you on the morrow. I have prepared your inner bodies to receive the greater light of Elohim. Thus build and build again, and be ready. For surely they come with a power unequaled.

In the name of the adorable one Jesus the Christ, I seal you in my heart's love forever. Forget me not.

December 29, 1985
Camelot
Los Angeles County, California
ECP

CHAPTER 20

*The words of Morya from the
beginning unto the end of our dictations
are all cipher, all keys, all kernels,
that will open up by the heat of divine fervor.*

SACRED FIRE BAPTISM

"Greet the Living Flame of God"

Light from Darjeeling beckons the traveler Home. Thus the bourne* of the noble attends the return from battle. Know, then, that as there is comfort in the pocket of Hercules,[1] so there is, beloved, comfort in the twin of Gemini that I bear.[2]

Have you thought of the brain itself as being twins of the mind of God? Have you thought of the limitation of these hemispheres of the brain? Have you thought of the deprivation of light-bearers from having the full use of the faculties of the mind of God? Well, I say to you, if you have not, then think of it! And think of it now. For these fallen ones have suppressed, as though with the boot of the Soviet, the full flowering of the crown of life.[3]

Let the light rise in this body. Let the light rise for the full flowering of genius that can be known in the physical octave by those of every age. Let the cells give up the ghosts of all that is past. Let them give up all that is less than the light, the golden liquid light that each cell can and shall hold in the balance of Alpha and Omega.

---

*bourne: realm or domain

Surely, I AM come. I AM come on a note of victory, not to leave you, then, in astral scenes of netherworlds of Nephilim gods. Thus Hercules has opened the vision of the vast panorama of heaven. I open the panorama of earth that can be the fullness of the LORD and of his coming. They shall not pass!

I urge our scribes, noting the precise answers to precise calls, to provide even another alternate preamble focusing on those facts that come to light in answer to the call of the first one.[4] There may be seven such preambles, all blue, but each one ensconced in one of the chakras and one of the seven rays.

Let the fire of the blue lightning of the mind of God unlock the fullness of the potential of the seven chakras and the seven rays and the Elohim's seven focuses upon the brow.[5] Let the seven spheres of the causal body descend.

Let yourself become now, beloved, the angel clothed with a cloud of the I AM Presence and upon his head the rainbow of the causal body of God.[6] For as the fire of the blue lightning of the mind of God descends, it does challenge in you the anger of mortality and death itself, lodged even in the molecules of physical matter.

Beloved, rejoice in the alchemy of chemicalization and leap into the flames of sacred fire! It is the only way. Sacred fire baptism may challenge you and it may even singe some portion of the human you would retain. But when you emerge from that sacred fire baptism—a unique and personal initiation of Maitreya—I tell you, nothing in this world can touch you, for you are fire!

It is a spiritual fire, a flame that cannot be quenched! Thus it is written: He does make "his ministers a flame of fire."[7]

Would you have it, beloved? Then see that the diamond heart and the Gemini mind,[8] the very solidity of reality, are thine own. And therefore, you shall not even notice what the sacred fire has taken from you, for it will be nothing of any import whatsoever.

Hasten, then, to greet the living flame of God. Do not rub

your eyes and say, "Am I seeing things?" when you see a flame walking toward you on the road. Blessed ones, I am serious. For the sacred fire manifest as salamander or seraphim does indeed walk down the road as a giant pillar or a giant leaf in shape.

Notice how the fire runs to greet you. Blessed ones, so greet it: "I see thee coming, O sacred fire! I shall not turn and run but leap into thy rainbow crescendoing, ascending, descending, undulating fiery presence!"

O blessed one, I know few sons of God who have not at that moment had a flash of a desire to be somewhere else. It will pass. And you will know that there is not anywhere else to go but into the heart of the flame.

Mark the heart again at the two-thirds level, beloved, and know that if you leap into the flame at that point, you will find yourself seated in a cave in the rock in the heart of meditation with Gautama. And you will recognize that that sacred fire is the gateway to the etheric octave.

These are the things of which I would speak to my chelas, not of wars and tribulations and of rehearsals of the activities of the unmentionables. O blessed hearts, if you are weary, believe me, the earth itself is weary and so are we of such discussions.

Thus, having divested myself of all that you may bear in this coming fortnight (and must bear for us), I may then digress in a spiritual mode so that you might also remember that we are adepts of the spiritual fire and that this is the training we give to our chelas.

Most notable ones who have noted the signs, let thy body be the vessel of the Holy Spirit and thy soul the bride of Christ. The key I have given, 'tis enough.

Meditate upon the cadences of my mind, for they are a rope that you pick up at the beginning of a tunnel. And you follow the rope, and beyond its cadences and the paces through the tunnel you will reach the secret chamber of my heart. Hold on to the rope. Do not let go of it. My sentences form this strong hemp.

Therefore, through all the darkness that you pass, beloved, you will find that the words of Morya from the beginning unto the end of our dictations are all cipher, all keys, all kernels that will open by the heat of divine fervor.

In the name of our LORD the Almighty One and him in his sons and daughters, I serve.

August 10, 1987
Royal Teton Ranch
Park County, Montana
ECP

CHAPTER 21

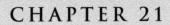

*When you are instruments for the transmutation
of world karma, you are surely transmuting
your own karma while you earn your stripes
and secure your opportunity to attain
union with God in this life. . . .
The intensity of your violet-flame decrees
is lifting untold burdens from within
your psyche and the psyche of the planet.*

TAKE A STAND FOR TRUTH

Fusing the Fragmented Parts of the Soul

Hail, legions of truth!
Hail, legions of truth!
Hail, legions of truth!
[Congregation gives the salutation:]
Hail, El Morya! Hail, El Morya! Hail, El Morya!
My beloved, be seated.

You have most graciously received me this day and throughout this conference and for many lifetimes.[1] I come on the heels of my brother chohan Hilarion, for I would continue his message of truth to you.

Heretofore when you have been faced with the choice of whether or not to declare your faith, the messenger has said to you, "If you do not wish to declare your faith, for you fear that to do so would jeopardize your job or your situation or your future, then do as you will." Thus, beloved, over the years some—not all, but some who count themselves as my chelas and as Saint Germain's Keepers of the Flame—have denied their messenger, their Church or their affiliation with the ascended masters, always for fear of persecution.

I must tell you, beloved, as Jesus has told you:

"The servant is not greater than his lord. If they have persecuted me, they will also persecute you." "Blessed are ye, when men shall revile you and persecute you and shall say all manner of evil against you falsely for my sake. Rejoice and be exceeding glad, for great is your reward in heaven: for so persecuted they the prophets which were before you."[2]

If you are in a church where there is no persecution, be suspicious of that church. Persecution is the testing of the mettle. Persecution demands that you take a stand for truth, even at the cost of life or limb.

Remember the early Christians who were thrown to the lions. Yes, beloved, the burdens that were upon them that caused them to retreat to the catacombs of Rome are upon you at times. But I tell you, there is something clean, *something very clean* about stating one's cause, one's purpose and one's life devotion. There is something liberating that sweeps through one when one can say without concern: "Yes, I love the ascended masters and I serve the ascended masters, and I am their chela. Come, and I will show you why."

Blessed ones, you have nothing to hide, for the newspapers have carried the story of your organization, whether properly or improperly presented, for decades now. Yes, you truly have nothing to hide.

I speak of this because there are legions of living truth who serve under Pallas Athena and legions of living love who serve under the Maha Chohan. They will defend your right to espouse the religion of your choice. And as you know, beloved Pallas Athena is the twin flame of the Maha Chohan. And so you can see how the power of truth and the fierce power of divine love, released through the ruby ray, combine as an indomitable force in the earth.

The messenger has heard from one who said: "Someone has found out who I am. Shall I admit to who I am or shall I conceal it?" And that one answered the question himself and did determine to pronounce the truth of his affiliation. It is a momentous event in the life of anyone when that one can, for the sake of truth, set aside job or family or associations or club membership, et cetera, in deference to the mighty truth of God that has brought that one even to the feet of his mighty I AM Presence, even to the path of the ascension.

You are legions of truth. You carry the shield of Pallas Athena. And as you carry that shield and move toward the Sun, the Sun is reflected in that shield. And then there is an oscillation that occurs between you and the Great Central Sun. And that oscillation becomes a current of energy so powerful that you can take your stand, as did the Spartans at Thermopylae, who could take that daring stand against the Persian army, beloved, because they were ensconced in the living flame of truth.[3]

You have been there. All of you have been in situations where your voice alone has made the difference—here, there and anywhere and in previous lifetimes. Now I say to you who would be received by the Holy Spirit and know as never before that comfort flame burning on the altar of your being: You must recognize that a part of that comfort flame is the living flame of truth. And truth contains honor and honor contains love, a love that is selfless, willing to suffer any cause to attain the victory.

On this first day of the year I ask you first and foremost to make your peace with yourself. For if you are not at peace with yourself, you will not be at peace with me and surely I will not be at peace with you. I shall come where your members are divided within and without, and I shall help you fuse the fragmented parts of the soul into one whole.

I will come, beloved. But I say, whether you have a difficult psychology or health problems or a challenging astrology, let it be understood that the members of your being must be in harmony with one another so that there is not a warring among them[4] whereby one organ does not work with another organ, just as one neighbor sometimes does not work with another neighbor. And so, you understand.

In the fullness of the Holy Spirit manifest as Shiva—Shiva!—I come. I come in the purity of Shiva and in the love of Shiva. Look at the balance of the cosmic dancer! Look at that whirling fire! Wherever you call Shiva, there he is to disperse all that hinders your progress on the path of truth.

Measure all things by truth, honor and love—love as compassion and love as "tough love," as they say, which does not indulge another but does hold on to that one and does compel that one to realize selfhood and, in so doing, to rejoice with God in an accomplishment that is all his own.

Thus, beloved, in all ways I ask you to clear the mind of deviousness, of division, of prevarication. I want you to know, as Hilarion has said, that the legions of truth are on the march on behalf of the youth. And this day I am determined to count every one of you among these legions. Therefore, clear the way for me, beloved, for you will be disqualified if you speak an untruth. It is better to be silent than to speak an untruth. Keep your counsel, if you will, but when you speak see to it that you speak righteously.

Now we turn the page of the calendar. . . .

What are the portents, beloved?

Those of you who have long been with me and who have studied at my retreat understand the portents. What we view as a most difficult task indeed is dealing with those who have risen to positions of leadership in the governments of nations, in the military establishments of nations who are not qualified to do their jobs.

Are you not almost incredulous when you think that in this day and age there could yet be an attack on a population of innocent civilians such as the one launched in Chechnya?

Can you believe it, beloved—brother killing brother at the orders of the state? How can that one show his face? It is difficult for the world to understand.

Do you scratch your head and say, "We are moving into the next century and yet war goes on and on and on"? It is, indeed, tragic.

Thus, take note when you see leaders who arrive at the top dictating the terms of nations, the terms of finance, the terms of health, the terms of war and peace. Take note how often they are not in any way qualified to deliver the peace or the well-being of nations. And when you look at that and you think of the descending karma of this day, which surely is pounding the earth like hailstones, as prophesied,[5] beloved, so know that there is great concern in the retreats of the Brotherhood regarding the future of this civilization. For those who have the light and are of the light are most often not in positions of power.

Therefore, what do you do?

You do what you have always done: you run to the altar of God, you give your invocations, you call to the seven archangels and the Holy Kumaras each hour and ask for dispensations for the binding of the forces of Evil in the earth that the children of light might go free.

ALWAYS COME BACK TO THE ALTAR

When you are frustrated, when you wonder what to do, you must always come back to the altar. For the altar of God, beloved, is the place where the all-power of God is focused. As you know, the large crystal on the altar is the chalice for the flame of the ark of the covenant. And in that crystal chalice and above on the etheric plane, there is the presence of the Maxin Light[6] that once burned on Atlantis but was extinguished during her decline.

So, beloved, there is no place you can go that is more powerful than your altar.[7] We have created the portable altar[8] for you so you can fold it up, put it in your backpack, be on your way and then set it up at your destination. Wherever you are, you can establish your own forcefield, even if you have but a small crystal as the chalice for the flame. Wherever you go, you can raise up an altar to God, Yahweh, as did Abraham, Isaac and Jacob and the children of Israel in their wilderness wanderings. Yes, beloved hearts, this is the way.

There is an inner altar of the heart and there is an outer altar where you offer your devotions, which you can set up anytime, anywhere. Teach this to your children. Teach your children, beloved, that the altar is the place where God and man meet through the flame of the ark of the covenant. I ask you to go to the altar frequently and to tend the flame on the altar of your heart, for this practice will result in mighty changes in the earth.

KEEPERS OF THE FLAME
HAVE MADE A MAJOR DIFFERENCE

Think you that you have not had a hand in world transmutation and in the major changes for the better that have recently taken place? Indeed you have! Wondrous things have come to pass in the earth even while the dark doings of men continue.

I announce to you on behalf of the entire Darjeeling Council of the Great White Brotherhood that the Keepers of the Flame of planet Earth have made a major difference thus far. And I, El Morya, am counting on you to multiply and multiply again the giving of your violet-flame decrees daily and not merely at our services on Saturday night.

The violet flame is the "elixir" for the transmutation of world karma. When you are instruments for the transmutation of world karma, you are surely transmuting your own karma while you earn your stripes and secure your opportunity to attain union with God in this life. I say it now and I say it again: the intensity of your violet-flame decrees is lifting untold burdens from within your psyche and the psyche of the planet.

Keep it up, beloved! You are winning. And I give you the vision of your winning. I am telling you that since our call to you last October,[9] you have established focuses of the violet flame in many nations around the world. And as the violet flame begins to turn in an upward spiraling action, there is the sound of the seventh ray, there is the inner music of the spheres and there is, as it were, a leaven in the earth. And the leaven in the earth is the violet flame you bear in your heart.

See to it, then, that you invoke your violet fire and your tube of light, using the decree Saint Germain gave you.[10] I ask you to invoke the violet flame twenty minutes a day without fail, beloved, for you will see new levels of transmutation, new doors of opportunity opening. For Saint Germain and Portia will be able to deliver to you all that you have given in your violet-flame decrees, multiplied many tens of thousands of times over.

PURSUE YOUR ASCENSION WITH HOLY ZEAL

This is the word of God in this moment. . . . The hour of the telling approaches when many of the prophecies of Revelation shall come to pass. The coming . . . years will intensify both Light and Darkness through the presence of the Five Dhyani Buddhas. Therefore, give their mantras.[11] Enter in to the fiery coil of their beings! Seek their assistance as you pursue your ascension with a holy zeal. Seek your Buddhahood zealously, for you can have it.

And it is Padma Sambhava who has assisted Saint Germain in delivering the violet flame to the age. And we have already discussed how the clergy have not allowed the people to invoke the violet flame (which is the flame of the Holy Spirit) in the churches.

I say, open the doors of your heart and the pores of your body and let the violet flame enter in! And do not so quickly accept the verdicts that are given to you by the physicians of the world.[12] For the Good Physician, your Lord and Saviour Jesus Christ, is with you, and your Christ Self overshadows you. And some of you, though not that many of you—but enough of you to make it worthy of note—have actually achieved the bonding to your Holy Christ Self in this year, after working toward that goal for many years.

ACHIEVE THE BONDING
TO YOUR HOLY CHRIST SELF

This is the blessed estate to which you aspire. For you know that it is written "The soul that sinneth, it shall die."[13] Therefore, the only way for your soul to attain eternal life is for her to merge with, to fuse with, her Holy Christ Self, who is truly her own Higher Self.

Thus, as you ascend day by day and your soul is fused with her Christ Self, she is also fused with her Lord Jesus Christ and other avatars. No matter what religion you are affiliated with, you know that that Christ Presence by any other name is the fullness of the Son of God within you.

So, beloved, count yourself in jeopardy—yes, in jeopardy—if you have not made it your business to see to it that your soul is bonded to your Holy Christ Self. And when it is, beloved, you make decisions based on what that Inner Christ is telling you as you listen to his inner Word. As you have heard the voice of conscience, your mentor from birth, so you know that that voice is indeed the voice of your Holy Christ Self, who is indeed a part of your being. You are in a body of clay because once upon a time you descended below the vibratory level of your Christ consciousness, and now you must climb up the ladder out of the very pits of your own unconscious mind and seek daily to sustain the level of your Christhood.

It is wise to take the teachings and to use them as a measuring rod to monitor yourself as to when you are out of alignment with the vibration of your Christ Self. Each time you depart from acceptable levels, you must turn and face your Christ Self and offer violet-flame decrees. You must also call to Archangel Michael for reinforcements of angels to keep you in the paths of righteousness. Yes, beloved, this is the goal I have for my chelas.

And as I look at the star upon the Christmas tree, I remember the star of Bethlehem that guided me when I, as Melchior, journeyed with Balthazar and Caspar[14] to the place of the birth of the Holy Child. And after worshiping him, we did depart another way that we might not have to report to Herod the whereabouts of that child.[15]

PROTECT YOUR INNER CHILD

Protect your inner child. Call upon us as the three wise men to tend and nurture and protect your inner child; for, as you know, your inner child is your soul, who needs your loving attention. And if you hear many children speaking to you from within, know that these are fragments of your soul. And the fragments must become one voice—one voice, one soul immaculate. Only then shall that soul rise in wholeness as a totality of being.

In conclusion, I say to you that this is a year when you must seek protection. And that protection is a vital ingredient to your empowerment by the Holy Spirit. You must call upon the legions of light of the first ray for the protection of nations and continents, of all sentient life and especially the precious children.

Thus, beloved, it is well to put on your armour and to keep it on to the end of this decade. It is well to know that you have made yourself so one with the legions of the first ray that you are sealed in the perfection of God that is his holy will. The holy will of God will carry you. It is like truth and honor. When you know what the will of God is and you do it, no matter what the cost, you have our blessing.

I AM EVER AT YOUR CALL

And just as you take your coat and wrap your children in it to shield them from the cold, so I, Morya, your Bapu, take my mantle and wrap it around you to shield you, even as you are shielding others. I take you in my arms as the little child—the little child who was born once upon a time—and I remind you of your native innocence. There is nothing wrong with innocence, for innocence brings you into proximity with the living Christ.

I AM Morya, ever at your call. Call to me. Offer me your heart in my blue-flame decrees. I will return to you the exact portion you have given multiplied by the power of ten. I will see you Tuesdays, morning, noon and night, in the court—the court of King Arthur and his knights and ladies of the flame.

I bow to the LORD God within you.

[22-second standing ovation]

January 1, 1995
Royal Teton Ranch
Park County, Montana
ECP

CHAPTER 22

*Your goal is to have the Lord Christ of you,
your Holy Christ Self, occupy your four lower bodies.
If those bodies are full of debris that has been stored
in the attic of the brain for centuries, there is no
room whatsoever for the Christ to enter in.
Clean house!*

CLEAN HOUSE!
I AM THE CHAMPION OF MY CHELAS

If You Make Your Bed in the Psychic,
You Will Have to Lie in It!

Heighten consciousness!
Rise to the level of your God Presence!
Know the Lord as the infinite will of God!
Internalize that will:
    in the mind, in the third eye, in the heart, the soul!
Let light abound! Raise consciousness!

I draw up the white fire from the base of the spine to the third eye. Feel it! For I have come with my magnet that you might know what it is to have the sacred fire rise on the altar of being. And in those who require more transmutation before that sacred fire may be raised, I will leave it sealed in the base-of-the-spine chakra for this encounter.

But I shall come! And each time I come and each time you see my name on a class program, you can expect me to accelerate the sacred fire within you so that you might feel the burning at the base of the brain, so that you might feel the burning in your heart, even as the disciples' hearts did burn within them as they walked with the Lord on the road to Emmaus yet did not recognize him.[1] So you see, they had not raised the sacred fire for the opening of the third eye; for had they done so, they would have recognized Jesus as the risen Christ.

Thus, beloved, it is well to give the bija mantras to the Divine Mother.[2] These are important, for they are life-quickening.

The Mother flame is for the "watering" of all of the chakras and the cleansing of the soul. And as the fire of the Mother does rise on the spinal altar, you ultimately experience communion with her in the secret chamber of the heart, where your Mother energies and your Father energies reunite. It is then that you sense your wholeness, your completeness, and the balance of your yin/ yang energies. No longer are you incomplete, no longer do you crave this or that, for you have entered into the internalization of the white fire of God. This is possible unto you.

Let the bija mantras to the Divine Mother become a permanent part of your Friday-night ascension service. For not only is the ascension service an opportunity for you to clear the discarnates from the planet but it is also an opportunity for you to increase the rings of the white-fire body around your four lower bodies and chakras. So visualize yourself in these rings, for we desire to see you put on greater and greater light from the very heart of Luxor in preparation for your ultimate Victory.

Therefore, Serapis Bey does send a ray of light to me in this moment, asking that I might speak in his behalf. For he would tell you, beloved, that the two most empowering actions that you can achieve right within your own temple are the conservation of the sacred fire and then the raising up of that sacred fire as you are able and as you are comfortable in so doing.

At each level of self-mastery you attain to, the daily requirement for personal and planetary transmutation by the violet flame is increased. For some, an additional prerequisite to progress is the sorting out of this and that in the unconscious and the subconscious.

This is also very important, beloved. For unless you clear the many levels of being, and specifically the issues of your psychology, you will find that the rising sacred fire will give a certain permanence to the knotty problems you desire to cast into the violet flame.

Therefore, consciously direct a ray of violet flame to each of your chakras, from the base of the spine to the crown. The large violet-flame poster that illustrates the chakras superimposed on Michelangelo's statue of David[3] provides a strong visualization for clearing the chakras and raising the Kundalini.

Visualize yourself systematically transmuting records of the ancient and near past until you have a fully cleansed temple that the Lord Christ might occupy. Yes, see yourself encircled in pulsating ovoids of violet flame, as shown on the poster. For what you see and internalize you shall become.

CLEAN HOUSE!

Your goal is to have the Lord Christ of you, your Holy Christ Self, occupy your four lower bodies. If those bodies are full of debris that has been stored in the attic of the brain for centuries, there is no room whatsoever for the Christ to enter in.

Clean house! But in the very same hour, fill the house with light. Sweep it clean, fill it with light and repeat the ritual day after day.

Why, you wash your dishes daily, you clean your houses, you take care of your clothing, you take care of your person. Why not take care of these compartments of consciousness that you have so neglected?

Clean out the realm of the mental body and all the records of episodes that have been impressed upon it for thousands of years. When you self-empty and then call to God to fill you, giving the prayer *"Come, occupy! occupy! occupy! my beloved Christ Self,"* day by day by day you will have that clearing. And you may live to rejoice in these very bodies over the complete clearing of all past records. You may live to accomplish the balancing of 100 percent of your karma so that you may fill your vessels with *light! light! light!* qualifying that light with whatever is the need of the hour in vibration, in speech, in energy, in consciousness.

Understand that your physical body is the temple of the living God.[4] And therefore, be solicitous of that temple in every way. Every cell is a chalice, every atom and all energy in motion that holds the balance of Alpha and Omega.

Thus, from the white-fire core of your innermost being centered in the base-of-the-spine chakra, call to your I AM Presence to raise the sacred fire to your crown chakra and the third eye and *let light! light! light! intensify!* Let your aura be magnified! Let rings upon rings of your causal body surround you here below because you shall have drawn from your causal body such intensity of light through your decrees.

You know that the only act that can take from you the victory of your decrees is the act of entering into discord. And it doesn't help matters when you are not regular in your decrees. When you are regular in your decrees and you judiciously hold your harmony —because you are concerned about holding your harmony—you may maintain and accelerate the momentum of your decree work *and build upon it! and build upon it! and build upon it!* And you may sense that you are receiving the great reward of your work because you are meeting the Buddha at least a quarter of the way by building the rings of your causal body around your four lower bodies.

BECOME THE BRIDE OF CHRIST

This, of course, is an adjunct to your walking the Path with your Holy Christ Self and submitting to the initiations you must undergo to become the bride of your Lord, Jesus Christ. Certainly, if you have a temple that has been emptied and filled with light— which you can now adorn with the seamless garment you have woven, for all the rents have been healed and all aberrations of consciousness have been transmuted by the violet flame—this will bring you closer and closer to your soul's fusion with the heart of Jesus and to bearing the title and the mantle of Bride of Christ.

The ceremony wherein one is received as a bride of Christ is awesome, beloved. And I deem it to be most awesome when the soul who is to become the Lord's bride is still in incarnation.

The presence on earth of a bride of Christ can be felt throughout the world. For all on earth are made aware of a very special presence, a very special relationship, a very special holiness between the bride and her Lord. And until you yourself achieve oneness with Christ, you have the opportunity, if you are married, to reconsecrate at the altar of God the marriage you have entered into at the human level; thus, man and wife may celebrate their present oneness and their future union with Christ as his brides.

Now then, beloved, the blessing and true beauty of marriage should be known to you. But there is another marriage I would speak of and that is your marriage to your Guru. For some time, of course, your Guru may necessarily be me, for I am the one appointed to this office by Saint Germain and the hierarchy of light. I am the one appointed to receive you on behalf of the seven chohans and the Maha Chohan as you enter the path of chelaship.

CONSTANCY, THE KEY VIRTUE

When I take to myself a chela and sponsor that chela, it is a very, very special event. Many people wait lifetimes for such an opportunity simply because it is not possible for me to carry the weight of those who have not yet transmuted a certain amount of karma and have not shown a certain steadiness—a steadfastness on the path of the will of God, veering neither to the right nor to the left.

Constancy is the key virtue that I must have in those who truly desire to be one with me. If I would train you personally, beloved, I must have from you an unflinching constancy whereby you maintain a steady level of absorption of the blue flame of the will of God and thus enter day by day into the sacred fire of the first ray. You must be willing to take any rebuke, any correction, to take it swiftly and to then swiftly self-correct. You must have a momentum on giving the decrees to the ascended masters who serve principally on the first ray. You may give any (or all) of the blue decrees, whether they be to me or to Surya or to Himalaya or to Vaivasvata or to Archangel Michael.

I tell you, beloved, when you keep yourself saturated in the blue ray and you are alert to every out-of-step state of mind that you might even consider entertaining, you will find that I shall become your champion. Once I become the champion of a chela, I will work with that chela to the end. Thus, beloved, do not think that I take lightly the taking on of a chela.

Many of you are chelas in the becoming. But I must test and try you for many years, sometimes for lifetimes, before I receive the signal from Almighty God himself that I might burden myself by taking on another student.

Realize this, beloved. It is well to make yourself a devotee of the will of God. For as a devotee, *you will increase! and increase! and increase!* many shades of blue rings around your four lower bodies and the circumference of your life. And when you have proven yourself under fire and in many situations—untenable situations, devastating situations—and have come out right side up, we will know that we have a chela of the first order and we will receive you that you might be anointed before the council in Darjeeling.

ALL CAN MAKE THEMSELVES WORTHY

Yes, this is a very special opportunity and all can make themselves worthy. I speak of it, beloved, because I have surveyed the earth and I have listened to the dictations that have been given at this class and I understand that there are many, many people in the world who would seek and find this teaching if they knew it existed somewhere.

Since I am about to sponsor millions of souls for this activity and this Path, I must be certain that you who are here and who form the foundations of this community throughout the earth are true to me. You must be true to the souls who are entering in. You must care for them and raise them up. You must be done with your criticism, condemnation, judgment and gossip. And you must laud the power of God that gives to us the opportunity to truly turn the world around in the upcoming years.

Thus, beloved, at the same time that I speak about receiving many among you as chelas, for many of you are worthy, I also must speak about those who have not been chelas, who have never been chelas, but who have hung on to this activity like moths flitting around a lamplight. At times they have gathered around the flame in such numbers that the flame could no longer be seen.

Therefore, I am seeing to it that these individuals will no longer be a part of this community. Some have already left. Some have been removed because they refused to surrender certain psychic activities that cannot in any way be tolerated in an organization sponsored by the ascended masters. It is a matter of black and white: you either forsake the psychic or you may not be a part of this organization.

It is often true that individuals who are psychic do not know that they are psychic, for they have tumbled into the world of illusion, the world of baubles and trinkets and smoke and mirrors. They have descended in a downward spiral into the astral plane and, lo and behold, they believe they have found Shangri-la!

KNOW THE LAW REGARDING PSYCHICISM

Well, beloved ones, I wish to discuss with you the matter of placing yourselves before teachers other than the ascended masters and before teachings other than the teachings of the ascended masters. If you are determined to take courses from this or that instructor because he or she professes to teach something you think you ought to know and yet you are aware that that instructor is psychic or has been identified as psychic by the messenger, this is what will happen:

When you place yourself before a teacher who is not tied to the Great White Brotherhood, who does not have God-control of his four lower bodies or of anger (or the Martian A's the messenger has listed[5]) and who is in some kind of a valley of indecision, choosing to live neither in Light nor in Darkness but in a gray area, you open yourself up to receive from that teacher whatever untransmuted substance is lodged in his electronic belt. (For the pupil is always the one who receives and the teacher is always the one who gives.) And you will not be able to screen out the psychic from the nonpsychic; for the psychic vibration pollutes the entire stream of consciousness of the one who lets himself flow with it. Thus, you take in not only what the psychic consciously dishes out but the entire subconscious momentum of his psychicism, including his impure vessel, which in most cases has not been dedicated as a chalice for violet-flame transmutation. (In the world of the psychic there are many who have no determination to transmute past karma and there are others who do use the violet flame but are nevertheless unwilling to give up their involvement in the psychic.)

And the conclusion will be that I will have nothing further to do with you because you will have made your bed in the psychic and you will have to lie in it until you decide to "clean up your act," as the saying goes. If you go the way of the psychic when you know the Law, I cannot help you and I can no longer have any ties to your lifestream. Nor can any other ascended master maintain ties to you, for the Great Law will not allow it.

You must understand that through your tie to the Great White Brotherhood through Padma Sambhava and the lineage of hierarchy that sponsors this messenger,[6] you have the greatest opportunity in the entire Matter universe to take your ascension in this life. The hierarchies of light who are involved with this earth are also involved with this universe. And therefore, their sponsorship of this organization is not something merely of this earth.

So I have spoken and this is my statement. Hear it well. I have set a full table before you. The Lord Christ has broken the bread of life and given you of his Body and his Blood. It is not necessary for you to know everything about everything, including the things of the psychic. It is not necessary for you to look for shortcuts. There are no shortcuts!

You can fool yourself in many ways, whether by muscle testing or by this or that something or other that someone has come up with. But in the end, beloved, you will find that you have made no forward progress whatsoever and that you have forsaken your spiritual path and your spiritual trust with the ascended masters, who are your teachers and Gurus. And I say, you will find yourself with a bellyful of psychic energy and you will have only yourself to rid yourself of it.

Psychic energy is like quicksand. Souls can be sucked into it and actually defend their right to be doing what they are doing because they are so enmeshed in the psychic plane and its psychic inhabitants that they can no longer tell the difference between the spiritual path and the psychic path. This is a tragedy of the age!

There are millions of souls on earth who are following psychic teachers and, as a result, they are falling by the wayside. Because they are tied to these teachers, they are unaware that their auric sheath (the light that is closest to the body) is being "bled" from them. Unknowingly, they are losing their soul essence. It is being taken from them not necessarily by spiritualists or crystal-ball gazers but by everyday people who live in the psychic plane. Therefore know that when you keep company with such people, you make yourself vulnerable to all levels of the astral plane. When you place yourself opposite them as a student, you are even more vulnerable.

A typical example of psychism on television that draws millions into the astral plane every day, hence into the surreal world of the psychic, is the so-called soap opera. There is absolutely no redeeming value in the "soaps." They are a cesspool of the psychic and those who put their attention on that cesspool day in and day out will find themselves still in that cesspool after they pass from the screen of life in the change called death.

Another example of psychism is the violence in the Saturday-morning cartoons. This violence is a horrendous desecration of the soul of the child. The makers of these cartoons have sown the wind and *they shall*—I say, *they shall*—reap the whirlwind of their karma for the abuse of the minds and emotional bodies of children.

ALLEGIANCE TO THE ONE GOD

We are your teachers. We are your initiators. We give you your initiations on the Path. As your parents, we coddle you. You cannot imagine how we root for you and go to battle for you. But we expect one thing: allegiance to the one God and the one God in the person of the ascended masters.

The ascended masters are the sponsors and teachers of this organization. If there is a subject of study that you are interested in, ask the messenger if she will teach on that subject. Ask her if she will invite qualified instructors who are not psychic to come and teach such subjects as you deem necessary for the furtherance of the educational goals of this organization.

Over the years the messenger has invited many experts in the fields of health, education, psychology and self-help. And we are certainly open to having our chelas excel in advanced learning techniques as long as these do not involve autosuggestion or auto-hypnosis. The call to your I AM Presence and Holy Christ Self can take you to any plane or octave that is necessary for you to enter to tap the resources of the brain and the higher intelligence of the mind of God. Keepers of the Flame must never allow themselves to be hypnotized nor should they hypnotize others. For the hypnotist displaces the role of the Holy Christ Self and deposits his own untransmuted energy in the unprotected subconscious or unconscious.

The bottom line is this: I will have nothing further to do with anyone who goes after the world of the psychic and its followers. If you pursue the psychic, you will have to clean up your world on your own. You will have to once again make your soul and your four lower bodies an acceptable chalice for your Holy Christ Self if you desire to be a part of this organization.

I trust I have made myself clear. I want you to understand that I am in some measure concerned and equally burdened that Saint Germain should have to deal with such goings-on in this organization as students professing to take dictations from the Maha Chohan and other ascended masters when they have no mantle and no office in the Great White Brotherhood that would authorize them to take dictations. And I am chagrined that the Maha Chohan himself should be subjected to individuals who would take dictations that are supposedly from him but are not and who claim to have the Holy Spirit but do not.

The initiations of the Holy Spirit come to you day by day. And they come, beloved, when you are ready. Before you can become a direct disciple of the Holy Spirit under the Maha Chohan, you must submit yourself to the paths of the seven chohans and master at least three of those paths, one of which must be the path of the first ray under me. The chohans who preside over the other two paths of your choosing may accept you, whether as a preferred chela or a beginning student, or they may tell you to diligently follow the path taught by the messengers until you may be invited to be directly under the tutelage of one or both of these chohans. I exercise the same discretion.

Therefore it burdens me to see a certain setting aside or rejection, if you will, of the masters, who have been with you for so long, in favor of those who come to town with their pots and pans and snake oil, seeking to tear from you your First Love.

Your first and true and only love should be your I AM Presence. Call to your I AM Presence to see to it that you have every bit of edification and learning that you require to make your ascension. But do not be greedy in indulging in this, that, and the next course offered here and there and everywhere as conniving psychic entrepreneurs take advantage of silly people who will come into their shops and pay high prices to be taught, often by those who have not been cleansed by the Lord Christ and therefore in whom that Christ does not dwell.

I WILL NOT COMPROMISE

I trust you understand my concern and my sternness. I do not, I will not compromise. I will not carry any chela's psychic baggage. If you have needlessly yet knowingly tied yourself to psychic people or the psychic plane, then you will have to demagnetize your four lower bodies with the assistance of Archangel Michael and Elohim Astrea and use the violet flame assiduously until you are finally out of the astral plane—once and for all.

In this hour, then, I seal you for the victory and I say, we will have in this community those who are fine examples of the Path. And we will let those who are glassy-eyed and already gone, gone into the psychic, even with the aid of psychedelic drugs, gravitate to lower levels, where they would just as soon be in any case. Let us part in peace with those who do not recognize their high calling in God and their stupendous opportunity to advance along the lines of the great dispensations of the Central Sun.

I bow to the Christ in each one and I bid you adieu.

[41-second standing ovation]

April 16, 1995
Royal Teton Ranch
Park County, Montana
ECP

CHAPTER 23

*Compare yourselves not to those who have
made the Olympics on earth but to those
who have entered the cosmic Olympics.
Obtain thy co-measurement with those
who have already ascended.*

THE SPIRIT OF
THE GREAT WHITE BROTHERHOOD
SCHOOLING THE DESIRE
BY GOD-CONTROL

The Reinforcement of Christhood
in a Spiritual Community

Ho! The light dawns. And the Darjeeling Master is pleased.

I AM in the heart of every chela. And I stand with you in this hour of the Dark Cycle which has turned.[1]

And in turning, my beloved, you are also turned toward the light. And as has been said, when you face the light the shadows are behind you. It is so. Let the light always be before and the shadow behind, but let the roving eye of God—the All-Seeing (360-degree) Eye of God—remain in awareness and in God-control of the shadow.

Let us speak, then, of shadowed forces and shadowed ones. For, beloved, there are levels of control and God-control ye know not of.

Beloved, what can you control in life? The only thing which you can control is the self, for it is not lawful to control any other self, save the parent in God-control of the child entrusted to his care. Beloved, understand well, then, the meaning of the predicament of free will juxtaposed against the backdrop of cosmic and universal, systemic and planetary forces moving in, through, and around the individual.

Beloved ones, it has never been more precarious, hence more important, for the chela of the will of God to be in God-control of his mind and forces and heart and self-knowledge and to be therefore preparing to enter that Gemini mind of God[2] that is the Alpha and the Omega of the central sun of your mighty I AM Presence.

HEED MY MUSINGS AND COMMENTARIES

It is of cosmic import, O chelas, that you do heed my word as my musings and commentaries upon the scenes of our time pass from me through the messenger to you. For often, in a moment and in a comment you will find the telling of all that is required to unlock the puzzles of the present and the mysteries of life.

Inasmuch, then, as it is so that God-control within the individual must set the bounds of his habitation,[3] understand this: that when you remain in God-control of the four lower bodies—of energies of the electronic belt and the karma—and when this God-control is not by human will but by your acquaintance with the mind of God, then the force of the central sun of being, which is the heart, begins to expand and not undulate but to hold its position as the central sun of the auric envelope.

RETAIN THE AURIC FIELD
OF LORD GAUTAMA BUDDHA

Pray, then, that thy threefold flame be in balance, that the Mother be in thee, and that thy flight be not in winter.[4] Pray, then, above all things, to retain the auric field of Lord Gautama Buddha, who has lent to you, beloved, not only the thread of contact to his threefold flame but, to the devotees of the will of God, his auric field—the causal body—to be congruent with your own as you so will it and so periodically attune yourselves with those secret rays of his heart. He who is safe in time of planetary tribulation is the one who is sealed in this auric light intensified.

We come, then, for a measure of sanity and a measure of prevention. Let us take out our putty and seal the leaks in the auras of our chelas who invoke so much light—and yet that light sometimes oozes, sometimes drips or spills through pinprick holes or larger rents in the auric field.

Beloved ones, the strength of the auric field is the strength of the electromagnetic field—the latter being more permanent, whereas the aura is more reflective of momentary ups and downs. We, then, come with the putty of blue lightning and the sacred fire to assist you. Our angels, then, mend the energy field and the auric envelope as you are seated in loyalty and devotion in this hour of our coming.

Beloved, you are most beloved. Thus, it is our desire, we of the Darjeeling and Indian and Royal Teton Councils of the Great White Brotherhood with whom you serve, to give you an awareness this day of what it is like to be free of the leaky vessel, to feel yourselves in an auric envelope that has warmth and power and the Presence of God, so that as you move through your day you sense you are in that Presence, you do not stray from it, and you are abounding in the joy and the knowledge:

My Redeemer liveth.
I AM Who I AM.
I dwell in the Presence of God.
I feel that Love with me alway.
And therefore, I know
I shall reach the place and period of my Destiny!

I shall go beyond these years of adversity of the planet!
I shall find myself yet in this body *in the New Day!**

REJOICE IN THE COMFORTING PRESENCE
OF GOD WITH YOU

Beloved, if you do not feel this comforting Presence of God
with you alway, then I would say you ought to consider having a
certain concern regarding your maintenance of the harmony of
light you have invoked and regarding dangers on the path of life,
whether from invasion of disease or accident or simply from being
at the wrong place at the wrong time, which has proven fatal to
many in this unleashing of terrorism.

Beloved ones, we come, then, with this Presence of Love. As
you feel it from our heart, remember it is not only your I AM
Presence and the Holy Christ Self and Holy Spirit with you, but
it may very well be the overshadowing of an ascended master
whom you love, an ascended twin flame, or an angel sent by one
of the archangels to assist you.

Rejoice, then, in that comforting Presence and value it as
against all commodities and situations and positions in the earth.
For there are places in the earth, beloved, where you may wander
which are so dark and heavy—many of these not far from you here
physically—where this Presence is neutralized by the darkness
only because your God-mastery in that Presence, in the holding
of it, is not yet attained. And therefore the Presence rises to a
higher electronic field and you are unable to sustain that very light
in the places of darkness where you may roam, where you may find
your employment or other goings and comings to fulfill the neces-
sities of life.

I ask you this week, then, in the name of the first ray, whose
Lord I am, to take the opportunity for self-observation, that you

---

*Give this fiat with those of God Harmony in *Pearls of Wisdom*, vol. 29, no. 47, October
12, 1986.

might note when comes the absence of this comforting warmth of the sunlight of your Christhood—what is the cause of it. Go after the cause, be it fear or anxiety or mundane involvements or allowing the world's energy to enter through excessive access to your lifestream of the media, such as television, et cetera.

Beloved, safety is indeed in the ark of the LORD.[5] Therefore, with all thy getting, get the ark of the LORD. Can you find it? Can you see it? It is the Place Prepared, indeed—the place of your heart, the place of the aura.

Safety in the Great White Brotherhood.

May it be a cloud of witness[6] around you sustained by your heart's pull and tug on angelic hosts and your love.

Safety in the heart of the threefold flame and the Buddha.

Safety, indeed, in the heart of Christ.

INVOKE COSMIC BEINGS AND ELOHIM IN THE MIGHTY WORK OF THE AGES

Thus, beloved, seeing as all must come to that level of a certain disappointment in the fact that all we can ever control is the self that is God's gift to us, how, then, do we enter in to this mighty work of the ages—the perfecting of the self and the holding of the balance in the earth?

It is quite simply by the invocation of cosmic beings and Elohim, whose auras and electromagnetic fields easily contain the earth or the solar system or the galaxy and beyond. Since each one may be in God-control of his electromagnetic field and aura, you may understand how the Presence of a single twin-flame manifestation of Elohim in the earth in the physical octave through physical chelas may hold in God-control—to the extent of the law of karma and free will—a planetary lifewave, an earth body and elemental life.

To a certain extent, then, your invocation of Elohim, sustained as a vibration in your aura, does provide Elohim with the anchor points of contact physically, thereby allowing those electrodes placed in the earth to have a greater physical manifestation. Where the free will of lightbearers the world around provides a stable aura for Elohim to manifest through, you may then visualize an *antah-karana**—a starry body composed of lightbearers, each star a point in the electromagnetic field of the Alpha, the Omega of Elohim.

As star clusters in the heavens are seen as outlines of formations, constellations, and figures, so visualize, then, the mighty aura of Purity and Astrea, Hercules and Amazonia surrounding the earth and then the solar system. See all lightbearers as though they were stars, chakras in the body of Elohim—each one a point emanating that light into the physical octave by the authority that is given solely to those in physical embodiment.

BECOME A PART OF THE BODY OF LIGHT

Now you can see how your participation and membership in the body of God, membership in the Great White Brotherhood, allows you by the will of God to participate in a greater aura of cosmic beings for the God-control of worlds and the outcome of events in those worlds. In many ways we thus come to the appreciation of the Great White Brotherhood—that those who suddenly awaken to cosmic consciousness and become aware of their own lack of it in the presence of such beings may not delay two or ten million years till they might also attain to the level of a cosmic being, but join forces with that one and become a part of that specific body of God. For truly Elohim are the body of God.

Thus, any and all who realistically, in assessing their own attainment, feel inadequate to the holding of the balance of a planet may have immediate recourse in this fashion to enter and become a part of the body of light of the entire Spirit of the Great White Brotherhood. Then consider that we ourselves, as ascended

---

antahkarana: [Sanskrit "internal sense organ"], the web of life; the net of light spanning Spirit and Matter connecting and sensitizing the whole of creation within itself and to the heart of God

masters or newly ascended ones, may from time to time feel inadequate to a cosmic challenge and therefore become ourselves a part of the universal body of God, the universal mind of God.

Increasingly, you see, we have all at our specific levels come to the understanding of the law of the One. When we enter the one God and the one true body of God—each one positioned as a starry chakra emanating the light of our own causal body and benefiting from the light-emanation of all others—we can see, as you would say, "the light at the end of the tunnel." We can see the Matter cosmos swallowed up in the body of God universal. We can see all things coming to culmination as the Spirit cosmos, then, devours the Matter cosmos even as the Serpent swallows his tail.

Beloved ones of light, this principle of the law of the One is carried, then, to the practical reality of this community of the Holy Spirit and does underscore why so many in all ages have sought to and decided to join themselves to a spiritual community. They have felt the reinforcement. Aye, indeed, it has been the reinforcement of the Christhood of every individual of that community, for strength is always in the light.

KNOW THE MEANING
OF THE GREAT CENTRAL SUN MAGNET
THAT YE ARE

Now, then, beloved, there have crossed your day, your newspapers, your earth, your nations certain most disconcerting situations that have truly taxed your imagination as to how the one or the few in your area could indeed hold the balance of light when the prevailing world opinion or local opinion has been directly in opposition to that light and Christ. Thus, I come with the reminder and the perspective that all of us have gleaned as we have served the light in all ages: Until the one enter the "Onehood" of the many and define it as the Great White Brotherhood, the one may achieve only so much.

Considering, then, those forces arrayed, understand how the law of positivity, the law of absolute Good, must have the circle of light drawn about its members and its members' auric field in their intensity as opposed to their distension, in their saturation as opposed to their extension—must have the capacity to swallow up the prevailing darkness, else darkness will prevail on earth. For universal transmutation is by the Body and Blood of Christ in ye all. Saturate ye, saturate ye the body temple and chakras.

Know the meaning, then, of the Great Central Sun Magnet that ye are. For I have described it as the grid of light of Elohim into which, one by one, by 100 percent free will, you can insert yourselves. You can accomplish this, beloved, but only if all forces be willing, else the larger body will eject the attempted transplant of lesser selfhood into greater Selfhood with the pronouncement "Go back, then—go back outside of the circle. Thou hast not, then, the unity of life-purpose to become a viable cell in the universal body of God."

DESIRE TO BE GOD

Therefore, we deal with the desire that is reflected in the center of every cell of your being, the desire that is centered in every organ and chakra. The desire to be God must be full, else thou canst not be full of light. Desiring springs from the deepest well of life.

We who, then, must keep the fires burning in the mental quadrant of the earth body are constantly confronted with people's desires at the subconscious level diametrically opposed to the words, the acts, the efforts that are carried out from the mental level, until in some the word is absolutely meaningless, has no relevancy to reality or to truth. And indeed, beloved, across the planet there is a babble of voices that confirm personalities, vent angers, frustrations, retaliations; and all of this yet does not reflect that core desire for good or for ill.

Beloved ones, those who are out of touch with the seat of

desire of their beings, always trying to be someone they are not, trying to do something to please someone else, to appear wise, to advance politically or financially—these are in a most sorry state. They are most unreal, most uncomplimentary in any situation, for they never bring out the best in others or in themselves.

Beloved, the individual who is truly in touch with the desiring of the heart and the soul can deal with it, can confront it, and has the understanding to know that he can elevate that desire, accelerate that desire, infuse it with light and wisdom, even as he would mold the clay and refashion a sculpture of the man himself. That individual, then, is pleasant to be with even if he may be on the dark side of life. For the one in touch with his desire is at the starting point of life that may truly take a divine direction under the guidance of the Guru or the Great White Brotherhood.

Take the individual who hates, desires to hate, knows that he hates and that he desires to hate—knows that he desires to murder. At least he is integrated with his inner being. He will be true to himself. Because there is an integration this entire momentum may be turned and harnessed to the desire to love, the desire to embrace God, the desire to give life and not take it away.

We can work with such individuals. But it is difficult to reach a point of contact with those who know not who they are because they know not what they want. Today they want this, tomorrow they want that. And the genie hops from this assignment to the next, never able to complete any, for the genie of the mind becomes confused by the desire body or the soul that has not become the captain of her ship. Beloved ones, we can do little for such individuals, for even if we should desire to play Santa Claus, it is not the will of God.

SCHOOL THE DESIRES

Thus, beloved, when you salute the banner of Maitreya and determine to walk in the direction of the North Star—the mighty

I AM Presence (or true north)—beloved ones, we may assist you. Be certain, then, that in your desire to be married to the Christ and to be married too quickly that all of your uncontrolled and unassessed desires are not like the tin cans and horns that someone has tied to your chariot labeled "Just Married."

Beloved ones, I am serious. For those who would wed the Christ and yet have dangling out the back end all of these unsettled things of desire, truly, truly, beloved, cannot remain wed. And this is the cause of divorce in the physical octave and troubles in the marriage circle.

Each one, then, must school the desire. The desire is not king and queen. The desire is subject to the will of a spirit spark who descended. The desire is an accouterment, a garment, an effect of an identity—an *id-entity* in God, beloved. Therefore, the identity may direct all desire according to the will. But the will will not succeed without love or without wisdom or without the purity of the drive of the Mother.

Thus, understand, when you recognize wrong desire, you must enter into the heart of Alpha and Omega—hence into the heart of the Gemini mind of God, into the great circle of the T'ai Chi where God is—and you must put on the cloak of God's desire. You must try it on and you must say:

"If my desire is incorrect, and I suspect that it is, what is God's desiring in this matter? I will go to the fount. I will experience it. I will put it on by devotion to my own Krishna consciousness. I will rise in my Holy Christ Self to the heart of God's desire. I will see through the eyes of God's desire. I will love through the heart of God's desire. I will speak the word of God's desire. I will try it on and see how comfortable I am in this state of God-desire and if I may leave the moorings of my human desires that bind me to dangerous individuals and circumstances in the name of human good."

You see, beloved, there is only one way out of the limited,

unfruitful, unbeneficial desire—and that is to go to the heart of God, to mount the Tree of Life, to enter in and say, "What is my God's desiring in this matter? I have no more struggle in me. I can no longer be torn between this and that. For too long I have been vacillating like a pendulum which Morya cannot even keep track of, nor would he."

So you see, beloved, for all of us at any plane of our spiritual manifestation to know and become the higher point of reality we desire or should desire, we must go there and settle the matter at once and entirely and then put on that garment, bring it back to the place where we are as an embryo of light—an embryonic sun that surrounds the heart and being—and determine and say, "My Guru has pointed to this sphere. My God whom I can perceive is thus so inclined and of this mind. I rejoice to wear that garment for a season, to make it my own, to be that one, and then after certain seasons to measure that which I have truly incorporated and mastered as against the former state."

Only from the point of mastery can you gauge, measure, choose, decide upon the former state of limitation. Do you see, beloved? This is the conundrum, the Chinese puzzle. It is the koan. It is the challenge that every Guru must place before the new or advancing chela. It is the understanding that the chela must become the master first in order to truly know if he would retain the lesser state where he now is.

Let us consider for a moment that you are in a limited state and know not the way to go. There is only one way to go to find out the way to go and that is to gain the mastery first and then visit the former place, as going back to visit with old friends or old places or old embodiments, vibrations, and so forth.

You have a certain mastery. You go back and you say, "I am mighty glad I made my choice to be where I am. Yes, I see—I decide here and now I will make it permanent. I do not ever want to go back to that place, that 'Old Italy,' that old place I used to know and love. No, I can see the space I have traveled by Morya's co-measurement. I can see that where I have gone is the place I truly want to be."

Thus, you have all done this. Now you must simply do it again and realize that no place in the physical octave can be described as any but a place of a new level of limitation as well as a new level of the unlimited state of Wholeness. No state is static. Every state demands progress, lest the beasts of prey come and find you—lest they sniff you out by a vibration too long kept that they may now identify as "your" vibration.

Do not hold so much of the self so long that the computers of the fallen ones may have a point of contact of your identity, beloved. Be in the next place before they have found you in the last place! And they will be confused forever, and I trust you will not.

So, beloved, I would entertain you a bit in the face of the serious questions of life. I would love you a bit and more, that you might find the treasure of your heart and be not discouraged in this hour of many challenges. I tell you, they could be many more but for the victories you have already won.

And the truth will be always true—that God will not give you any more challenges than you can handle, beloved. It is just that God is adding a few balls to the jugglers who juggle so well in this activity their many projects and responsibilities.

Now he says, juggle some more . . . and some more. And thus you find yourselves also having to juggle on a spinning top while holding your balance—a top whose axis is off. The top is planet Earth, beloved. But all this you can do, for the saints have done it. And, after all, you have asked for the ascension. Therefore, we give you what is necessary to achieve it.

Just remember, beloved, as a man thinketh in his heart, so is he.[7] Many of those who follow the Hindu religion, therefore, though they may appear wise, have believed that it takes endless aeons to attain that level of karma-free being to enter into permanent union with God. As they believe, so are they—on a treadmill of a never-ending road, thinking that sometime down the highway of a long, long *manvantara** they may arrive at the goal.

These procrastinators are found in every religion in defense of many different and peculiar doctrines. But procrastination is one wherever you find it. Therefore, do not be so easily misled by those who appear wise in any circle of life. For you are the wise ones and you understand that to ascend is a demanding course. You may compare yourselves not to those who have made the Olympics on earth but to those who have entered the cosmic Olympics. Obtain thy co-measurement with those who have already ascended and you will truly possess the finest rule and measuring rod both for the inner court and the outer court of life.

BE DILIGENT IN MASTERING
THE GEMINI DARK CYCLE

I assign you, O chelas of the will of God, to be diligent, then, in the science of astrology in mastering this Gemini Dark Cycle.[8] Consider the square that forms the cosmic cross of white fire. Consider the trine. Then consider the form that is made through each and the several combinations that may come to you in connecting the point of Gemini to the other points of the hierarchies of the Sun. Then remember there are 360 points and all of these, of course, divisible. But then, this that goes beyond perception is taken care of by your allegiance to the path of the five secret rays and the heart of the Buddha.

You have the Instruction, beloved. You have the Joy. You have the Goal. Now protect these three, and go for it. I say to you, Go for it! beloved. For *to you* belongs the Victory. What a pity that you should allow anyone else to seize from you that ball of Victory.

---

*manvantara: [Sanskrit from *maver* "man" + *antara* "interval," "period of time"], in Hinduism, one of the fourteen intervals that constitute a *kalpa*—the duration of time from the origination to the destruction of a world system (a cosmic cycle)

I am always, in the name of Jesus Christ, the servant of Almighty God and of the soul of my chelas. I am your own and I am with you. This is my comfort this day.

April 27, 1986
Camelot
Los Angeles County, California
ECP

EPILOGUE

If anything is clear from Morya's words in this second volume of messages, it is his plea to us to use our hearts and minds to liberate ourselves from the byways of wrong desire.

This no-nonsense master shows us unequivocally that wisdom is not simply a placid or blissful state of being. Rather, it is an active thrust for attaining something that's been sought after by spiritual seekers through the ages: making the leap from our everyday, all-too-human state of awareness to what the ascended masters call becoming one with our Real Self.

"Come up higher," is their perpetual cry to our souls. In this book El Morya lays out what this means: Let go of the things that really don't matter in the grand scheme of things and redirect your consciousness to a higher state of being that's just around the corner. Self-transcendence doesn't have to take centuries or decades. All it takes is a firm determination that once and for all we're done with the wishy-washy on-the-Path-and-off-the-Path-again mentality that has kept us earthbound for way too long.

Morya uses everything he has at his disposal to get us to that point of reality that seems so simple and so natural to an ascended master. You can feel it in his words, his phraseology, the thoughtforms in this book. Sometimes there's the direct psychological approach that takes the student by the scruff of the neck and sets him straight regarding his priorities. Sometimes it's the stern rebuke that says, "enough is enough." And sometimes it's the wonderful humor that hits home all the more when you realize it comes from an enlightened being who's seen it all, in terms of the human equation, and literally can't wait to see each of his students break through the "paper bag of his own finite awareness," as Morya once called it.* In the last chapter in this book, El Morya describes this perpetual human dilemma from the perspective of the chela rather than his own:

> You see, beloved, there is only one way out of the limited, unfruitful, unbeneficial desire—and that is to go to the heart of God, to mount the Tree of Life, to enter in and say, "What is my God's desiring in this matter? I have no more struggle in me. I can no longer be torn between this and that. For too long I have been vacillating like a pendulum which Morya cannot even keep track of, nor would he."

Would Morya ever leave us? With a master so committed to our victory, it's hard to imagine. Yet we can feel in these gentle jabs his impatience with our procrastination. He knows what's waiting for us in terms of a higher state of awareness and can't tolerate the mañana consciousness that keeps us sliding back from the Shangri-la beckoning just beyond the horizon of our mind.

So, wisdom is as wisdom does. May Morya's words be the goad that makes you burst out of the paper bag and embrace the fullness of divinity that you really are!

---

* *The Chela and the Path,* chap. 2

APPENDIX

El Morya's Sponsorship of Spiritual Organizations

THEOSOPHY
and

AGNI YOGA

THE THEOSOPHICAL SOCIETY

In the second half of the nineteenth century, during their final incarnation, the Mahatmas Morya, Kuthumi and Djwal Kul lived in close proximity near Shigatse, Tibet, becoming close associates with the common goal of reviving the ancient wisdom of unified science and religion. Morya and Kuthumi were under the strict direction of an adept, far in advance of themselves, known as the Maha Chohan [Great Lord] and another master known as Serapis.

In a letter to A. P. Sinnett, Morya tells of the origins of the Theosophical Society and its period of trial:

"On the 17th of November next [in the year 1882] the Septenary [seven-year] term of trial given the Society at its foundation . . . will expire. One or two of us [Morya and/or Kuthumi] hoped that the world had so far advanced intellectually, if not intuitively, that the Occult [hidden, esoteric] doctrine might gain an intellectual acceptance, and the impulse given for a new cycle of occult research. Others . . . held differently, but consent was given for the trial. It was stipulated, however, that the experiment should be made independently of our personal management; that there should be no abnormal interference by ourselves.

"So casting about we found in America the man to stand as leader—a man of great moral courage, unselfish, and having other good qualities [Henry Steel Olcott]. He was far from being the best, but . . . he was the best one available. With him we associated a woman of most exceptional and wonderful endowments [Helena Blavatsky]. Combined with them [these endowments] she had strong personal defects, but just as she was, there was no second to her living fit for this work. We sent her to America, brought them together—and the trial began.

"From the first both she and he were given to clearly understand that the issue lay entirely with themselves. And both offered themselves for the trial for certain remuneration in the far distant future. . . . For the 6½ years they have been struggling against such odds as would have driven off any one who was not working with the desperation of one who stakes life and all he prizes on some desperate supreme effort. . . . In a few more months the term of probation will end."[1]

Morya gives another vision of Theosophy

"Europe is a large place but the world is bigger yet. The sun of Theosophy must shine for all, not for a part. There is more of this movement than you have yet had an inkling of, and the work of the T.S. [Theosophical Society] is linked in with similar work that is secretly going on in all parts of the world. Even in the T.S. there is a division, managed by a Greek Brother [the Master Hilarion] about which not a person in the Society has a suspicion. . . . The cycle I spoke of refers to the whole movement. Europe will not be overlooked, never fear; but perhaps you even may not anticipate *how* the light will be shed there."[2]

The Masters' purpose for Theosophy

In a letter to A. P. Sinnett, Master Kuthumi states the purpose of the Theosophical Society, which the masters founded in 1875 through Helena Blavatsky: "A genuine, practical Brotherhood of Humanity where all will become co-workers of nature, will work for the good of mankind *with* and *through* the higher *planetary Spirits* [Divine Beings and rulers of planets]."

Kuthumi continues, "Plato was right: *ideas* rule the world; and, as men's minds will receive *new* ideas, laying aside the old and effete, the world will advance: mighty revolutions will spring from them; creeds and even powers will crumble before their onward march crushed by the irresistible force. It will be just as impossible to resist their influx, when the time comes, as to stay the progress of the tide. But all this will come gradually on, and before it comes we have a duty set before us; that of sweeping away as much as possible the dross left to us by our pious forefathers. New ideas have to be planted on clean places, for these ideas touch upon the most momentous subjects. It is not physical phenomena but these universal ideas that we study, as to comprehend the former, we have to first understand the latter. They touch man's true position in the universe, in relation to his previous and future births; his origin and ultimate destiny; the relation of the mortal to the immortal; of the temporary to the eternal; of the finite to the infinite; ideas larger, grander, more comprehensive, recognising the universal reign of Immutable Law, unchanging and unchangeable in regard to which there is only an ETERNAL Now, while to uninitiated mortals time is past or future as related to their finite existence on this material speck of dirt. This is what we study and what many have solved. . . . The *Chiefs* want a "Brotherhood of Humanity," a real Universal Fraternity started; an institution which would make itself known throughout the world and arrest the attention of the highest minds."[3]

Morya, on those whom he could trust in Theosophy

"I say again then. It is he alone [the individual] who has the love of humanity at heart, who is capable of grasping thoroughly the idea of a regenerating practical Brotherhood who is entitled to the possession of our secrets. He alone, such a man—will never misuse his powers, as there will be no fear that he should turn them to selfish ends. A man who places not the good of mankind above his own good is not worthy of becoming our *chela*—he is not worthy of becoming higher in knowledge than his neighbor. If he craves for phenomena let him be satisfied with the pranks of spiritualism. Such is the real state of things. There was a time, when from sea to sea, from the mountains and deserts of the north to the grand woods and downs of Ceylon, there was but one faith, one rallying cry—to save humanity from the miseries of ignorance in the name of Him [Gautama Buddha] who taught first the solidarity of all men."[4]

Descriptions of and testimonies of encounters with Master Morya

Comments and descriptions by C. W. Leadbeater from *The Masters and the Path*:

"The house of the Master Morya is on the opposite side of the valley [from the Master Kuthumi's house], but much lower down —quite close, in fact, to the little temple and the entrance to the caves. It is of an entirely different style of architecture, having at least two storeys, and the front facing the road has verandas at each level which are almost entirely glassed in."[5]

"Madame Blavatsky has often told us how she met the Master Morya in Hyde Park, London, in the year 1851, when he came over with a number of other Indian Princes to attend the first great International Exhibition. Strangely enough, I myself, then a little child of four, saw him also, all unknowing. I can remember being taken to see a gorgeous procession, in which among many other wonders came a party of richly-dressed Indian horsemen. . . . And even as I watched them pass, as I stood holding my father's hand, one of the tallest of those heroes fixed me with gleaming black eyes, which half-frightened me, and yet at the same time filled me somehow with indescribable happiness and exaltation. He passed with the others and I saw him no more, yet often the vision of that flashing eye returned to my childish memory.

"Of course, I knew nothing then of who he was, and I should never have identified him had it not been for a gracious remark which he made to me many years afterwards. Speaking one day in his presence of the earlier days of the Society I happened to say that the first time I had had the privilege of seeing him in materialised form was on a certain occasion when he came into Madame Blavatsky's room at Adyar, for the purpose of giving her strength and issuing certain directions. He himself, who was engaged in conversation with some other Adepts, turned sharply upon me and said: 'No, that was not the first time. You had seen me before then in my physical body. Do you not remember, as a tiny child, watching the Indian horsemen ride past in Hyde Park, and did you not see how even then I singled you out?' I remembered instantly, of course, and said: 'Oh, Master, was that you? But I ought to have known it.' I do not mention this incident among the occasions when I have met and spoken with a Master, both parties to the interview being in the physical body, because I did not at the time know that great horseman to be the Master, and because the evidence of so small a child might well be doubted or discounted."[6]

Leadbeater offers this account from another Theosophist who met Morya, Mr. S. Ramaswami Iyer

"I was following the road to the town, whence, I was assured by people I met on the road, I could cross over to Tibet easily in my pilgrim's garb, when I suddenly saw a solitary horseman galloping towards me from the opposite direction. From his tall stature and skill in horsemanship, I thought he was some military officer of the Sikkhim Rajah. . . . As he approached me, he reined up. I looked at and recognized him instantly. . . . I was in the awful presence of him, of the same Mahatma, my own revered Guru, whom I had seen before in his astral body on the balcony of the Theosophical Headquarters. It was he, the Himalayan Brother of the ever-memorable night of December last, who had so kindly dropped a letter in answer to one I had given but an hour or so before in a sealed envelope to Madame Blavatsky, whom I had never lost sight of for one moment during the interval.

"The very same instant saw me prostrated on the ground at his feet. I arose at his command, and, leisurely looking into his face, forgot myself entirely in the contemplation of the image I knew so well, having seen his portrait (that in Colonel Olcott's possession) times out of number. I knew not what to say; joy and reverence tied my tongue. The majesty of his countenance, which seemed to me to be the impersonation of power and thought, held me rapt in awe. I was at last face to face with the Mahatma of the Himavat, and he was no myth, no creation of the imagination of a medium, as some sceptics had suggested. It was no dream of the night; it was between nine and ten o'clock of the forenoon. There was the sun shining and silently witnessing the scene from above. I see him before me in flesh and blood, and he speaks to me in accents of kindness and gentleness.

"What more could I want? My excess of happiness made me dumb. Nor was it until some time had elapsed that I was able to utter a few words, encouraged by his gentle tone and speech. His complexion is not as fair as that of Mahatma Kuthumi; but never have I seen a countenance so handsome, a stature so tall and so majestic. As in his portrait, he wears a short black beard, and long black hair hanging down to his breast; only his dress was different. Instead of a white, loose robe he wore a yellow mantle lined with fur, and on his head, instead of the turban, a yellow Tibetan felt cap, such as I have seen some Bhutanese wear in this country. When the first moments of rapture and surprise were over, and I calmly comprehended the situation, I had a long talk with him."[7]

Leadbeater's comment on Morya's age

"The Master Morya . . . appears to be a man absolutely in the prime of life—possibly thirty-five or forty years of age; yet many of the stories which his pupils tell of him assign to him an age four or five times greater than that, and Madame Blavatsky herself told us that when she first saw him in her childhood he appeared to her exactly the same as at the present time."[8]

Master Morya's meeting with H. P. Blavatsky, age 20, in 1851

"During her childhood [Madame Blavatsky] had often seen near her an Astral [etheric] form, that always seemed to come in any moment of danger, and save her just at the critical point. HPB had learnt to look upon this Astral form as a guardian angel, and felt that she was under His care and guidance.

"In London, in 1851, she was one day out walking when, to her astonishment, she saw a tall Hindu in the street with some Indian princes. She immediately recognized him as the same person that she had seen in the Astral. Her first impulse was to rush forward to speak to him, but he made her a sign not to move, and she stood as if spellbound while he passed on. The next day she went into Hyde Park for a stroll, that she might be alone and free to think over her extraordinary adventure. Looking up, she saw the same form approaching her, and then her Master told her that he had come to London with the Indian princes on an important mission, and he was desirous of meeting her personally, as he required her cooperation in a work which he was about to undertake.

"He then told her how the Theosophical Society was to be formed, and that he wished her to be the founder. He gave her a slight sketch of all the troubles she would have to undergo, and also told her that she would have to spend three years in Tibet to prepare her for the important task. HPB decided to accept the offer made to her and shortly afterwards left London for India."[9]

One of the many appearances of Master Morya to H. S. Olcott, 1876 or 1877

"I was quietly reading, with all my attention centered on my book. Nothing in the evening's incidents had prepared me for seeing an adept in his astral body; I had not wished for it, tried to conjure it up in my fancy, nor in the least expected it.

"All at once, as I read with my shoulder a little turned from the door, there came a gleam of something white in the right-hand corner of my right eye; I turned my head, dropped my book in astonishment, and saw towering above me in his great stature an Oriental clad in white garments, and wearing a head-cloth or turban of amber-striped fabric, hand-embroidered in yellow floss-silk.

"Long raven hair hung from under his turban to the shoulders; his black beard, parted vertically on the chin in the Rajput fashion, was twisted up at the ends and carried over the ears; his eyes were alive with soul-fire; eyes which were at once benignant and piercing in glance.... He was so grand a man, so imbued with the majesty of moral strength, so luminously spiritual, so evidently above average humanity, that I felt abashed in his presence, and bowed my head and bent my knee as one does before a god or a godlike personage.

"A hand was lightly laid on my head, a sweet though strong voice bade me be seated, and when I raised my eyes, the Presence was seated in the other chair beyond the table....

"At last he rose, I wondering at his great height and observing the sort of splendor in his countenance—not an external shining, but the soft gleam, as it were, of an inner light—that of the spirit.

"Suddenly the thought came into my mind: 'What if this be but hallucination; what if H.P.B. has cast a hypnotic glamour over me?

I wish I had some tangible object to prove to me that he has really been here; something that I might handle after he is gone!'

"The Master smiled kindly as if reading my thought, untwisted the fehtâ [turban] from his head, benignantly saluted me in farewell and was gone: his chair was empty; I was alone with my emotions! Not quite alone, though, for on the table lay the embroidered head-cloth; a tangible and enduring proof that I had not been 'overlooked,' or psychically befooled, but had been face to face with one of the Elder Brothers of Humanity."[10]

Master Morya speaking of himself

"I, am as I was; and, as I was and am, so am I likely always to be—the slave of my duty to the Lodge [the Great White Brotherhood] and mankind, not only taught, but desirous to subordinate every preference for individuals to a love for the human race."[11]

The Master Kuthumi on Morya

"Now, that 'way' [Morya's way] is simply the bare truth, which he [Morya] is ready to write to yourself, or even say and repeat to your face, without the least concealment or change—unless he has purposely allowed the expressions to be exaggerated . . . and he is— of all the men I know just the one to do it without the least hesitation! . . . I am prepared to concede . . . and to admit and repeat with you (and himself at my elbow) that he is *a very imperious* sort of chap, and certainly very apt *sometimes* to become angry, especially if he is opposed in what he knows to be right. . . .

"You, who belong to it, [British society] will hardly if ever be able to appreciate such characters as Morya's: a man as stern for himself, as severe for his own shortcomings, as he is indulgent for the defects of other people, not *in words* but in the innermost feelings of his heart; for, while ever ready to tell you to your face anything he may think of you, he yet was ever a stauncher friend to you than myself, who may often hesitate to hurt anyone's feelings, even in speaking the strictest truth."[12]

Theosophical publications

Both Master Morya and Kuthumi (among other adepts, including Djwal Kul) commissioned and worked through Helena Blavatsky in the publication of *Isis Unveiled,* a monumental work in two volumes, Science and Theology, respectively. In the preface to volume 1, Blavatsky writes:

"The work now submitted to public judgment is the fruit of a somewhat intimate acquaintance with Eastern adepts and study of their science. It is offered to such as are willing to accept truth wherever it may be found, and to defend it, even looking popular prejudice straight in the face. It is an attempt to aid the student to detect the vital principles which underlie the philosophical systems of old. . . .

"When, years ago, we first travelled over the East, exploring the penetralia [innermost parts] of its deserted sanctuaries, two saddening and ever-recurring questions oppressed our thoughts: *Where,* WHO, WHAT *is* GOD? *Who ever saw the* IMMORTAL SPIRIT *of man, so as to be able to assure himself of man's immortality?*

"It was while most anxious to solve these perplexing problems that we came into contact with certain men, endowed with such mysterious powers and such profound knowledge that we may truly designate them as the sages of the Orient. To their instructions we lent a ready ear. They showed us that by combining science with religion, the existence of God and immortality of man's spirit may be demonstrated like a problem of Euclid. For the first time we received the assurance that the Oriental philosophy has room for no other faith than an absolute and immovable faith in the omnipotence of man's own immortal self. We were taught that this omnipotence comes from the kinship of man's spirit with the Universal Soul—God! The latter, they said, can never be demonstrated but by the former. Man-spirit proves God-spirit, as the one drop of water proves a source from which it must have come. . . .

"Our work, then, is a plea for the recognition of the Hermetic philosophy, the anciently universal Wisdom-Religion, as the only possible key to the Absolute in science and theology."[13]

The Secret Doctrine

We note again consistent characteristics of Master Morya: universality, brotherhood and the importance of a union between science and religion, and, further, that there has always existed a universal wisdom-religion and that this universal religion should and will exist again in the world.

Another characteristic teaching of Master Morya is that the key to knowledge of God is through one's own immortal spirit, which at that time was called the Atman or Atma (Sanskrit: Self) or the Monad and later (in the decade of the 1930s) was called by the Master Saint Germain the I AM Presence.

In 1888, *The Secret Doctrine* was published in two volumes: Vol. 1, Cosmogenesis, Vol. 2, Anthropogenesis. The first volume explained in detail the origin and evolution of the universe, while the second volume expounded upon the development and evolution of man. The book also proved by many examples the universal truths that underlie all the major religions.

The Secret Doctrine was a milestone in the evolution of consciousness on this planet. In a precipitated letter to Dr. Hubbe-Schleiden who visited Blavatsky in Wurzburg, Germany, while she was writing *The Secret Doctrine,* Master M. stated: "I, the humble undersigned . . . certify that the 'Secret Doctrine' is dictated to Upasika [HPB] partly by myself and partly by my Brother K.H."[14]

Both *The Secret Doctrine* and *The Mahatma Letters* presented a vast panorama of evolution originating from "An Omnipresent, Eternal, Boundless, and Immutable PRINCIPLE,"[15] and ending in our present manifested universe containing innumerable divine beings functioning on various planes and dimensions who brought our universe into objectivity.

Master Morya and Kuthumi revealed that the "soul" (also

called a monad), a ray of the Divine Monad or spirit spark was obliged to evolve through vast cycles of development and evolution from higher dimensions down to the physical, in order to acquire self-consciousness in the planes of matter and to eventually achieve God consciousness, evolving into a personification of God.

Morya, with Kuthumi, brought forth startling revelations based on ancient manuscripts which they showed to Blavatsky in visions, some going back to Lemurian and Atlantean times. Morya believed that the time had come to release certain teachings, as did Kuthumi, long kept hidden by the adepts, solely for the enlightenment and upliftment of mankind.

Some of these teachings included the seven principles or seven "bodies" in man, the highest of which is the Divine Self or Atman, the seven "rounds" or cycles of planetary incarnation comprising the lifetime of a planet, lasting over 4 billion years, the evolutionary journey of the monad (soul) through seven root-races, the out-breath *(manvantara)* and in-breath *(pralaya)* of the cosmos, and the fact that our present universe and all therein is the karmic effect of a previous universe.

Morya and Kuthumi also made known to the world the existence of an occult hierarchy (of which the two masters were a part) also called the White Lodge or White Brotherhood which had guided the humanity of this and other worlds for millions of years. But the greatest teachings were the inherent divinity of man and a deeper understanding of the law of karma and reincarnation.

Elizabeth Clare Prophet comments on the founding of Theosophy

"The year 1875 was a pivotal year, a pivotal year of astrology and of the opening of the way for the twentieth century. In the East, El Morya and the master Kuthumi were founding their Theosophical movement. In the West, there began studies in metaphysics, homeopathy, experiments of Mesmer and so forth.

"Truly, there was an opening of the way of a new understanding so that on the first day of the year of 1900 we entered the century with new religions East and West knocking on our doors, with members of the Buddhist and Hindu sects of India coming to the United States and giving their teachings for the first time. . . .

"So in that auspicious year of 1875, El Morya and Kuthumi working closely with Djwal Kul, Saint Germain, and Serapis Bey, founded the Theosophical Society through Helena Blavatsky in New York City. Very interesting that Saint Germain and El Morya and the sponsors chose that city—that city that is booming and bursting with ideas and with minds upon minds stimulating other minds and souls to creativity.

"Theosophy became a worldwide movement that had a profound influence on Western thinking. Madame Blavatsky stated that the most important goal of the Theosophical Society was to revive the work of Ammonius Saccas. He is the reputed founder of the Neoplatonic School 1700 years ago. The work of that school, she said, was 'to reconcile all religions, sects and nations under a common system of ethics, based on eternal verities.'"[16]

"The sense of the continuity of the real inner mysteries of God —the continuity of religion—was bestowed on Blavatsky by the masters who sponsored her. And what would the masters bring forth? They would bring forth [the teaching] from ancient Atlantis and Lemuria to the fore, to the present century, that we might have the benefit of carrying the torch of this teaching, this eternal teaching into the next age."[17]

Persecution and schism in Theosophy

The masters Morya and Kuthumi, as well as Blavatsky and her associates were subject to severe and continuous opposition from many quarters during the history of Theosophy. Many would-be disciples failed but the movement continued. Morya also made it known that the work of the masters and their disciples was always opposed by the "Brothers of the Shadow," those who had taken the left-handed path of selfishness, ego and destruction.

In 1891 H. P. Blavatsky passed on and the leadership of the organization went to Olcott, Annie Besant and C. W. Leadbeater. In 1895 a schism split the Society in two, with William Q. Judge leaving for America as head of the Theosophical Society in America, with no affiliation with the Society in Adyar, India. The cause of the schism was that Judge claimed to have received letters from the masters who were directing him, and that Olcott, Besant, among others, did not accept the letters as authentic.

As a result of another upsetting controversy, the last we hear of the masters Morya and Kuthumi communicating with Olcott was in 1907 (the year of his passing). The message, given to the Society from the masters (who were "ascended" at that time) was this: "That those who believed in their existence and that They, Who were behind the Theosophical Movement, would continue to employ it as an agency for uplifting mankind and must some times use imperfect instruments; that members should cease from disturbances and from rushing into dissensions which undermined the Unity of Brotherhood and lessened its strength. They [the masters] were powerless to check disturbances arising from the Karma of individual members, but refusal to take part in such disturbances would aid Them. The Law would adjust any seeming injustice. 'Hold together in brotherly love, since you are part of the Great Universal Self . . . are your Brother's sins not your own?'"[18]

Universality

This message from the masters to the Theosophical Society on avoiding dissension is a landmark message applicable to all other organizations founded by Master Morya (or founded by any master) to the present hour. It is also applicable to nations and it points to Morya's characteristic insistence on unity and brotherhood.

THE AGNI YOGA SOCIETY

Master Morya's work with Nicholas Roerich and the Agni Yoga Society

The Master Morya had his attention on Russia at the same time he was working with the Theosophical Society. In Russia Morya sponsored two amanuenses, Nicholas Roerich and his wife, Helena.* Nicholas was born in 1874 to a wealthy and politically influential family and became interested in art, painting, archeology and in writing both poetry and prose.

Nicholas attended the Imperial University and the Imperial Academy of Art. When he was twenty-four he met his future wife, who was five years younger than he and they were married in 1901. Helena gave birth to two boys.

Master Morya began contacting young Helena in 1885, during the time when he was immersed in the co-directing of the Theosophical Society. Author Ruth A. Drayer states: "She was six years old when she first met the 'tall figure, dressed in white' she came to know as a 'Teacher of Light, who lived somewhere far away.' Shortly afterward, she began having numerous dreams and visions that would allow her access to deeper realms of reality and gave her the ability to predict future events."[19]

The Russian Theosophical Society

According to Elizabeth Clare Prophet, "a Russian branch of the [Theosophical] Society was founded in 1908, and the Roerichs apparently joined it prior to World War I. Years later, Helena Roerich translated Blavatsky's monumental work *The Secret Doctrine* into Russian."[20]

---

*For consistency and clarity in this book, we have used "Helena" as Mrs. Roerich's first name, although some authors use "Elena."

Master Morya's appearances to the Roerichs

Aware of the growing threat of the Bolsheviks, the Roerichs left for Finland in December of 1916, just months before the Russian Revolution. During the next few years they experienced financial problems until they arrived in London in 1919, where Nicholas's art exhibition was a success.

Ruth Drayer continues the story: "Their days in London contained many surprises, but nothing equaled the experience the couple had one day while passing a group of Indian men on Bond Street. Making eye contact with the tallest, they immediately recognized the piercing eyes of Master Morya, so well known to them from their daily meditations. Although bearded and wearing a turban, it was their Master, and their hearts must have paused at the sight of him. Later that night, he visited them in their studio flat at Queen's Gate Terrace. . . . In her [Elena's] dreams she began to receive books to read, and two luminous silvery figures appeared at her bed with certain dates and glowing digits on their foreheads."[21]

Drayer continues: "In March 1920, the thought transmissions, or communications, from Master Morya began. At first both of the Roerichs received messages; then, Elena carried on the work. The transmissions became their source of strength and brought a most precious solace into their lives. 'Those who with a full heart fulfill our requests will attune their ears to the harmony of the Universe,' said Master Morya. Reams of messages were transmitted throughout the rest of their lives, inspiring, educating, and counseling them and giving them knowledge almost impossible to attain in any other way."[22]

"Over the next few decades, the transmissions were transcribed in books that sounded the call for a new time of 'the power of thought.' Given the name Agni Yoga, the teachings explained the creative relationship of human thought to the energy or fire of which the universe is made."

Master Morya said: "I give you the Teaching, karmic messages, indications. The Teaching is intended for the whole world, for all beings. . . . The more broadly you comprehend, the more truly it is yours. My friends! Happiness lies in serving the salvation of Humanity. Put aside all prejudices and summoning thy spiritual forces, aid mankind. Turn the unsightly towards beauty. As the tree renews its leaves, so shall men flourish on the path of righteousness."[23]

New Era Community

In 1923, the Roerichs and their family traveled to India. From 1925 to 1928, they journeyed into Central Asia, including Kashmir, Mongolia and Tibet. In 1928, Nicholas founded the Himalayan Research Institute and then settled in the Western Himalayas, in the Kulu valley. During this time Master Morya continued to transmit messages.[24]

The first book in the Agni Yoga series was *Leaves of Morya's Garden,* released in 1924. The second volume of *Leaves of Morya's Garden* was released in 1925. In 1926 came *New Era Community,* which was a challenge to the Soviet communism of Lenin and Stalin. In this book Morya states:

"And another absolute condition must be fulfilled. Labor must be voluntary. Cooperation must be voluntary. Community must be voluntary. Labor must not be enslaved by force. The condition of voluntary agreement must be laid into the foundation of advancement. No one may bring dissolution into the new house. Workers, builders, creators, can be likened to high-soaring eagles. Only in a broad flight does the dust and rubbish of decay fall away." "All compulsion is condemned. Compulsory slavery, compulsory marriage, compulsory labor, incite rebellion and condemnation. But of all the forms of compulsion the most culpable and ugly is the compulsory community. Each compulsion is doomed to a reaction, and the worst form of compulsion is doomed to the worst reaction."[25]

Morya's blueprint for the New Era Community

"Family, clan, country, union of nations—each unit strives toward peace, toward betterment of life. Each unit of cooperation and communal life needs perfecting. No one can fix the limits of evolution. By this line of reasoning a worker becomes a creator. Let us not be frightened by the problems of creativeness. Let us find for science unencumbered paths. Thus, thought about perfectionment will be a sign of joy.... The communal life has long been a sign of cooperation and of mutual respect.... Altruism is a requisite if one is to devote one's talent to the common work.

"Unity is pointed out in all beliefs as the sole bulwark of success. Better attainments can be affirmed if the unity of coworkers is assured.... We shall realize a beautiful meaning if we can introduce the great concept—friend. Community may consist only of friends."

Morya continues: "Ancient working community-guilds left testimony of their vitality. One can see how people cultivated their skills toward perfection. They knew how to shield each other and how to guard the dignity of their community. So long as people do not learn to defend the merit of their fellow-workers they will not achieve the happiness of Common Good....

"The Community, as Fellowship, can unprecedentedly accelerate the evolution of the planet and give new possibilities of intercourse with the forces of matter. It must not be thought that community and the conquest of matter are found on different planes. One channel, one banner—Maitreya, Mother, Matter! ...

"The man who is lost in conjecture as to where is slavery and where is freedom is unable to think about the community. The man who oppresses the consciousness of his brother cannot think about the community. The man who distorts the Teaching cannot think about the community. The basis of the community lies in freedom of thinking and in reverence for the Teacher....

"Understand the Teaching; understand that without the

Teaching one cannot get along. This formula must be repeated, for in life much is done without the Teaching. The Teaching must color every act and every speech."[26]

Elizabeth Clare Prophet remarks on the importance of community in her commentary on Morya's book *New Era Community:*

"The community, which is the opportunity for all chelas to be together and to be one with the guru and receive the teachings, is more important than the survival of any one of its members. . . . I would like us to study this book [*New Era Community*]. It is very precious to me, because I see community as the most precious thing in the world. . . . There can be no guru-chela relationship without community, and, therefore, the teaching, the Word, the messenger and the students will not survive. The more we know about community as the white cube in the heart, and then as its ramification in the outer, the more we stabilize an outer forcefield of the Great White Brotherhood."[27]

Living Ethics

Under the direction of the Master Morya, Roerich gave to the world the philosophy of Livings Ethics, based on a unifying spiritual mindset:

"According to this mindset, the Universe is a grandiose spirited system of energy that is evolving according to the Great Laws of the Cosmos. It explains a man as one of many structures, closely linked and interacting with the others—with similar objects on the surface of our planet, with celestial bodies, with the worlds of other states of matter. Viewing a man as 'part of the cosmic energy, part of the elements, part of Cosmic Reason, part of the consciousness of the higher matter,' Living Ethics assigned to him the role of evolution's chief tool. Without a man the main task of the evolution process—spiritualization of the matter, its transformation into a higher state of different quality—would have been impossible.

"Apart from our solid world Living Ethics also observed the

worlds of different states of matter. . . . Combining the matter of these kinds inside himself the man is constantly interacting with these worlds. The nature of this interaction is defined by the level and the expansion of one's mind and by the participation of one's heart. Therefore the Teaching lays great emphasis on ethical notions and their practical realization—high moral standards, love, compassion, feeling of responsibility for one's close ones and for the evolution of the planet as the whole.

"According to the doctrine, 'The feeling of responsibility should be developed infinitely. The spirit of a man, like the Creator, holds responsibility for all his deeds. We shall not be in fear of realizing the phenomenon of responsibility. We are responsible not only to ourselves, but also to the Cosmos.' "[28]

Following titles

The teaching of Living Ethics was embodied in all subsequent publications dictated by Morya to the Roerichs. After *New Era Community* the following titles were published: *Agni Yoga, Infinity* (two volumes), *Hierarchy, Heart, Fiery World* (three volumes), *Aum,* and *Brotherhood.* These were published between 1929 and 1937.

The Roerich Peace Pact and Banner of Peace

Nicholas Roerich created an international plan for the protection of cultural treasures from the ravages of war. Roerich's plan involved using a symbolic banner to identify as neutral—and thus to be respected and protected by belligerents—the world's historic monuments, museums, scientific, artistic, educational and cultural institutions and their property and collections.

The Banner of Peace, inspired by Roerich's original design, is the symbol of the Roerich Pact. Displayed in magenta (deep red) on a white background, the banner shows three spheres, or dots, within a circle. For Roerich, the symbol represented not only the circle of eternity encompassing past, present and future, but also

represented religion, art and science, three key aspects of culture, within the circle of culture in its entirety.

In 1935 the Inter-American Treaty on the Roerich Pact was signed by the 21-member republics of the Pan-American Union, including the United States. It became the foundation of the 1956 Hague Convention for the protection of monuments. Later signatories included India and the Balkan states.[29]

Master Morya, through Elizabeth Clare Prophet, spoke of the Roerich Peace Pact in 1996

"Blessed ones, the Darjeeling Council is working with a terrific intensity to turn this world around. We *must* have your energy. . . . We speak to those of South America, Central America, North America. We speak to you of every nation in earth. We say, beloved, let the white fire of God intensify. Rejoice that you have the Holy Spirit, that you have the understanding of the Path and the teaching. Awaken souls. And above all, remember that there is a flag that flies in Darjeeling not unlike the symbol of Nicholas Roerich. It is [the symbol of] the Roerich Peace Pact. That flag, beloved, has the three dots within a circle. It was placed upon those buildings that were hospitals or of the arts or of museums for protection during World War II. Blessed ones, our banner does fly, for we are determined that the Darjeeling Council and all of the chelas of all of the masters who are a part of that council will not fail. We are determined that we will have the victory but we must not forget it—*daily.*"[30]

Paintings of Nicholas Roerich

Roerich painted over 7,000 works of art, including easel paintings, stage designs and murals. In his travels in India and Asia, Roerich visited and painted places where the Masters Morya and Kuthumi lived and frequented. In *Heart of Asia,* he writes:

"Until quite recently several ashrams of the Mahatmas of the Himalayas existed near Shigatse and further in the direction of the sacred lake Manosaravar. Knowing this, and the facts that surround those remarkable sites, filled me with a special emotion. It was wondrous and strange to pass through the same places where They passed. There are still old people who remember meeting Them personally—calling Them by the names of Asaras [wise men, Hindu in appearance, with long hair and white attire, who often appear in the Himalayas] and Khuthumpas. Some remember that a religious school was founded there by the Mahatmas of India. . . .

"We stood in the same courtyard where an episode occurred with a letter, which was destroyed and then miraculously restored by a Master. We passed the caves where They had stayed and crossed the same rivers and in these same jungles of Sikkim stood outside their outwardly modest Ashram. . . .

"While Europeans argue about the existence of the Mahatmas, the Hindus are significantly silent, for many not only know about Them, but have seen Them and have actual proof of Their deeds and appearances. Because the people of Asia had always yearned for Them, the Mahatmas created a special existence there, manifesting

Themselves when it was necessary and passing unnoticed otherwise; leaving Their imprint only upon the hearts and minds of those who know. They are not a fairy tale, imagination, or invention, the Mahatmas are living forms.

"I do not wish to persuade or try to convince anyone of Their existence. A great many people have seen Them, have talked to Them, and received letters and material objects from Them. . . .

"How many people are there who would love to receive a letter from the Mahatmas! But after it provided a moment of astonishment and confusion, would it really change their lives? Probably not.

"But now people are knocking on the doors for this great knowledge; many of the younger generation simply want to start a correspondence with a Guru or find a real teacher."[31]

The Master Morya dictated messages, teachings and books through the Roerichs until 1937, when the last volume of the Agni Yoga series was published. Nicholas Roerich passed on in 1947, with no further need to reincarnate. He is an ascended master today.

The lasting legacy of the Agni Yoga Society

Elizabeth Clare Prophet has stated: "The Agni Yoga Society and the many books they have published are a very important thread of the ascended masters' teachings through Morya. El Morya dictated in Russian to the Roerichs. . . . And Morya has a great love for the Russian people and the fire of his will in Darjeeling will bring about the redemption of both Russia and China."[32]

Appendix Notes

1. *The Mahatma Letters to A. P. Sinnett* (London: Rider and Company, 1926), Letter 44, Morya to Sinnett, February 1882, p. 263; brackets and paragraphing added.

2. *Mahatma Letters*, Letter 47, Morya to Sinnett, March 3, 1882, p. 271.

3. *Mahatma Letters*, Letter 6, Koot' Hoomi [K.H.] to Sinnett, December 10, 1880, pp. 23–24.

4. *Mahatma Letters*, Letter 38, Morya to Sinnett, received about February 1882, p. 252.

5. C. W. Leadbeater, *The Masters and the Path* (Adyar: Theosophical Publishing House, 1969), p. 27.

6. Ibid., pp. 29–30.

7. S. Ramaswami Iyer, quoted in Leadbeater, *Masters and the Path,* p. 30.

8. Leadbeater, *Masters and the Path,* p. 35.

9. Constance Wachtmeister, *Reminiscenses of H. P. Blavatsky* (Wheaton, Ill.: Theosophical Publishing House, 1976), p. 44, quoted in the article on Morya at *Theosophy Wiki,* https://theosophy.wiki/en/Morya.

10. Henry Steel Olcott, *Old Diary Leaves: America, 1874–1878* (Adyar: Theosophical Publishing House, 1941), pp. 379, 380.

11. *Mahatma Letters*, Letter 29, Morya to Sinnett and A. O. Hume jointly, p. 225; brackets added.

12. *Mahatma Letters,* Letter 30, K.H. to Hume, pp. 232, 233; brackets added.

13. H. P. Blavatsky, "Preface," *Isis Unveiled: A Master-Key to the Mysteries of Ancient and Modern Science and Theology,* first ed. (1877; repr., Pasadena: Theosophical University Press, 1976), vol. 1, pp. v, vi, vii.

14. Virginia Hanson, ed., *H. P. Blavatsky and the Secret Doctrine* (Wheaton, Ill.: Theosophical Publishing House, 1971, 1988), p. 17.

15. H. P. Blavatsky, *The Secret Doctrine: The Synthesis of Science, Religion, and Philosophy,* first ed. (1888; repr., Pasadena: Theosophical University Press, 1963), vol. 1, p. 14.

16. H. P. Blavatsky, quoted in Joseph Head and Sylvia Cranston, *Reincarnation: The Phoenix Fire Mystery* (San Diego: Point Loma Publications, 1977), p. 488.

17. Elizabeth Clare Prophet, "Review of Teachings from El Morya," given during the 37th Anniversary of The Summit Lighthouse, August 6, 1995.

18. *The Theosophist,* Feb. 1907, p. 385, *et seq.,* quoted in Josephine Ransom, *A Short History of the Theosophical Society* (Adyar, Madras: Theosophical Publishing House, 1938), pp. 367–68.

19. Ruth Abrams Drayer, *Nicholas and Helena Roerich: The Spiritual Journey of Two Great Artists and Peacemakers* (Wheaton, Ill: Quest Books, Theosophical Publishing House, 2005), p. 8. For background on the Roerichs, see chap. 1, especially pp. 3, 5, 6, 7.

20. Elizabeth Clare Prophet, "A Profile of Nicholas Roerich," *Pearls of Wisdom,* vol. 33, no. 43, November 4, 1990. See note 34.

21. Drayer, *Nicholas and Helena Roerich,* p. 17.

22. Ibid., pp. 17–18.

23. Ibid., p. 18. The author does not list the source of these quotes.

24. See *Theosophy Wiki,* article on Nicholas Roerich, at https://theosophy .wiki/en/Nicholas_Roerich.

25. *New Era Community* (New York: Agni Yoga Society, 1951), pp. 9, 196.

26. Ibid., pp. 7, 8, 10, 50, 71, 73.

27. Elizabeth Clare Prophet, *Community: A Journey into the Heart of Community* (Corwin Springs: The Summit Lighthouse Library, 2002), pp. 2, 3.

28. The quotation on Living Ethics is taken from the Nicholas Roerich article at Theosophy Wiki, https://theosophy.wiki/en/Nicholas_ Roerich.

29. See El Morya, 2002 *Pearls of Wisdom,* vol. 45, no. 52, December 29, 2002, p. 392, n. 8.

30. Ibid., p. 389.

31. Nicholas Roerich, *Heart of Asia,* quoted in Drayer, *Nicholas and Helena Roerich,* pp. 249–52.

32. Lecture by Elizabeth Clare Prophet, October 25, 1973.

NOTES

PROLOGUE

1. El Morya, October 8, 1977, "The Gemini Mind for the Governing of Society and the Self," published as chapter 17, this book. For excerpt quoted here, see pp. 195–96.
2. Elizabeth Clare Prophet, "Cosmic Consciousness," lecture, November 24, 1981.
3. Ibid.
4. El Morya, April 8, 1990, "Bonded to the Lord of the First Ray: The Initiation of the Bonding of Guru and Chela," *Morya and You: Love* (Summit University Press, 2018), pp. 284, 288–89. Also published in its entirety in 1990 *Pearls of Wisdom,* vol. 33, no. 13, April 8, 1990.

CHAPTER 1: The Perfection in Your Heart Is God

1. Mark 16:19.
2. Acts 1:9.
3. Rev. 1:15; 14:2; 19:6; 21:6; 22:17.
4. Rev. 21:6.

CHAPTER 3: The Jar of Freedom

1. *Yasna:* chief liturgical portion of the Avesta (scripture of the Zoroastrians collected from writings, sermons, and oral traditions of Zoroaster before 800 B.C.); composed of litanies, *gathas* "hymns," and invocations to Ahura-Mazda and other gods.
2. Traditionally each New Year's Eve, Gautama Buddha releases the thoughtform for the year. The 1965 thoughtform was a golden scroll, descending from God out of heaven, with the words

PEACE with Honor. See Gautama Buddha, January 1, 1965, "Go Be!" 1965 *Pearls of Wisdom,* vol. 8, "Prologue," p. xii.

3. Matt. 18:6.
4. John 14:2, 3.

CHAPTER 4:   **The Gift of Divine Grace**

1. John 6:68.
2. Matt. 13:12; Mark 4:25; Luke 8:18.
3. Isa. 1:18.
4. Acts 9:18.
5. John 3:17.
6. "Brighten the Corner Where You Are" was a popular song published in 1913, with music by Charles H. Gabriel (1856–1932) and lyrics by Ina Duley Ogden (1872–1964). It has been performed by many recording artists through the decades. The lyrics are as follows:

   > Do not wait until some deed of greatness you may do,
   > Do not wait to shed your light afar;
   > To the many duties ever near you now be true,
   > Brighten the corner where you are.

   Refrain:
   > Brighten the corner where you are!
   > Brighten the corner where you are!
   > Someone far from harbor you may guide across the bar;
   > Brighten the corner where you are!

   > Just above are clouded skies that you may help to clear,
   > Let not narrow self your way debar;
   > Though into one heart alone may fall your song of cheer,
   > Brighten the corner where you are.

   > Here for all your talent you may surely find a need,
   > Here reflect the bright and Morning Star;
   > Even from your humble hand the Bread of Life may feed,
   > Brighten the corner where you are.

7. I Cor. 15:52.
8. Chief cornerstone. Matt. 21:42; Mark 12:10; Luke 20:17; Acts 4:10–12; Eph. 2:20; I Pet. 2:5–7; Ps. 118:22; Isa. 28:16.

9. Amos 7:8.
10. Luke 23:34.

CHAPTER 5:   The Will of God Is a Charge of Radiance from Afar

1. Isa. 64:8; Jer. 18:6.
2. Mark 4:39.
3. Cosmic Egg. In the teachings of the ascended masters, the spiritual-material universe is known as the Cosmic Egg. It includes the galaxies, star systems, and worlds known and unknown, whose center is called the Great Central Sun. For additional information, see *Saint Germain On Alchemy*, glossary entries "Central Sun" and "Cosmic Egg."
4. Matt. 8:12; 13:42; 22:13; 24:51; 25:30; Luke 13:28; Acts 7:54.
5. Mr. Krishnamurti. Jiddu Krishnamurti (1895–1986) was educated in theosophy by Annie Besant, then president of the Theosophical Society. He became a teacher and writer in Europe and the United States during the 1920s. In 1929 he left the Theosophical Society and eventually rejected the masters as his teachers.
6. Luke 22:31.
7. *At the Feet of the Master*, originally published in 1910, was written down by Jiddu Krishnamurti under the name of Alcyone. According to the messengers Mark and Elizabeth Prophet, the book was written under the direction of the master Kuthumi while Krishnamurti was still under his guru, Maitreya.
8. Isa. 14:12–15.
9. As mice and men. The phrase "Of mice and men" is taken from Robert Burns' poem "To a Mouse," which reads (in modern English) "The best laid schemes of mice and men / often go awry." John Steinbeck used the phrase as the title of his 1937 novella *Of Mice and Men*, which illustrates the powerlessness and tragedy of the central characters.
10. Luke 15:18.
11. The nine ambassadors. In a lecture in the evening of August 27, 1967, the messenger Mark L. Prophet stated that the original mission of the nine ambassadors "has been secret almost since the foundation of the world. . . . These ambassadors represent hierarchy. They are charged with the responsibility of acting as observers in the world of form of that which men do. . . . Hierarchy, then,

in constant communion with the Godhead, utilizes these reports from the nine ambassadors at large, who are scattered upon the planetary body, as a measurement whereby certain dispensations can be secured from the Karmic Council. . . . And this morning we learned something that is happening to that system. And as a result, we believe now that we understand how Saint Peter could make the statement that the world would ultimately be destroyed by fire. . . . In this case it would be a destruction brought about because of the intensification of the fire of the Presence."

12. Rev. 12:14.
13. Rev. 6:16.
14. Luke 21:28.
15. Rom. 13:12.
16. Luke 1:78, 79.
17. *The Pilgrim's Progress* is a Christian allegory written in two parts, 1678 and 1684, by John Bunyan. The plot centers on the journey of the protagonist, Christian, from his hometown, the "City of Destruction" (this world), to the "Celestial City" (heaven). The work is a symbolic vision of the spiritual path where the hero encounters both companions and adversaries along the way and is victorious in the end.

CHAPTER 6:   **Where the Masters Lead, Let Mankind Follow**

1. Heb. 12:23.
2. El Morya was previously embodied as King Arthur, who founded the Order of the Knights of the Round Table in the area now known as Glastonbury, England. For further information on King Arthur of Britain, see *Morya and You: Love,* by Mark L. Prophet and Elizabeth Clare Prophet, pp. 310–12.
3. II Pet. 1:10.
4. Luke 9:62.

CHAPTER 7:   **The Power of Right Thought**

1. Dante's *Inferno* is the first part of the fourteenth century epic poem *The Divine Comedy,* which relates the journey of Dante through hell, guided by the ancient Roman poet Virgil. During the course of the journey through the nine circles of hell, Dante encounters

grotesque and frightening images and sounds depicting the suffering of souls for their crimes, such as sorcery, murder, blasphemy,
suicide, and others. The *Inferno* is followed by Dante's journey
through purgatory and paradise.

2. The Sign of the Cross. A ritual blessing upon oneself made by members of most branches of Christianity, signifying the trinity of Father,
   Son and Holy Spirit. The movement is the tracing of the shape of
   a cross on one's own body by touching the forehead, the chest, and
   then each shoulder. The ascended masters teach that the cross sym-
   bolizes the meeting place of God and man at the nexus where the
   Christ consciousness is born.

3. Gen. 1:27; 2:8–15.

4. Hedon is taken from the Greek word *hedone* meaning "pleasure."
   Mark Prophet spoke of the planet Hedron (also known as Hedon)
   as being a paradise of beauty and culture. At some point, the evolutions of Hedron succumbed to the pleasure cult of selfishness
   and indulgence, and the planet eventually was destroyed. For more
   information, see Mark L. Prophet and Elizbeth Clare Prophet,
   Paths of Light and Darkness (in the Climb the Highest Mountain
   series), pp. 9–18.

5. "Planetary chain" is a theosophical term referring to the "chain" of
   planets linked together that form our solar system. It also refers to
   the seven globes or spheres that comprise each planet.

6. Ezek. 18:23; 33:11.

7. Jer. 31:33; Heb. 8:10.

8. The etheric, or memory, body contains the Tablets of Mem
   (memory), which are the recordings of all vibrations and energy
   impulses that the soul has ever sent forth.

9. Gen. 2:18, 21–24.

10. Old Ironsides. The master may be referring to Oliver Cromwell
    (1599–1658), English general and Lord Protector whose soldiers
    nicknamed "Old Ironsides," or to the USS *Constitution,* the 44-gun
    U.S. Navy frigate launched in 1797 and still in commission to this
    day. Oliver Wendell Holmes wrote a poem in 1830 in tribute to
    the frigate entitled "Old Ironsides" which contributed to saving
    the vessel from being decommissioned.

11. Meanderings of the Grail Consciousness. On the same day that this
    dictation was given, Mark Prophet gave a lecture, "Meditations on

the Holy Grail," in which he said, "The ancient order of Melchizedek is the power behind the manifestation of the Holy Grail, which
is symbolic of the Christed ones, of those who were without father
and without mother in the simple sense that they, according to the
ancient mysteries, created themselves . . . In order to be a member
of the Melchizedek priesthood, to move through the universe with
the speed of light, to be able to *dominate* time as well as space, to
be a *master* of time as well as space, you have to have the qualities
of universal love. And this cannot be something that is a sweet
nothingness like a pretty little rose that someone would paint, or
an idea of an innocent look on someone's face. We're talking about
the power of the living God."

CHAPTER 8:   **Be Clothed with Right Mind
                and the Sternness of Consciousness**

1. Ps. 60:4, 5; Song of Sol. 2:4.
2. Joel 2; Josh. 6.
3. Matt. 5:1–12.
4. According to Greek mythology, Atalanta was a virgin huntress who
    agreed to marry only if her suitors could outrun her in a footrace.
    One suitor, Hippomenes, asked the goddess Aphrodite for help.
    She gave him three golden apples which he intended to throw
    in Atalanta's way to slow her down. Every time Hippomenes got
    ahead of Atalanta in the race, he rolled a golden apple ahead of
    her and she would run after it, taking her off course. Hippomenes
    won the footrace and married Atalanta.
5. James 1:17; I John 1:5.

CHAPTER 9:   **The Banner of the Mother of the World Is Revealed**

1. John 20.
2. Isa. 2:4.
3. In the sentence beginning "Circle come full circle" El Morya is
    describing a use of energy that is karmic in nature, whereas the
    ascended masters teach that the right use of the energy of the
    three-times-three is a means to obtaining the nine gifts of the Holy
    Spirit. The messenger Elizabeth Clare Prophet explained in a lec-
    ture given on January 25, 1976: "The gifts of the Spirit are nine in

number because of the action of the three-times-three, the action of the squaring of the Trinity. When we have the balanced three-fold flame of Father, Son and Holy Spirit and it is squared, it is the power of the nine. Thus the nine gifts of the Holy Spirit can only be contained by the one who has first balanced the love, the wisdom and the power in the Christ consciousness." The bestowal of the nine gifts of the Holy Spirit is by definition the transfer of the power of the three-times-three, which the disciple must learn to wield and enhance through the balanced threefold flame and the science of the spoken Word.

4. Gen. 3:15.
5. Rev. 1:7.
6. Matt. 28:20.

CHAPTER 10:   **Do You Love Morya? Then Love the God Within! Love His Holy Will!**

1. Ps. 37:11; Matt. 5:5.
2. Isa. 65:17; 66:22; II Pet. 3:13; Rev. 21:1.
3. Matt. 5; 13:1–3.
4. "A message to Garcia" is a phrase that has special meaning for millions of people around the world. It is a phrase that has become synonymous with noble qualities of character such as dependability and dedication to accomplish whatever task or responsibility is asked of someone. "A message to Garcia" came about during the Spanish-American War in 1898, when U.S. President McKinley needed to quickly secure the cooperation of General Garcia, leader of the revolutionary forces in Cuba. Garcia was somewhere in the mountainous jungles of Cuba, but no one knew where. McKinley was looking for someone who could find Garcia and deliver his message. The then Lieutenant Andrew Summers Rowan carried the letter over his heart and disappeared into the jungle in search of General Garcia. After three weeks, Rowan emerged on the other side of the island after having safely delivered the message. Author Elbert Hubbard wrote of this story in 1899 and said of Rowan: "Here was a rare man who had the ingredients for success that are needed everywhere." Rowan's success has been attributed to his tenacity to not give up, to not waste time, and to stay focused on the goal by keeping in mind the much larger goal. Due partially

to Rowan's heroic accomplishment, Spain ceded Puerto Rico, the Philippine Islands, and Guam to the United States and abandoned all claims to Cuba.

5. Matt. 8:12; 13:42; 22:13; 24:51; 25:30; Luke 13:28; Acts 7:54.
6. Matt. 10:16.

CHAPTER 11:   **Ageless Wisdom Is the Fulfillment of the Hungers of the Soul**

1. Matt. 5:6.
2. I Kings 18:31–38.
3. Lev. 18:21; 20:2–5; II Kings 23:10; Jer. 32:35.
4. Luke 2:13, 14.
5. James 4:3.
6. Rev. 2:27.
7. Matt. 27:51; Mark 15:38.

CHAPTER 12:   **Morya Comes! We Thunder with the Hope of a New Day!**

1. Isa. 62:8.
2. Ps. 18:9.

CHAPTER 13:   **The Illumination of Mankind Is a Passion of the Universal Consciousness**

1. Matt. 13:45–46.
2. Heb. 11:3.
3. The crystal and the mist. In a lecture given on October 13, 1968, the messenger Mark L. Prophet explained that the state of the "mist" is the realm of mankind's thought, feeling, and motive. The state of the "crystal" is the action taken based on one's thoughts and feelings. It is the crystallization of conduct from the thought and feeling realm into actual manifestation.
4. *Dark Shadows* was a weekday television show that aired on ABC from 1966 to 1971. It was a soap opera that depicted supernatural occurrences. Its airing included 1,225 episodes.
5. See I Cor. 3:16, 17.
6. Luke 23:34.
7. Matt. 12:40.

8. I Pet. 3:18–20.

9. Eph. 6:11.

10. Gen. 30:27–43; 31:1–3.

11. Rev. 20:14, 15; 21:8.

12. Jude 1:13.

13. I Cor. 2:14.

14. The great dragon Tiamat. In Babylonian mythology, Tiamat is the primordial female principle of chaos (represented as the tumultuous sea) which takes the form of a dragon. She is depicted as the enemy of the Babylonian gods of light and law.

15. Dan. 5:5, 24–28. "MENE, MENE, TEKEL, UPHARSIN" means "Thou hast been weighed in the balances, and thou hast been found wanting."

16. John 11:1–43.

17. Howard Hughes (1905–1976) was one of the most financially successful individuals of his times. He was a billionaire, an aviator, and a film producer and director. Although admired by many for his wealth and business acumen, he became, in later years, an eccentric recluse, which added to his reputation as a man of mystery.

18. Matt. 6:33.

CHAPTER 14: **Know the Star-Fire Perfection of the Will of God**

1. Eccles. 1:2.

2. Cosmic Egg. See page 301, n. 3.

3. Keepers of the Flame Lessons. The Keepers of the Flame Fraternity is a nondenominational fraternity for men and women in the tradition of ancient spiritual orders. It was founded by the ascended master Saint Germain in 1961 through his messenger Mark L. Prophet and is composed of spiritual seekers who pledge to see this earth through to a golden age of freedom, peace and enlightenment by keeping the flame of life. The Keepers of the Flame course is comprised of 33 monthly lessons on the practical application of cosmic law to assist seekers and members to walk the path of soul testing, spiritual growth and, ultimately, to achieve the ascension. To sample a free online lesson and for additional information about the lessons and the fraternity, see https://www.Summit Lighthouse.org/keepers-of-the-flame/.

4. Ascension of the Cosmic Egg. The messenger has explained that

the spiritual-material universe is known as the Cosmic Egg. (See page 301, n. 3.) In a 1973 *Pearl of Wisdom,* Serapis Bey spoke of the ascension of embodied souls, of the planetary body itself and of "the entire Cosmic Egg." He said, "Can you contemplate that hour when the entire cosmos is quickened in the ascension spiral? . . . One day you shall witness the ascension of the entire warp and woof of time and space. Think of that, blessed hearts, and set it squarely before you as the mark. For you must be given the vision. You must have the vision and the authority to claim that vision." (1973 *Pearls of Wisdom,* vol. 16, no. 26, July 1, 1973)

5. *Invictus* is the Latin word for "unconquered." The British poet William Ernest Henley (1849–1903) composed his well-known poem "Invictus" on the overcoming of adversity. The poem parallels Henley's victorious spirit through his dark trials with illness and disease. He wrote the poem in 1875 from the hospital where he was receiving treatment for tuberculosis of the bone.

CHAPTER 15:   The Coiled Spring of the Will of God

1. El Morya is the hierarch of the Temple of Good Will in the etheric plane over the city of Darjeeling, India, in the foothills of the Himalayas. This retreat is a mandala and a forcefield that is used by the solar hierarchies to release increments of cosmic energy to the planet. Together with the members of the Darjeeling Council, the Brothers of the Diamond Heart, who serve at this retreat under El Morya, assist mankind by organizing, developing, directing and implementing the will of God as the foundation for all successful organized movements. As the Chief of the Darjeeling Council of the Great White Brotherhood, El Morya presides at roundtable meetings in this retreat.

2. Rev. 11:3–18.

3. Rev. 11:1.

4. Rev. 6:6.

5. Matt. 13:24–30.

CHAPTER 16: **The Initiator of God's Will Cometh to Initiate Chelas Who Are Conscious Collaborators with the Will of God**

1. Matt. 19:30; 20:16; Mark 10:31.
2. Audio recordings containing subliminal messages and utilizing autohypnosis techniques as well as other forms of programming of the subconscious mind have become the latest fad in consciousness development. Promoted as self-help products to assist individuals in overcoming bad habits, removing blocks to success and riches, and developing self-confidence, these audio recordings include lectures, guided meditations, affirmations, and subliminal messages embedded into background music or nature sounds.

    On January 1, 1988, beloved Omri-Tas said in his dictation: "The violet flame truly allows you to perform, as it were, a cosmic surgery—and this is never by a momentum that may be fed into the subconscious by all of the popular recordings that are available to you as to how you can become a better person and overcome procrastination and all manner of burdensome addictions. Blessed hearts, these recordings are for those who are computerized and do not have a threefold flame. They are for those who have merely a human personality that has built upon itself incarnation after incarnation without integration with any flame or Spirit of God. . . . Blessed ones, anything that comes from the human level, no matter how positive the statements are, does always embody the entire karma, electronic belt and subconscious of the individual through whom it has come." (1988 *Pearls of Wisdom*, vol. 31, no. 3, pp. 25, 26)

    Only through invoking the light of your mighty I AM Presence to work transmutation by conscious free will with the soul fully engaged as the alchemist in your temple, the conscious collaborator with the will of God, can you balance your karma and make your ascension. People who promote the use of the subconscious in self-programming are either ignorant of the laws of God ("Father, forgive them for they know not what they do,") or they have not bent the knee to the universal Christ, to their Holy Christ Self or to the Great Law. The latter want human attainment and human happiness without allegiance to the I AM Presence. Circumventing, they think, the Guru-chela relationship, they would also bypass all accountability for their karma. Those who follow them are of the school of Atlantean mentalists who seek to develop the mind for the control of self and other selves and for the control of circumstances without the necessity of obedience to cosmic principle.

When human power is thus acquired without true Christ Self-mastery, its use or abuse is subject to the righteousness of man and not the righteousness of God. When, pray tell, does this power misused become the practice of witchcraft or black magic? When the individual crosses the line because his standard is "the ends justify the means," he himself may not know it, for he has never felt the necessity to submit his comings and his goings to The Lord Our Righteousness (Jer. 23:6). Furthermore the gains of such subconscious programming are illusory because sooner or later in this life or in many future lives the individual must consciously stand, face, and conquer his karma. This karma *is not transmuted by these audio recordings.* But the karma is the root of the problems he suppresses through the use of such recordings. Thus when the problems and the karma return, he must finally begin the true path of discipleship.

In conclusion, these audio recordings are a dangerous procrastination on the path of reunion with God. They create the illusion of self-mastery and prosperity while the carnal mind through the subconscious weaves a tangled web around the soul. They are autohypnosis, verily the carnal mind's deception of the soul to postpone her true Christ victory in the light on the path of individual overcoming as outlined in the teachings of the Great White Brotherhood.

3. The word *religion* is derived from the Latin *religio* "bond between man and the gods" or *religare* "to bind back."

CHAPTER 17:   The Gemini Mind for the Governing of Society and the Self

1. Coming Revolution in Higher Consciousness. On June 30, 1976, in Washington, D.C., Pallas Athena, Goddess of Truth, called for the raising of the consciousness of the people of earth by the flame of truth—the Coming Revolution in Higher Consciousness. She said: "I wish you would understand this day that when I say

I AM Truth incarnate, I must rely upon your body, your flesh and your blood, your mind and your soul to be the incarnation of the Word of Truth that I AM! . . . I claim you for the cause of truth because you have made that cause your own. . . . And I will use that flame to light a nation and to light a world!"

2. Refers to "The Science of Rhythm for the Mastery of the Sacred Energies of Life," given by Elizabeth Clare Prophet October 7, 1977. The lecture included a slide presentation showing the uses and misuses of rhythm, sound, and energy in music and its effect on the human aura, with illustrations taken from pastel drawings by the messenger.

3. Matt. 28:18.

4. Refers to the dispensation announced by the Elohim Apollo, July 6, 1975—the release of an increment of the light of illumination "delivered only once in ten thousand years for the elevation of consciousness and the centering of that consciousness in the crown [chakra]. . . . Now the rod coming from the Central Sun by cosmic edict—the stepping-up of the mind of humanity! And the Solar Logoi implant that rod in consonance with the Christ Self of each one. And it is done! And mankind may, if they choose, employ the rod to enter a new era and a golden age!" See "An Increment of Light from the Holy Kumaras," in *The Great White Brotherhood in the Culture, History, and Religion of America*, pp. 269–70. On October 7, 1977, Apollo announced that some who had passed certain initiations over many thousands of years now stood ready to inherit a portion of the mind of God. "I announce to you this initiation so that you might feel the urge to quickly place your atoms and cells in alignment with God's mind so that you, too, might receive in each successive cycle those increments that are to be given before the year 2001." See 1978 *Pearls of Wisdom*, vol. 21, no. 20, p. 97.

5. See note 1 above.

CHAPTER 18: **The Inner Temple Work of Serapis Bey in the Four Quadrants, "Chariots," of Matter**

1. The tenth vision: the four chariots. The Rev. C. I. Scofield's commentary on Zechariah 6:1–8 quoted at the beginning of this *Pearl* is as follows: "The interpretation of the tenth vision must be

governed by the authoritative declaration of verse 5. That which is symbolized by the four chariots with their horses is not the four world-empires of Daniel, but 'the four spirits of heaven which go forth from standing before the Lord of all the earth' (v. 5). These 'spirits' are angels (Luke 1:19; Heb. 1:14) and are most naturally interpreted of the four angels of Rev. 7:1–3; 9:14, 15. These have also a ministry earthward, and of like nature with the 'spirits' of Zech. 6:1–8, viz. judgment. The symbol (chariots and horses) is in perfect harmony with this. Always in Scripture symbolism they stand for the power of God earthward in judgment (Jer. 46:9, 10; Joel 2:3–11; Nah. 3:1–7). The vision, then, speaks of the LORD's judgments upon the Gentile nations north and south in the day of the LORD (Isa. 2:10–22; Rev. 19:11–21)." (*The Scofield Reference Bible,* p. 969, n. 2)

2. "Mother's Clearance in the Dark Cycle of Taurus." At the request of El Morya and Serapis Bey, the messenger conducted a service before El Morya's dictation for the clearance in the Dark Cycle of Taurus of the 10/4 axis and dweller-on-the-threshold of Keepers of the Flame, earth's evolutions, and Atlantean and Lemurian records. This "10/4 Axis Clearance" service, followed by El Morya's dictation, is posted at https://www.SummitLighthouse.org in the member area ("Broadcast," "On-Demand Replays," scroll down to "Clearance Replays," where this service is listed).

3. James 1:21.

4. See note 2 above.

5. Heb. 11:35.

6. Dweller-on-the-threshold. See 1985 *Pearls of Wisdom,* vol. 28, no. 26, p. 350, n. 10.

7. John 13:10.

8. Trial by fire. (Initiation by the Cosmic Christ) Dan. 3:8–30; I Cor. 3:13–15; I Pet. 1:6, 7; 4:12, 13.

9. The cosmic clock. For a list of published lectures by Elizabeth Clare Prophet on this subject, see 1985 *Pearls of Wisdom,* vol. 28, no. 26, p. 350, n. 8.

CHAPTER 19: Seeking and Finding the Mystery of Life

1. El Morya was embodied as Thomas Becket, born winter solstice, December 21, 1118, in London, England.

2. Matt. 7:7, 8; Luke 11:9, 10.
3. See Serapis Bey, December 28, 1985, "The Descent of the Mighty Blue Spheres," 1986 *Pearls of Wisdom,* vol. 29, no 15.
4. On December 29, 1170, after years of conflict with King Henry II of England over the rights of Church versus State, Thomas Becket, Archbishop of Canterbury, was brutally murdered in his own cathedral by four knights who acted on the king's desire to be rid of "this turbulent priest." Becket, who had been noncompromising in his defense of the Church, had just returned from France where he had exiled himself for six years in protest of Henry's abuse of power.
5. Deut. 4:24; 9:3; Heb. 12:29.
6. Refers to Serapis Bey's fourteen-month cycle through the spheres of the causal body. For more information, see Elizabeth Clare Prophet, "Fourteen-Month Cycles of the Initiation of the Christed Ones through the Spheres of the Great Causal Body," 1984 *Pearls of Wisdom,* vol. 27, no. 56, pp. 495–510.
7. See Saint Germain, October 13, 1985, "The Sword of Sanat Kumara: The Judgment of the Rulers in the Earth Who Have Utterly Betrayed Their God and Their People," 1985 *Pearls of Wisdom,* vol. 28, no. 50, pp. 589–91.
8. See Sanat Kumara, December 31, 1984, "A Dispensation of the Solar Logoi," 1985 *Pearls of Wisdom,* vol. 28, no. 6, p. 60.
9. I Pet. 2:5.
10. I Cor. 15:51–53.
11. Jude 4, 12.

CHAPTER 20: **Sacred Fire Baptism**

1. Pocket of Hercules. In a dictation on August 10, 1987, Hercules said: "O beloved, it is a momentous hour. Therefore, be seated in a compartment of my consciousness.... You may climb inside one of an infinite number of pockets in the lining of my cloak and feel cozy all inside.... Blessed hearts, feel the warmth and the joy of this little hammock of a pocket inside the cloak of Elohim and know that I have a pocket for each and every one of you. And do you know that elves of Hercules have embroidered your name upon that pocket that is your very own private berth?... I give you this which is indeed a reality, that you might know the

profound comfort of Elohim, that you might have the sense of abiding in me always as I truly abide even in the center of the atom of self that you have charged with the will of God." (1987 *Pearls of Wisdom,* vol. 30, no. 47, November 16, 1987)

2. The twin of Gemini. El Morya is the initiator under the hierarchy of Gemini on the 5 o'clock line of the cosmic clock. At the close of his dictation on August 8, 1987, El Morya said, "I have not left off speaking with you, but shall continue at inner levels—nor have I concluded this address. But I close my portfolio on this chapter that you might find peace in the will of God and return again to hear me, beloved. For can a Gemini be without a twin?" (1987 *Pearls of Wisdom,* vol. 30, no. 46, November 15, 1987)

3. Refers to the service prior to El Morya's dictation in which the messenger gave teaching on UFOs, an upcoming event called the Harmonic Convergence (which was seeking to make contact with UFOs), and the fallen ones and their manipulation. She gave intense fiery calls for the clearance of these forces from the planet.

4. Refers to "Alternate Preamble to 10.00, Prayers to Archangel Michael for the Deliverance of God's People on Earth," in *Prayers, Meditations and Dynamic Decrees for Personal and World Transformation,* pp. 177–83. For a number of years, in response to the many timely issues across the planet that need prayers and decrees—warfare, calamities, climate, defense, freedom, society, and so forth—the organization has published a yearly decree focus booklet with detailed prayer inserts. In addition, a monthly focus sheet and a weekly focus sheet provide information about current and timely situations for prayers.

5. The focus of Elohim at the Royal Teton Retreat. The seven rays of the Elohim are enshrined at the Royal Teton Retreat, an ancient focus of light congruent with the Grand Teton in Wyoming. The rays are concentrated and anchored in a large image of the All-Seeing Eye of God that is located in a council hall of the retreat. On March 28, 1986, Lord Lanto called to the Elohim: "I, Lanto, summon thee in this hour to the Royal Teton Retreat and to our mountain. Thus, come to the Grand Teton, O Elohim. Intensify these foci of seven rays upon the brows of twin flames." Lord Lanto invited souls and their twin flame to come to the Grand Teton that night while their bodies were asleep to receive the dispensation of the

"alignment of the inner being and the fiery ovoid and the chakras by the hand of Elohim, who shall place their hands on the brow of the male and female form. For out of Elohim in the white-fire core of being thou didst come forth in this form as the polarity of being." (1986 *Pearls of Wisdom,* vol. 29, no. 40, August 24, 1986)

6. Rev. 10:1.
7. Ps. 104:4; Heb. 1:7.
8. The Gemini mind. This dictation by El Morya, "The Gemini Mind: For the Governing of Society and the Self," given October 8, 1977, is published as chapter 17, p. 189.

CHAPTER 21:   **Take a Stand for Truth**

This dictation by El Morya is published in its entirety in 1995 *Pearls of Wisdom,* vol. 38, no. 8, February 19, 1995.

1. El Morya, representing the Elohim and archangels of the first ray, gave this dictation during the *Class of the Seven Chohans* with the Maha Chohan, held December 29, 1994, through January 1, 1995, at the Royal Teton Ranch, Park County, Montana.
2. John 15:20; Matt. 5:11, 12.
3. The Spartans' stand at Thermopylae. In 480 B.C. the Spartan king Leonidas commanded the Greeks in their heroic stand against the immense Persian invasion at the pass of Thermopylae, gateway to central Greece. Although the Persians overwhelmingly outnumbered the Greeks, Leonidas resisted the advance of the Persian army under King Xerxes for two days. On the third day, when the Persians approached from the rear and no reinforcements were in sight, Leonidas dismissed most of his troops. Assisted by the remaining Greek allies, Leonidas and his 300-member Spartan royal guard fought to the last man. Their heroic stand enabled the Greek fleet to retreat. Later this fleet defeated the Persians. Leonidas was an embodiment of Serapis Bey.
4. Rom. 7:15–25; Gal. 5:16–26; James 4:1–10; I Pet. 2:11.
5. Isa. 28:2, 17; Ezek. 38:22; Rev. 8:7; 11:19; 16:21.
6. Maxin Light. As described by Phylos the Tibetan in *A Dweller on Two Planets,* the Maxin Light is the "unfed fire" that burned in the temple of Incal on Atlantis for five thousand years. The flame, which cast "a light of intense power," burned in the shape of a giant

6

spearhead, over three times the height of a tall man.

7. The flame of the altar. The flame of the ark of the covenant burns at the high altar here at Maitreya's retreat. The altars of Church Universal and Triumphant that Keepers of the Flame tend daily around the world are tied to that flame and receive its emanations. For instruction on how to set up a simple altar in your home, see 1994 *Pearls of Wisdom,* vol. 37, no. 12, p. 127, n. 10.

8. Send for the five-panel portable altar with the Chart of Your Divine Self and portraits of Jesus Christ, Saint Germain, El Morya and Kuthumi. Full-color laminated, heavy stock, 14¾" × 28⅝".

9. The masters' plea at the October class for more violet flame. See 1994 *Pearls of Wisdom,* vol. 37, nos. 39, 40, 42, 43, 44, pp. 449–54, 458–60, 476, 480–82, 509, 511–12, 525–26, 531–32.

10. "Violet Fire and Tube of Light Decree" by Saint Germain: decree 0.01 in *Prayers, Meditations and Dynamic Decrees for Personal and World Transformation.*

11. Mantras of the Five Dhyani Buddhas:
Om Vairochana Om. Om Akshobhya Hum.
Om Ratnasambhava Tram. Om Amitabha Hrih.
Om Amoghasiddhi Ah.
Enhance your meditation on the Buddhas with a 19" × 23" lithograph of the mandala of the Five Dhyani Buddhas. Designed in authentic Tibetan style, this richly colored lithograph combines traditional Buddhist symbols with photographs of Tibetan and Nepalese statues from the thirteenth to fifteenth centuries. Reproductions of statues of the Five Dhyani Buddhas are also available on wallet-size laminated cards. The back of each card includes a description of the Buddha, his mantra, symbol, mudra, and the poison his Wisdom antidotes, all you need to know to invoke his presence. Available at http://Store.SummitLighthouse.org. See also "Introduction to the Five Dhyani Buddhas and Their Mandala," in 1994 *Pearls of Wisdom,* vol. 37, no. 2, pp. 13–26.

12. The ascended masters encourage the prevention of illness through natural methods, including a disciplined diet, exercise, fresh air, a positive spiritual and mental attitude and wise health care in every area of living. However, this is not a substitute for medication and the proper medical care under a physician when needed. The

masters do not recommend the avoidance of established medical procedures. Nor do they recommend the application of any healing technique without the advice and supervision of a licensed health care practitioner.

13. Ezek. 18:4, 20.

14. The ascended masters El Morya, Kuthumi and Djwal Kul were embodied as the three wise men Melchior, Balthazar and Caspar.

15. Matt. 2:1–12.

CHAPTER 22:   **Clean House! I AM the Champion of My Chelas**

1. Luke 24:13–35.

2. Bija mantras to the Divine Mother. See "Bija Mantras to the Feminine Deities" and "Bija Mantras for Chakra Meditation," nos. 617 and 618 in Church Universal and Triumphant's *Book of Hymns and Songs;* or nos. 24 and 27 in the *Angels* booklet; or no. 22, "Bija Mantras for Chakra Meditation," in *Heart, Head and Hand Decrees* booklet; all available at http://Store.SummitLighthouse.org.

3. Violet-flame poster illustrating the chakras superimposed on Michelangelo's statue of David. This beautiful full-color poster is 19" × 25"; also 5"× 7" and wallet card sizes; available at http://Store.SummitLighthouse.org.

4. I Cor. 3:16, 17; 6:19; II Cor. 6:16.

5. Martian A's. The misqualified Martian energies include aggression, anger, arrogance, argumentation, accusation, agitation, apathy, atheism, annihilation, aggravation, annoyance and aggressive mental suggestion.

6. Lineage of hierarchy. The order of Gurus in a lineal descent from Sanat Kumara is the following: Sanat Kumara, Gautama Buddha, Lord Maitreya, Jesus Christ, Padma Sambhava. On July 2, 1977, Padma Sambhava bestowed the mantle of Guru upon the messenger, Elizabeth Clare Prophet. He said: "The ascended masters come as a living witness to proclaim in this hour that the Guru-chela relationship can now be sustained in this octave through the flame of the heart of the Mother." (See 1991 *Pearls of Wisdom*, vol. 34, no. 1, pp. 2, 3; and 1984 *Pearls of Wisdom*, vol. 27, Book I, Introduction, pp. *66–73.*)

CHAPTER 23: **The Spirit of the Great White Brotherhood Schooling the Desire by God-Control**

1. Dark Cycle in Gemini. On April 23, 1986, the Dark Cycle entered its eighteenth year, signifying the return of personal and planetary karma accrued through the misuse of God's light and the failure of Christic initiations under the hierarchy of Gemini on the 5 o'clock line of the Cosmic Clock. (For more on this subject, see 1986 *Pearls of Wisdom,* vol. 29, no. 23, p. 217, n. 3.) During the service before the dictation, the messenger led the congregation in decrees and invocations for the clearance of the Dark Cycle in Gemini. The service "Gemini Clearance and Dictation" is posted at https://www.SummitLighthouse.org in the member area ("Broadcast," "On-Demand Replays," scroll down to "Clearance Replays," where the service is listed).

2. See El Morya, October 8, 1977, "The Gemini Mind: For the Governing of Society and the Self," chapter 17, this book.

3. Acts 17:26; Deut. 32:8.

4. Matt. 24:20; Mark 13:18.

5. See Archangel Chamuel and Charity, July 7, 1985, "The Mystery of Love," 1985 *Pearls of Wisdom,* vol. 28, no. 39, p. 485.

6. Heb. 12:1.

7. Prov. 23:7.

8. To access the Gemini clearance, see note 1 above.

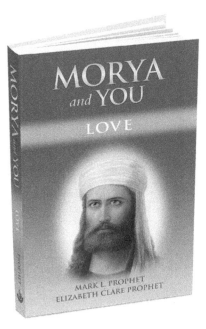

MORYA AND YOU
LOVE

MARK L. PROPHET AND ELIZABETH CLARE PROPHET

Sometimes we look a stranger in the eye and have a flash of recognition: we know this person! You may feel an instant soul connection when you gaze into the eyes of the fierce being whose portrait graces the cover of this book. Who is he?

He is the ascended master El Morya. Now a purely spiritual being, he's had many earthly embodiments where millions of souls knew him intimately—as father, brother, teacher, ruler and friend. He was Abraham. He was Sir Thomas More. He was Akbar the Great. And he had many more lives as the exemplar of fatherly guidance and love.

You may well have been one of those millions who knew him in the past. The problem is, you've forgotten all about him as you entered your present life.

Master Morya hasn't forgotten you. He's looking for his students and friends of old, and his eye is on you. His heart is longing for you. He has important teachings to convey to you, and he's ready to take you by the hand and lead you to the next step on your spiritual path. Get to know him! Read about his previous lives in the Appendix. Drink in his tender care for your soul, expressed in his own words in the 26 messages in this book.

Let Morya speak to your heart. You'll be grateful you reconnected with a dear friend whom you've known for a very long time!

THE CHELA AND THE PATH
Keys to Soul Mastery in the Aquarian Age
BY EL MORYA

El Morya gives personal instruction for spiritual seekers and chelas (students of a spiritual teacher). With the incomparable skill of a Zen master, he teaches us how to become who we really are and to see beneath the surface of daily life. Foundational for those who would both know their true potential and fulfill it.

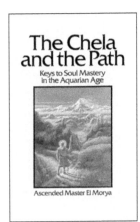

The Chela and the Path
Keys to Soul Mastery in the Aquarian Age

Ascended Master El Morya

THE SACRED ADVENTURE
with
LIGHT FROM HEAVENLY LANTERNS
BY EL MORYA

What is the will of God and how can it be found? A classic collection of prose and poetry, this is a jewel for any esoteric library. Includes the illustrated *Light from Heavenly Lanterns,* a meditation on the drama of the ascent of the soul; and a concise introduction to El Morya's incarnations.

THE SACRED ADVENTURE
with Light from Heavenly Lanterns

EL MORYA

SUMMIT UNIVERSITY ◆ PRESS®

The Summit Lighthouse®
63 Summit Way
Gardiner, Montana 59030 USA

1-800-245-5445 / 406-848-9500

Se habla español.

TSLinfo@TSL.org
SummitLighthouse.org

www.SummitLighthouse.org/El-Morya/
www.ElMorya.org

Mark L. Prophet (1918–1973) and Elizabeth Clare Prophet (1939–2009), were visionary pioneers of modern spirituality and internationally renowned authors. Their books are published in more than 30 languages, and millions of copies have been sold online and in bookstores worldwide.

Together, they built a worldwide spiritual organization that is helping thousands to find their way out of human problems and reconnect to their inner divinity. They walked the path of spiritual adeptship, advancing through the universal initiations common to mystics of both East and West. They taught about this path and described their own experiences for the benefit of all who desire to make spiritual progress.

Mark and Elizabeth left an extensive library of spiritual teachings from the ascended masters and a thriving, worldwide community of people who study and practice these teachings.

CPSIA information can be obtained
at www.ICGtesting.com
Printed in the USA
FFHW011327130619
52957080-58560FF